C0-AJZ-252

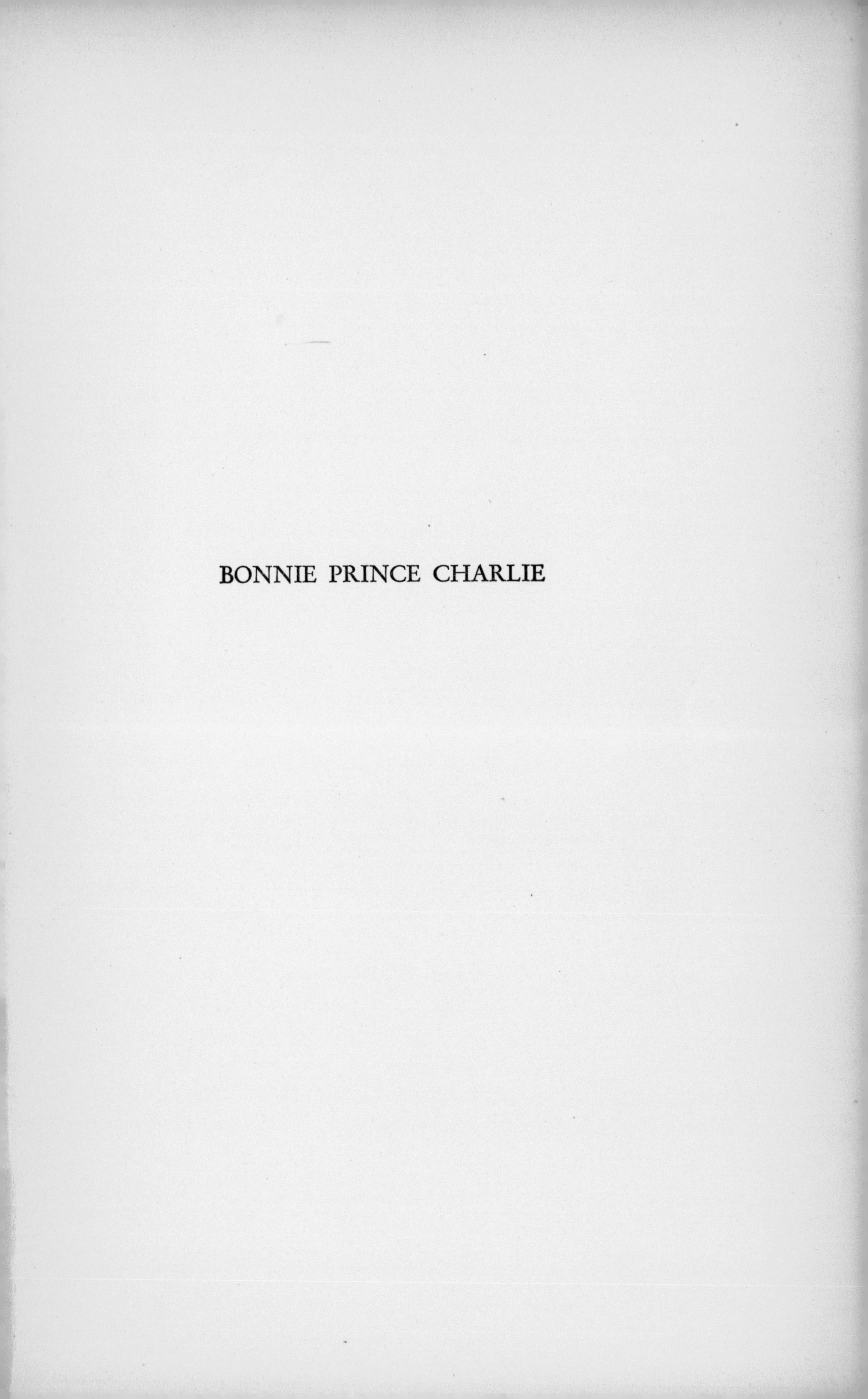

BONNIE PRINCE CHARLIE

CHARLES EDWARD STUART

From a Painting by John Pettie

Bonnie Prince Charlie

A Biography of the Young Pretender

by Donald Barr Chidsey

The John Day Company
New York

FIRST PUBLISHED, SEPTEMBER, 1928

PRINTED IN THE U. S. A.
FOR THE JOHN DAY COMPANY, INC.
BY J. J. LITTLE AND IVES COMPANY, NEW YORK
BOUND BY J. F. TAPLEY CO., LONG ISLAND CITY, NEW YORK

To

GLEN ALAN CHIDSEY, JR.

the hope of the family

ABOUT THE AUTHOR

DONALD BARR CHIDSEY was born May 14, 1902, in Elizabeth, N. J. Since his graduation from Battin High School in 1920 he has been in newspaper work, in a variety of capacities. He has also trouped as bit actor and assistant stage manager, has worked at various times and in various places as bookkeeper, waiter, bellboy, road gang foreman, ship steward, pin boy, golf caddy, iceman, and has done theatrical publicity. At present he is living in New York City and devoting himself to writing. His work has appeared in the old Smart Set magazine, the American Legion Magazine, the New York Sunday Times Magazine, Judge, and Life. *Bonnie Prince Charlie* is his first published book.

PREFACE

THIS is unlike most biographies in that it is the story of a failure, one of the world's greatest disappointments.

I do not apologize for Charles Edward Stuart. His vices were more numerous than his virtues, and they weren't so picturesque. But the world has been kind to him; he is remembered (when he *is* remembered) by the virtues; and it is difficult even for the student, doubly difficult for the layman, to think of him as anything but that dashing young prince who led a forlorn hope, laughing at danger, and charming every person he met.

Yet he did ever so much more than fight in the uprising of 1745. He fought all his life, and against soul-sickening odds too. He was not one of your single-accomplishment heroes: he did not swim a channel, take a trench, or rescue a ship's crew, and then retire quietly into private life. The drunken, smelly, ugly old wife-beater of Florence, when you get to know him, is as fascinating a figure as the handsome young athlete who scared three kingdoms out of their official wits, played hide-and-seek with an army through the wilderness of the Scottish Highlands, and caused half the world to fall in love with him.

Here the worst is told with the best, after the modern manner. And if it all sounds incredible to you, best and worst, I can only protest that it is backed by impressively dull books which represent the labor of many, many patient men. For there are no new discoveries reported in this volume, which is little more than the rendering into common language of a story previously broken up, stuffed with dates and figures, and scattered through dozens of volumes, many of which it is no longer convenient to obtain.

Earlier writers were not given to telling the complete career of Bonnie Prince Charlie. When they could not hear the rattle of musketry in the background they were no longer interested in him. History, to them, was a matter of battles. On the other hand, more recent biographers have been inclined to confine themselves to the obscurer details, apparently on the assumption that everybody knows the principal facts anyway.

But we all have our theories of how history ought to be retailed, just as we all have our theories of how children ought to be brought up; and I believe that the tale should be started at the beginning, carried through the middle, and dropped at the end. I hope you find this such a tale.

The book is not strewn with reference footnotes, but this is only to spare you the annoyance of stumbling over these things in every other paragraph. But I have to thank many previous students and scribblers. Original reporters like Neal MacEachain, Lord Elcho, Chevalier Johnston, John Macdonald, Arthur Henderson, James Ray, Vittorio Alfieri, John Home, etc., etc., have given the groundwork—although it was necessary to accept some of their statements with pursed lips, for MacEachain was obviously in love with Charles, Ray and Home were soldiers of King George, Elcho had tried in vain for many years to collect a considerable sum of money Charles owed to him and the bitterness of his failure in this warped his memory when he came to write his memoirs, while Alfieri's prejudice is instantly understandable to all who know of his *grande amour*.

A little later, such men as Bishop Forbes, Sir Walter Scott and Robert Chambers, did notable work in straightening details and saving for posterity many fascinating side-stories which without these men would have been permitted to die without benefit of type.

More recently, Herbert Vaughan, Bernard Kelly, Vernon Lee, Winifred Duke, Andrew Lang and others, have, generally, concentrated upon dimmed parts of this history. Lang, for example, set himself to disentangle the almost innumerable strings of the story after the spectacular disappearance of

Prince Charles from Avignon in 1749, and thanks to his labors a great hole in the narrative has been filled with substantial matters, and much guesswork previously indulged in by careless writers has been discountenanced.

Much of this book, too, is drawn from that great mass of personal and diplomatic correspondence, for years neglected by research workers, which within the past fifty years has been examined and admirably edited by such students as Alexander Ewald, Lang, Lord Mahon, Professor Terry and the late Dr. Blaikie.

In the death of Dr. Blaikie (which occurred while this book was being prepared for publication) the world lost one who was unquestionably the greatest living authority on Charles Edward Stuart. Without his "Itinerary," whole chapters of this book would have been hopelessly vague: indeed, it is debatable whether I could have done the job at all.

Such bits of sensational journalism as "Ascanius, or a True and Authentick Account, etc." I have read with amusement but not with note paper. Even when they were published, many years ago, they were not generally accepted as anything even remotely resembling the truth; and they have since been wholly discredited. In this class fall the works of the late Brothers Allen, or, as they called themselves, the Sobieski-Stuarts.

Contemporary political pamphlets have given me nothing of value. They are almost without number. I have read many, but it is impossible to credit any of them; for pamphleteers in those days, by reason of their very profession, felt strongly about politics, and the falsehood was an accepted weapon, no more reprehensible, even in the highest circles of statesmanship, than the street speech.

Above all, I have tried to give you a clear, well-rounded view of a complicated but, I think, thrilling situation. I hope I have succeeded.

THE AUTHOR

CONTENTS

LIST OF ILLUSTRATIONS

The decoration used on the binding case is from the Targe carried by Prince Charles at Culloden. (From the original in the possession of Cluny Macpherson, Cluny Castle, Inverness-shire.)

BONNIE PRINCE CHARLIE

CHAPTER ONE

His Consecrated Diapers

THEY made a great to-do when he was born. Salvos were fired from the Castle of Sant' Angelo. Members of the Sacred College, ambassadors, distinguished exiles, great nobles and their ladies, all came bearing gifts and bowed before the babe. The Pope visited the palace in person and provided material for the royal diapers—sixty thousand scudi worth of the finest linen available, all previously consecrated by His Holiness. Congratulations poured in from every corner of the earth. Thousands got drunk on the strength of it. And the really enthusiastic Jacobites affirmed that a new star had made its appearance in the heavens precisely at the moment of the child's birth.

They named him Charles Edward Louis Philip Casimir Stuart, and he grew up to stride and stumble through some of the most extraordinary adventures that have ever befallen any person in this world.

There was good reason for all this excitement. When, thirty-eight years before, William of Orange, at the head of a strictly Protestant army, marched upon London, King James the Second fled, panic-stricken. James was never a warrior. But he was a gentleman; and, before he himself escaped, he made certain that his wife and his one son were safely out of the country.

It was three o'clock on the morning of December 10, 1682. M. Saint-Victor, a Provence adventurer, bearing the Prince of Wales wrapped in a cloak, followed Queen Mary out of Whitehall, down the wet and slippery steps to the Thames, and into an open skiff. The river was churned up in a million whitecaps; the rain was icy cold. Marie-Beatrice d'Este of Modena, Queen of Great Britain and Ireland, attended only by a few of her foreign ladies, sat in the stern, probably praying, for she was very devout. She was also very beautiful. The Prince was less than six months old.

The party landed at Lambeth. A common coach was to carry them down the south road to Gravesend, where a yacht, the property of that most audacious of all lovers, Antonine, Count of Lauzun, awaited them. The horses were not yet harnessed. It was deemed advisable that Lauzun and Saint-Victor go inside while this was being done; but Mary and her ladies, who might be recognized, dared not enter; instead, they crouched in the shadow of the tower of old Lambeth church. The babe was in Mary's arms.

Across the turbulent water she could see the lights of London. All England was astir that night. If she were caught, she knew, her child would be taken from her. Anything might happen. She was horribly frightened. Whenever the 'ostler passed near her with a lantern, she jumped nervously. Several times she was almost discovered. Had the Prince cried just then, he would have altered the course of history. But he was a well-behaved baby.

The Queen and her party escaped, and Saint-Victor carried the tidings back to Whitehall. Soon afterwards, King James himself stole quietly out of England. Did he thereby abdicate? The Parliamentarians never could decide. At any rate, he was not in the country, and William of Orange was; and William of Orange, well aware that the Parliamentarians were not unmindful of his army, circuitously offered his services as King. It was all very embarrassing. Something must be done and that promptly: so much was evident. So they declared the throne vacant, and then elected William and his Stuart wife, King and Queen, co-regents. Then England looked the other way, and tried to pretend that nothing had happened.

King James joined his wife in France, and Louis the Fourteenth, his cousin, greeted both of them with honors truly regal. Louis gave them St. Germains, a palace just outside of Paris; he also gave them money and household troops and jewels and encouragement galore. He couldn't do enough for them. Indeed, the presence of these royal exiles in France just then was convenient for Louis. It gave him a mace he might at any time swing menacingly toward England. Yet the magnificent monarch seemed sincere in his greetings, and probably he was. No doubt his heart went out to his cousins. They were persons of royal blood and they must be kept in regal state lest people in France begin to question the theory of the divine right of kings. No honor that Louis could show them was too great for James and Mary. And when James went to Ireland, to try to win back his throne via that country with an army Louis had lent him, the French monarch said, "Adieu! the best wish I can make you is that I may never see your face again."

However, Louis did see his cousin's face again, many times. For the Irish uprising was put down, the Catholics were routed, and James scurried back to exile.

James, as king, had been harsh, cruel, bigoted. He had ruthlessly violated the laws of both England and Scotland. Yet he was a Stuart and, when he died, thousands wept.

Louis wept, of course. So did Mary of Modena; and so did the well-behaved baby, who had grown to be a well-behaved boy with pretty eyes and an aristocratic, if somewhat spiritless, face. King Louis, at the prompting of one of his mistresses, comforted the boy with a proclamation recognizing the male Stuarts as the only legitimate heirs of the English and Scottish thrones. Spain and the Papal states also recognized James the Third. But England clung to her Dutchman.

Queen Mary, William's spouse, died. And William himself was getting old. They had no children. The nearest Protestant heir to the throne was Anne, half-sister of the exiled boy king, and daughter of James by a previous marriage. Nobody objected to Anne, who was stupid, amiable and a good Church of Englander. But although she had borne no less than nineteen children, she was, at this time, childless.

So Parliament passed the Act of Settlement, proposed in the lower house by Sir John Bowles, who, Stanhope says, "was thought even then disordered in his senses; and who soon afterwards entirely lost them." The act wandered through the two houses: nobody seemed to object to it, but nobody was enthusiastic. At last it went to William, who signed it.

The Act provided that the crown should pass from William to Anne, when William died; and that when Anne died, assuming that she did so without having produced a twentieth child, it should pass to the nearest Protestant heir. This was the Dowager Duchess of Hanover.

On February 20, 1702, William was thrown from his horse. On March 8 he died. That same morning the houses of Parliament proclaimed Anne regent, and on April 23 she was formally crowned.

For a time, things looked brighter for the exile. With William dead, James might hope for a restoration. But the people liked Anne. She was an ideal British monarch—slow, stupid, good-natured, truly devout—and she didn't try to run the government. Anne was thirty-seven years old at this time. She had a husband whom she loaded with honor, creating him Generalissimo of all her armies and High Chief Lord Admiral of her navy. He was small and asthmatical, and excessively stupid. He collected coins and medals. He was fat and grew steadily fatter; and he was very fond of drink. "If there were in England at this time any person duller than Her Majesty," writes Stanhope, "that person was Her Majesty's consort, Prince George of Denmark."

James' heart beat high now. It was the year 1707, and apparently his best opportunity. England was weakened, for most of her troops were fighting on the Continent. The people did not have the same hatred of this James that they had felt for his father. France was eager to see England crippled, so that the Continental troops would be withdrawn; and Louis was willing to help James with money and with men. Five or six thousand soldiers under Comte de Gasse, one of the ablest generals of his day (he later became Marshal de Matignon), were assembled at Dunkirk; and the fleet set sail for England, with James, then twenty years old and not yet recovered from an attack of the measles, confident of victory.

Before the sailing, Louis presented James with his maiden

sword, saying, as he had said to the lad's father, "The best wish I can make you is that I may never see your face again."

Alas! Louis was doomed to see the Stuart faces many more times. It was singularly difficult, he was beginning to learn, to be rid of these tall, handsome sovereigns. Hard luck had pursued them since the second Robert of Scotland. Always it was something. . . . This time it was the English fleet, which caught the expedition as it was sailing into the Firth of Forth, where the Stuart supporters eagerly awaited it. The English fleet greatly outnumbered the French fleet, and the French commander was as responsible for James' life as though James had been his own king. So the French boats turned back. They tried once again to land, at Invernesshire, but a storm blew them out of their course and, before they could reassemble, the English fleet was again between them and Britain. There was nothing to do but return.

James' maiden sword was still unblooded. Eager to be busy at something kingly, he took a command in the Household Guards and fought gallantly at Oudenarde and Malplaquet.

Then came the Peace of Utrecht. France managed to place the Bourbons upon the throne of Spain; and England secured Gibraltar, the slave trade, and a clause demanding that the Stuart Pretender be forced to move out of France. Louis was polite in carrying out the treaty, but James refused to embarrass him by lingering. James went to live with the Duke of Lorraine at Bar-le-Duc and, when England insisted that he be moved from there, he went to Avignon. Still England insisted. So James crossed the Alps, wandered around in Italy for a while, and finally settled in Rome.

In due time Anne's consort, the distinguished Generalissimo of the British Armies and Chief Lord High Admiral of the British Navy, Baron Wokingham, Earl of Kendal, Duke of Cumberland, Warden of the Cinque Ports, Constable of Dover Castle, etc., etc., died. This ended whatever hopes optimistic persons might have had for a twentieth baby from Anne. The Queen was aging, too. She was by nature inclined to the cause of her brother, whose sad plight touched her tender, if not very deep heart. She must have wept when she read the letter he wrote to her:

". . . and you may be assured, madam, that though I can never abandon, but with my life, my own just right, which you know is unalterably settled by the most fundamental laws of the land, yet I am most desirous rather to owe to you than to any living the recovery of it. It is for you that a work so just and glorious is reserved. The voice of God and nature calls you to it; the promises you made to the king, our father, enjoin it; the preservation of our family—the preventing of unnatural wars—require it; and the public good and welfare of our country recommend it to you, to rescue from present and future evils; which must, to the latest posterity, involve the nation in blood and confusion till the succession be again settled in the right line." He begged her not to leave the throne "to the Duke of Hanover, the remotest relation we have; whose friendship you have no reason to rely on, or be fond of; who will leave the government to foreigners of another language, of another interest; and who, by the general naturalization, may bring over crowds of his countrymen to supply the defect of his right, and enslave the nation."

But Anne died rather abruptly; and the Duke of Shrewsbury and a few other adroit politicians arranged the matter so that the Elector of Hanover took over the English throne and scepter as quietly as though he had just dropped in for a call and found them lying there (the Dowager Duchess of Hanover, the heir apparent, had died only a few weeks before), and there was nothing for Scotland to do but follow suit.

George the First was short, fat, and pop-eyed, with a fondness for heavy food and heavy wines, with a greasy face, and also with a "seraglio of hideous prostitutes." These women ruled Britain for him. Two of them particularly, known as the "Elephant" and the "Beanpole" because of their figures, did a rushing business in office-selling and title-selling. All George's women were Germans. Not until near the end of his reign did he condescend to make love to an English woman. Moreover, he did not know a word of English and did not want to learn.

CHARLES EDWARD AS A BOY

He was still Elector of Hanover. England and the English bored him; and every time he got any sort of excuse he waddled back to his insignificant German province, Great Britain paying all the expenses.

No wonder he was not popular! The Stuarts, at their very worst, had been at least dignified, and the Stuarts had usually shown good taste in the matter of women.

So hope once again stirred in the breast of the exiled James. He was in correspondence with the discontented nobles of Scotland and England, who assured him that there were thousands of Jacobites ready and eager to rally round him. France would help. The clans could be called out. Ormond, Mar, Bolingbroke, and other powerful personages had offered their active support. The crowds of Edinburgh were singing, "The Auld Stuarts Back Again," and most of George's troops were in Flanders.

The Uprising of 1715 broke rather unexpectedly. The Earl of Mar, angry because he thought King George had slighted him, called out the clans ahead of schedule. There was every reason to believe that Mar would be successful. But, although a clever politician, he was one of the worst generals in history. Decisive action would have won at least Scotland for him. But he vacillated. He did not seem to know which way to move. And while he loitered, the House of Argyll summoned the Campbells to arms, the regular troops were called back from the Continent, the militia was raised, Marlborough ran true to form by going back on his promise again; and not long after James had been officially proclaimed King of England, Scotland and Ireland, Mar fought the Battle of Sheriffmuir.

Technically that battle was not decisive. Actually it was a victory for the established government. Mar had waited too long: the spirit had evaporated from one of the most enthusiastic and warlike armies ever assembled in Britain. The Campbell of Argyll—Ian Roy nan Cath, Red John of the Battles—knew his business. He avoided open conflict until Mar and his generals had defeated themselves. James was called over, landed, and was formally proclaimed King. But after Sheriffmuir everything was lost. The army broke up. James slipped back to France. The redcoats erected gallows galore; the slaughter commenced; and many a poor fellow who ought to have been led to glory, was left instead to dangle from a hempen rope. Mercy was nowhere in evidence.

James, however, tried again. Again it looked as though he simply could not lose, and again he did lose. Early in 1718, Charles the Twelfth of Sweden, who was exasperated because England had taken Bremen and Verdun, agreed to send 10,000 trained fighting men into Scotland. The clans were to be raised: the clans, slaughter or no slaughter, were always ready to fight for a Stuart. And Peter the Great of Russia, for reasons of his own, had practically promised to help.

That plot collapsed when King Charles fell dead in front of the fortress of Frederickshall. The trigger finger of an unknown soldier determined the destiny of three crowns.

James tried again. He was a persistent man; and a throne like that of England was worth the effort. Moreover, royalty was his profession, his whole life. The Stuarts had always subscribed, literally and fully, to the doctrine of the divine right of kings. James would have thought that he was disregarding a heavenly command had he neglected to try to recover the throne; and the duty was the more imperative because of the debt of gratitude he owed to those men, noble and otherwise, who had risked their lives and their properties for his restoration.

Cardinal Alberoni, in Spain, was a staunch supporter of the Stuart pretensions, and Spain was angry with Britain. James visited Philip the Fifth at Madrid, and soon fresh plans were afoot. An army of between 5,000 and 6,000 men was assembled at Cadiz—rather, two armies, a large one for England and a small auxiliary for Scotland. The Duke of Ormond was in command. They sailed without James, who was not able to be on hand at the time.

Off Finesterre they encountered a terrific storm. In Ireland men called it "the Protestant wind." Only two of the frigates, conveying the auxiliary army, managed to get through; the others were obliged to turn back. Only 300 Spaniards were landed on the Island of Lewis. Plans there had not been well made. Lord Seaforth appeared with a few hundred Mackenzies, and there were small groups of other clansmen; but most of the chieftains, lacking definite instructions, did not know what to do. Was the revolution on, or wasn't it? While they hesitated, an army of English regulars, reinforced by men from the Monroes, the Rosses and a few other clans loyal to the Hanoverian succession, marched against them. There was a skirmish in Glenshiel. As far as figures went, dead and wounded, the Highlanders and Spaniards won handily. But the uprising was obviously a failure. Without foreign troops the clansmen were doomed. They escaped as best they could; and the Spaniards gave themselves up next day and were sent back as a gift to Philip.

By this time James was getting rather downhearted in spite of himself. To arouse his interest by providing for an heir, his followers urged him to marry. He had probably never given much thought to the subject, and he was not excited when they proposed it to him. In effect he said, "Find the woman and I'll consider it."

So his followers made search among the eligibles and finally decided upon Clementina, daughter of Prince James Sobieski and granddaughter of King John Sobieski, the Polish general who had saved Europe by defeating the Turks before Vienna. There was no better stock in the Christian world. Clementina was beautiful, only sixteen years old, and a devout Catholic. But it was necessary that the greatest secrecy surround any proposal made to her, since the English government was watching affairs on the Continent closely and a set of spies reported everything the exiles did. Some go-between of great courage and discretion was needed.

The man selected was Charles Wogan of Rathcoffey, a dare-devil Irishman. He could talk like a poet, fight like a demon, drink like Panurge and, when the occasion suggested, could use right nimbly the brains God had given him. He had fought for James' restoration in 1715, had been captured, tried, and sentenced to hang; but he had broken jail at Newgate and escaped to France to rejoin the man he believed should be King. He was, at this time, only twenty-two years of age.

Charles Wogan of Rathcoffey wandered away from James' mock court—wandered through the various small German courts, flirting, fighting, dancing, gambling. Apparently he was just an adventurous blade, grown tired of fidelity to a king without a country and seeking some genuine excitement. The spies thought this, anyway, and dropped off one by one; so that, by the time Wogan had reached Silesia, he was alone. He had little difficulty getting the ear of the princess, and even less difficulty persuading her that she ought to become Queen of Great Britain and Ireland. Her parents did not object.

But there was the Emperor of Austria, whom England would ask to intervene. And since it was the presence of English warships at Sicily which alone was keeping possession of that desirable place for the Austrian throne, undoubtedly the Emperor would comply with the request.

In fact, that is exactly what happened. Wogan returned to Rome. But Clementina took too long in getting ready, and the secret leaked out. The princess and her mother were arrested at Innsbruck in the Tyrol, while they were on their way over the Alps from Poland to Bologna. They were detained in a convent, and Prince Sobieski was deprived of his government of Augsburg and imprisoned. The bridegroom was left waiting at the altar.

But Charles Wogan of Rathcoffey was not to be defeated so easily. He hurried to Urbino, got James' permission to make another trip, disguised himself as a traveling merchant carrying concealed pistols but no sword, and went to Innsbruck. It happened that Dillon's regiment, composed of Irishmen who couldn't find enough fighting in their own country, was stationed at Schelestadt, near Strasbourg. Wogan took into his confidence three compatriot officers—Misset, Gaydon and O'Toole. Lang has called them the Three Musketeers and likened Wogan, not inaccurately, to D'Artagnan.

This quartet somehow obtained passports for "Count Cernes and Family," who were supposed to be returning to Loretto from the Low Countries. Then they put their heads together.

On an afternoon in April, 1719, a cold, dark afternoon with more than a hint of snow to come, one Chateaudeau, gentleman-usher to the Princess Clementina, sauntered out to whisper with the porter of the convent gate. This Chateaudeau was a handsome, affable chap. "You wouldn't object, would you, if a pretty wench slipped in here to see me to-night?" The porter grinned, and grinned the broader when some gold coins were dropped into his palm.

Jenny, employed as a maid by Major Misset's wife, was chosen to gain access to the princess but was told only at the last minute the exalted rank of the person she was to help rescue; then, frightened, she refused to go through with the business. Wogan had to part with a few more gold coins before Jenny could be induced to change her mind.

She applied at the gate. The porter was not supposed to let anybody in or out; but one could hardly blame the court gentleman for wanting a bit of fun at night, in a lonesome place like this.

Jenny reached the apartment of the Princess and changed clothes with her. Clementina had given word that she was suffering from a headache and must not be disturbed. A sufficient time was allowed to pass . . . for the benefit of the porter. Afterwards, Clementina went to the gate in company with Chateaudeau. While the grinning porter watched, Chateaudeau bade her an affectionate but curiously loud farewell.

The snow had come and was still coming. The wind was rising. It was a dark and stormy night, exactly as it should have been. Down the road, near the gate, Charles Wogan of Rathcoffey and his Three Musketeers, waiting with the frightened Mrs. Misset, had heard that loud farewell. The Princess, poor girl! staggered blindly down the road. She was in a strange country, in pitchy darkness, trusting to strange men whom, now, she could not even find. One pocket of her apron contained the celebrated Sobieski rubies; in another pocket was a case containing some of the crown jewels of England, James' gift to her.

As soon as they dared, the Irishmen approached and bundled her into a coach, and the dash for the border began. They stopped first at an inn, to get dry, and there Clementina carelessly left behind her the crown jewels! If these were discovered the whole secret was out. O'Toole, a blonde, blue-eyed giant, galloped back to the inn, found it dark, couldn't awaken the landlord, smashed in the door by throwing his weight against it, and returned with the jewels.

Six relays of picked horses had been previously posted. But the Princess of Baden, a very important personage indeed, happened to be traveling just ahead of Wogan's party, and the Princess of Baden demanded, and of course got, the best post-horses. Wogan's party had to take second-rate animals. All that night they drove, eating almost nothing and sleeping only in snatches. Meanwhile, in the convent, Jennie was holding off pursuit by sending out word that her headache was worse and that she could not see anybody. She gained them twenty-four precious hours with this strategem. In time, however, the escape was discovered. A courier was dispatched to warn the troops at the border to stop the princess. The courier arrived at an inn just as the Princess and her Irishmen were quitting the place. What could they do to stop him? He was well mounted and had stopped only for a drink.

O'Toole strolled up, smiling an Irish smile. A pistol shot now would spoil everything, but there were pleasanter means. The blonde giant suggested a drink. The courier accepted. O'Toole suggested another. The courier accepted. . . . And so it went. O'Toole was the better man: in time he staggered outside, mounted, and galloped off after the rest of the party. But the courier was on the floor, and the landlord couldn't seem to wake him up.

After three days and three nights of hard traveling, they crossed the border. Twice their carriage had broken down, and the second time, in the village of Alla, six miles from the border, it was found to be beyond repair; so they hired a calash, a sort of cart, and made the rest of the trip in a blinding snow-storm. It was five o'clock on the morning of Sunday, April 30, when they awakened the Princess and informed her that she was safe.

James was in Spain, arranging for the Glenshiel fiasco. But Clementina was married to him by proxy, in Bologna, and as soon as James returned, they were married in fact. James was pleased with her. He caused a medal to be struck in honor of the event; he made the Three Musketeers Senators of Rome, and Wogan he knighted and obtained for him, appropriately, the governorship of La Mancha, in Spain. The girl Jenny was not prosecuted but was permitted to return to Mrs. Misset, who remained in the service of Clementina. Chateaudeau was arrested and held at Innsbruck until August when, at the intercession of the Empress-Mother, he was released. The bride and the bridegroom repaired to the Eternal City, where on December 20, 1720, after six days of labor, she bore him a son. And thereby hangs our tale.

CHAPTER TWO

The Great Adventure Begins

THE Jacobite leaders were taking no chances that this child should be declared the fruit of a fraud. His father, according to certain political enemies, was a common child who had been smuggled into the Queen's bed in a warming pan after Mary had shown herself unable to produce a child (William's wife and Anne were James' children by a previous marriage). So there was a goodly crowd present to witness the birth of Charles Edward Stuart. This gallery may have embarrassed Clementina, but her delivery was a state affair.

Exiles of noble name were there, by the dozen, along with many Cardinals, particularly their Eminences Cardinals Paolucci and Barberini, representing the Holy See; Gualtieri, the Protector of England; Sacripanti, Protector of Scotland; Imperiali, Protector of Ireland; Ottoboni, Protector of France; Aquavivi, Minister of Spain; and Panfili, the Senior Cardinal Deacon.

The babe, promptly wrapped in the consecrated swaddling clothes and placed on a couch under a magnificent canopy of red velvet, presided over his first levee. The Cardinals blessed him, the fanatics crouched before him muttering prayers, and the exiles and soldiers of fortune kissed his tiny red hands.

Outside, cannon were booming, crowds were cheering, coachmen and chairmen swore, the Pope hurried over from St. Thomas'. It was a great occasion.

Charles was a rather weak baby, but this was not amazing. His father had never been vigorous, and his mother was usually ill.

And his political heritage was equally ill-starred. From the beginning, even from the moment it became known that Clementina was pregnant, there were plots hatched about him. He was prenatally doomed to intrigue. He was born into scheming, and lived through scheming, and died in the midst of schemes.

You must know something of this extraordinary court in Rome, in order to understand why there were so many mad plans with this baby for an innocent centerpiece. It was a court without a country. Laws were issued from it, but they meant nothing except to a few sycophants. It was officially recognized by France, Spain and the Vatican, but even these governments could not pretend that James was an actual, ruling sovereign. He knighted persons who pleased him, or conferred upon them patents of nobility, but they were not recognized in Great Britain. He called his wife Queen and his first-born Prince of Wales; but these titles, too, were not officially recognized in the nations to which they were supposed to apply. James had no navy, and no troops except the swanky Papal cuirassiers who mounted guard at the gloomy old Palazzo Muti—a palace the Pope had given him. He had a cabinet, but its work was chiefly correspondence and its powers were purely mythical. He had a revenue, but only because certain friends and political well-wishers were pleased to be kind to him financially: the Pope, for example, allowed him 12,000 pounds a year, the Court of Spain also gave him a generous allowance, and he picked up odds and ends from other Courts and from faithful adherents in England and Scotland or from politicians who believed themselves to be far-sighted. He struck coins, but they were curiosities rather than currency. He issued proclamations, but only his devoted followers read them and, in England and Scotland, and in Ireland too, those followers did so in the secrecy of their bedchambers. The people of Rome were strictly enjoined by the Pope to call him King: and when he rode out, even informally, it was with a retinue of about forty titular officials, pages, postilions, and the like. He was, in short, a King Without a Country. The Romans called him "The King Here," and called George "The King There."

It was not that James had nothing to do. He worked harder than George, the actual monarch. He was continually in correspondence with his friends abroad and on the Continent, trying always to stir up rebellion; he was at his writing-desk hours and hours every day; he received all sorts of visitors, and listened to all sorts of wild plans; he was generous, seeing to it that the poverty-stricken exiles were treated well.

These exiles—his courtiers, ministers, officers of state—were of all types. Some of them were honest believers in the divine right of kings and particularly of Stuart kings. Some of them were Catholic bigots who intensely desired to see James on the throne so that England might be brought back into the fold. Some of them were political outcasts with whom the established court of St. James would have no traffic and who were thus obliged to turn to the next best thing. Some of them were romantic dreamers. Many of them were just plain adventurers, or unscrupulous schemers, who sought only their personal advancement. The fact that there were no definite rewards to be had did not cause them to cease scheming; rather it stimulated them. It was as though they gambled desperately for poker chips which were worthless counters but which, by a twist of fate, might become lawful coin.

All this was made still more confusing by the advent of Charles. There were those among the Protestant supporters of James' pretensions who believed that the only way to recover the throne for the legitimate line was through Charles. James, they estimated, could never be the actual king unless he abjured his religion; and this he had repeatedly refused to do. But perhaps Charles would not be so finicky.

Others believed that the public of Britain was disgusted with James and his repeated attempts to regain his throne by the use of foreign troops. But the public would have nothing against the new prince. To carry the child into Scotland and show him to the clansmen would be to precipitate a victorious uprising, these schemers thought.

Some of these plans were proposed to James. Others were kept secret from him. But almost every one of the exiles had some scheme tucked away in a corner of his brain, and each one believed that only his could be successful.

Meanwhile, Clementina languished, disappointed, in the cold palace. James was engrossed in business. Nor was he as romantic as he had first seemed. True, he was tall, and certainly he was distinguished. But he was also, to borrow Walpole's adjective for him, "meager." He was rather stupid to talk with: and, like every Stuart, he was inordinately stubborn. Clementina must have found things dull. For this was a court of hopeless dreams, of whispers, of sinister eyeings and secret, fantastic plots. It was a small, slow court, with great dignity, but absolutely empty of reality.

On March 6, 1725, she bore Henry Benedict Maria Thomas, etc., Duke of York.

Soon after this second birth, a marital quarrel which had long been smoldering, broke into flame. In itself it was a cheap and silly business, but it gravely prejudiced the Stuart cause.

James had the family weakness for favorites. He could not seem to stand alone but must needs attach to himself certain persons he believed to be true friends. One of the tutors he had appointed for the two princes was the Chevalier Andrew Ramsey. Ramsey was not sufficiently orthodox to please Clementina, and James, reluctantly, and probably only after some privately spoken harsh words, replaced him by Sir Thomas Sheridan—a sterner Roman Catholic but a man of much less learning and not so much common sense—and by James Murray, a Protestant! It was James' idea that his sons should be brought up to understand both the Protestant and the Catholic faiths, although it cannot be doubted that James sincerely hoped they would always adhere to Rome. James also said, explaining the Murray appointment to his Queen, that it would please the Protestants among his followers and dispel reports that he was himself a bigot.

But Clementina thought it was horrible. She said she wouldn't stand for it! Her husband was trying to bring up her children to be heretics!

There were other things she said she wouldn't stand for,

notably the appointment of Colonel John Hay as Secretary of State. James had created Hay, Earl of Inverness and Murray, Earl of Dunbar. He appears to have been sincerely fond of both.

But it was the third member of this little group, Hay's wife, Murray's sister, that Clementina hated most. She openly accused her husband of adultery with the Countess of Inverness; and, at the time, almost everybody seems to have believed her.

James said that the Countess was not and never had been his mistress; and in spite of all insinuations, there is not a shred of evidence to prove that she was. It may be that Clementina had reasons of her own for believing this. At any rate, she was hysterical about it, and was in the hands of certain schemers who were interested in promoting a royal breach. So she told James that unless he sent Hay and Mrs. Hay and Murray out of the court, she would no longer live with him. For answer the stubborn James took Mrs. Hay to the opera. So Clementina, with her ladies-in-waiting, retired to the Convent of St. Cecelia at Transtevere.

The little court was in a turmoil. The Queen of Nowhere had quit her job! Almost everybody took the woman's side, as is usually the case in affairs of this sort. The British spies worked day and night to keep up sympathy for the weak, overwrought woman; and they did their work so well that many an historian since has been ready to believe anything of the exiled king.

The Pope was indignant. Clementina pleased him politically because she was such an ardent Catholic. Nobody, certainly, had ever been tested more thoroughly in that ancient faith than James. But Clement XI did not seem to take this into consideration.

James had been planning a trip to Spain, on another hopeless political errand; but the Queen of Spain sent him a tart letter warning him never to set foot within her domains unaccompanied by his wife, and incidentally vituperating him with vigor. The emperor at Vienna, who had tried to stop the match in the first place, wrote to the same effect. And there were dozens of similar letters from Rome and from London and Edinburgh and Paris.

James wrote to the Queen, earnestly begging her to return to him, but not offering to accede to her demands. Probably he reasoned that, if he showed the world he could not handle his own wife, the world would never believe that he could handle three kingdoms. Besides, he was, as previously mentioned, a prodigiously stubborn man.

Clementina replied that she would not return until he had banished Murray and the Hays. So James, wearied of the whole business, decided to move to Bologna.

When the Vatican learned of his plans, three cardinals were sent with a remonstrance. They waited upon James, who received them with perfect good humor. They told him that the Pope had no objection to his going to Bologna for a few weeks, but he must not suppose that the Holy Father would consent to his living there, where the princes might be brought up as heretics. Of course, nothing was said about the fact that the Pope held the strings of James' money bags.

James did go to Bologna, but only for a short stay. Meanwhile, he was writing to Clementina, and once he even went to visit her, in an effort to induce her to return.

Eventually there was a reconciliation. This was in June of 1727, a year and a half after the Queen had gone to the convent. James was then at Avignon, on still another attempt to incite an uprising. George the First, on one of his many trips back to Herrenhausen, had overeaten once too often: numerous melons, for which he had a great fondness, brought about his death. His oldest son, who was also his bitterest personal enemy, succeeded him.

George the Second was another short man, though not fat. He was a spirited fellow, irritable, superstitious, and stingy. He had plenty of courage, numerous mistresses, a charming wife, and a nasty temper. He could talk at least a smattering of English; but, considered as a King of Great Britain and Ireland, he was quite as grotesque as his father. He hated books and art. Even when he was sober, he was wont to fall into rages at his ministers; and, on such occasions, it was his habit to kick his hat, or sometimes his wig, back and forth across the floor.

At the news of George the First's death, James had hurried to Nancy; and when the English government had remonstrated with France, and James was asked to leave, he had gone to Avignon. Here there was a burst of correspondence, of reports, of attempted bribes, of fantastic plots. Nothing came of it. James was gone almost a year.

Clementina had refused to join him in Avignon, but she was in Rome waiting for him on his return. There they lived fairly happily together for the rest of her life. James did not dismiss his favorites, and Clementina seemed to consider herself something of a martyr. She suffered from asthma, and also from a touchiness which must have been trying for James. But in time she turned her whole soul toward the church and became fanatically devout.

As for Charles, he was a lively lad, with large violet eyes and a mischievous manner. He was, from the very beginning, fond of all sports: he boxed and fenced, went shooting the covers at the Villa Borghese, rode for hours on horseback, spent much time at shuttlecock, went boating with his brother on the lake at Albano, and played an excellent game of golf. He didn't get on well with his tutors, for he had a sharp temper which was not improved by the lack of discipline resulting from the marital troubles of his parents. Murray he particularly disliked.

But he studied too, a little. He learned French and Italian and English. His father usually addressed him in English, which language they used in their later correspondence. James, long and lean and melancholy, affected things English about the palace: he went in for roast beef and March ale instead of Italian foods and wines.

At ten, the Prince had a slight attack of smallpox, but it did not leave him pockmarked.

At twelve, he was taken before the Pope and rattled off his

catechism in fine style, afterwards answering promptly all questions put to him. This pleased his Holiness, and thereafter Charles was well liked at the Vatican.

At fourteen, he went to war. Battles were an important part of any royal education in those days. Charles' experience was not lengthy. Another Charles, Emperor of the German States and King of Naples and of Sicily, was being attacked by the Spaniards, the French, the Sardinians, and others. The Spaniards, who wanted Don Carlos to be King of Naples, were throwing troops into Austrian Lombardy. The Imperial forces after having been defeated on several fields, were finally cooped into two fortresses, Capua and Gaeta, and these were besieged.

The Duke of Liria, son of the Duke of Berwick—one of James the Second's bastards—passed through Rome on his way to join the Spanish forces and, while visiting his uncle, he suggested to James that Prince Charles be permitted to accompany him to the war. Prince Henry, although a quieter lad, wanted to go also; but this permission was denied.

The Pope gave Charles a purse, and caused prayers to be said for his safety at all the churches of Rome. On July 27, 1734, accompanied by Murray, Gore, Sheridan, a confessor, a couple of friars, a surgeon, and four liveried servants, but strictly incognito, the Prince started for the front.

There he had a wonderful time. The soldiers were enthusiastic about him. The officers fell in love with him. The Duke, his cousin, was frightened about his safety, for Charles wanted to get in where the gunfire was heaviest. He all but forgot to write to his father, and was reprimanded for his negligence. Apparently he did not like to write letters, being too busy studying things military. He was shortly made a General of Artillery and given a salary of 1,000 crowns a month. And after many pleadings and teasings, he finally was permitted to go right down into the trenches where he was with the Duke, on August 6, when they ran up the white flag at Gaeta.

After that he wanted to go with the Spanish army into Sicily for a little more gunfire, but this James would not permit. And the Prince, who had been traveling as the Chevalier de St. George, returned early in September, laden with gifts and all excited.

The following year, the wearied Clementina died. Toward the end, she and her husband had been on something like endearing terms again; and he remained so long on his knees before the *prie-dieu* in her bedchamber that he swooned, while the two princes, it is said, wept themselves into sickness.

The funeral was truly magnificent. For three days the body lay in state in the Church of the Holy Apostles, while the Papal Guards stood patiently by with drawn swords and the populace gaped. Then came the procession, in which no less than thirty-two cardinals marched, and the final ceremonies at St. Peter's. Thirteen thousand pounds of wax tapers were burned. And of course another medal was struck.

It is not likely that his mother had any profound influence on Charles. She was a sad, distant sort of person, enwrapped in her religious meditations, constantly praying or distributing charity. Unquestionably she was very fond of him, and he was probably fond of her. But he doubtless thought more often, as a boy will, of his games and sports. She gave him his Sobieski blood: that was her principal contribution.

We learn very little about Charles during the next two years. He continued to live in the Palazzo Muti, to play the violincello, to shoot and golf and box and fence, to study British history, and to listen to the wild plots which over-ambitious exiles were constantly concocting for the restoration of his family. His father, thinking to insure Spanish assistance when The Day came, proposed to marry him to the Infanta: but the Castilian court did not approve the match and it fell through. His father, it seems probable, had taken Charles into his confidence concerning the numerous webs of intrigue that were being woven about the palace and about Europe generally. The Prince was beginning to understand his unique position in the world, and to realize its possibilities. It was pleasant to be called Prince of Wales, to have people kneel to you and kiss your hand, to occupy an armchair when you called on the

Pope, to be the darling of Roman society and the hope of all Jacobites the world over; but it would be much more pleasant to occupy St. James' palace and ride through the streets of the city of London, while crowds cheered.

Rome was the most cosmopolitan city of the world at that time, the world's art center, too. It was at all seasons thronged with English visitors on the Grand Tour. Some were Whigs, some Jacobites. All, by British law, were forbidden to have any contact with James, the "Old Pretender." But there was no law against meeting Charles and Henry, charming lads, good sportsmen, good dancers, and highly popular in Roman society. Charles, particularly, was notable for his spirit. But even a prince could have too much spirit. James knew that. James, for all his belief in the divine right of kings, knew that no monarch could succeed who was not also a politician, and the essence of politics, as somebody—probably Macaulay—said, is compromise. Charles needed broadening travel. James arranged for it.

At the age of seventeen, again incognito, this time as the Count of Albany, Charles set out for a tour of the Italian capitals. With him were Murray, Sheridan, and twelve other persons, five of them in livery.

The Prince was received with enthusiasm at Bologna, at Parma, at Piacenza, at Genoa and Milan and Venice. In Venice, despite his incognito, royal honors were officially paid to him: and, as a result, Businiello, the Venetian Resident at London, was asked to pack his things and depart.

Official England, in fact, was extremely annoyed to hear that the "Young Pretender" was so well received wherever he went. Charles traveled through Padua and Ferrara to Florence. Before he arrived in Florence, the English envoy there, Mr. Fane, exerted himself in every way to prevent a royal reception and official recognition of the Prince. Fane finally succeeded, although his victory was purely technical. The Count of Albany was greeted and entertained with all the magnificence and enthusiasm that the Prince of Wales could possibly have been accorded.

Visits to Pucca, Pisa and Leghorn followed, and then Charles returned to Rome.

The trip had smoothed him out. His manners were better. Moreover, the receptions and dinners and balls had thrilled him. He was beginning to wonder: What would it be like to be the Prince of Wales *in England?*

The time was again propitious for such thoughts. After many idle years, Jacobite hopes were rising. In Scotland, where the Stuarts always had been esteemed and the Hanoverians disliked, a group of powerful noblemen and clan chiefs, in 1740, agreed to strike a blow for the restoration of the exiled line provided France would assist. Certain Englishmen, notably Lord Barrymore, Sir Watkin Wynn and Sir John Hinde Cotton, also expressed their willingness to assist when an invasion was made, although they would not, like the Scots, put the promise in writing. The project hung, then, on French assistance; and there was good reason to believe that this would be forthcoming. Louis the Fourteenth, who had originally recognized the Stuart claims, was dead; and his successor, Orléans, the Regent, was friendly to the House of Hanover. But he had been unseated when Louis the Fifteenth came of age. When Charles, Emperor of Austria, died, and Maria Theresa ascended to that throne, half the nations of Europe unchivalrously decided that this would be an excellent time to declare war on Austria and regain some of their lost lands. Poland, Bavaria, France and Spain launched the attack. But the leading spirit, and the one which would get the lion's share of the spoils, was France.

But England did not dare to permit France to win, so she sent troops to the continent to assist Maria Theresa and also to protect George's Hanover. If the Stuarts were to inspire another uprising, England would undoubtedly forget her altruism and withdraw her troops to defend her own island; and this would leave France a clear field on the Continent. So that, aside from family reasons, Louis was interested in having the Stuarts try again.

John Murray of Broughton, who had been appointed James'

Secretary of Scottish Affairs, was busy talking to Highland chiefs; Lord Semple was falsifying elaborately in Paris; and, in half the other capitals, agents of the exiled line whispered requests for gold and for men, while monarchs and ministers were making cautious, qualified promises. In Paris, the vacillating Cardinal Fleury died: he had been a believer in peace at any price. James hurried to the Vatican and managed to secure the appointment of Cardinal Tencin to the post; and Tencin, owing his hat to James, was naturally favorable to the Cause. James continued to write graceful letters all the time he was not saying his prayers, and the young princes, Charles and Henry, whispered with courtiers and learned many curious things.

It looked as though The Day were truly coming, as though a Stuart plan might actually succeed. James was assured that 1,500 French soldiers would land at Invernesshire and pick up the Frasers, whom Lord Lovat, their chief, had promised to call out; that 1,500 more French soldiers would land on the West Coast of Scotland and pick up the Macleans, the Macdonalds, the Camerons and a few other clans; and that these two groups, united, would take Edinburgh and then march south. Meanwhile, Marshal Saxe was to land 12,000 more French soldiers at a place a few days' march from London, take the capital, and then march north. The two armies would then unite, and would proclaim James, King of Great Britain and Ireland, Defender of the Faith, etc., the cannon would boom, the crowds would cheer, the masses would be celebrated, the medals struck, and everybody would be happy, except, possibly, German George.

James was not entirely taken in by this pretty picture. He had seen it before, in many forms, and always it had faded away like mist before the morning sun. He was tired. . . . They wanted him to send his first-born to France to accompany the London army; but careful James demanded first the certain news that troops were assembled at Dunkirk and that the fleet was prepared to move. He would not send Charles until he was reasonably sure that France meant what she was saying. Finally, the reluctant father was convinced; and, on January 8, 1744, James and Charles said farewell.

Charles was tall, sturdy, handsome, alight with enthusiasm. The Great Adventure was about to begin! James, thin, exquisitely dignified, too wise for his own good, gazed proudly but sadly upon the lad. An oval face, smooth and good-humored, a beautiful smile, James saw, a high forehead, large light-blue eyes, a small mouth and small pointed chin. It was a proud face, not strong, perhaps, but high-spirited, boyish, lovable. The Prince's light-brown hair, yellow at the tips, was combed down in front of his peruke. There were a few shy freckles on his nose.

"Sire, I go in search of three crowns. . . ."

James shook his head. Why did every lad think that these grand dreams were unique with him? Why was there no way to check youth, to keep it from harm, without spoiling it? James recalled his own youth . . . There were lackeys, no doubt, and even obsequious courtiers, who—behind his back—called him a dull old fool. But he had been as young as this lad once, and as self-confident. He had not forgotten the thrill that had shaken his very soul when, from the deck of a French ship, he had watched the shores of Scotland come nearer and nearer, at last. For all his letter writing and cautious councils, he had not forgotten the crash of musketry at Oudenarde; the way he had led in his horsemen again and again at Malplaquet, finally routing the Germans in one glorious dash; the way that sweating, pop-eyed swordsman, seeing the light blue ribbon of the Garter (James had disdainfully refused to cast it aside before the battle), had slashed at him, wounding him in the arm. . . . They might call him a dull, slow-scheming fool. But he, too, had known what youth is like. This boy of his was not the first person to feel its thrill.

But James could not forget, either, those crushing disappointments that fell upon him one by one, each more bitter than the one before. He could not forget how his spirit had been wearied and sapped and exhausted by the nagging pettiness of politics and the dreadful persistency of religious hate.

And now here was this boy of his—this brave, handsome boy—going out, probably, almost certainly to the same miserable fate. . . .

"I go in search of three crowns, Sire, and I will bring them back and lay them at Your Majesty's feet."

There were tears in James' eyes, and a monster lump in his throat, as he threw his arms around the lad's neck.

"Heaven forbid that all the crowns in the world should rob me of my son! Be careful, Carluccio. . . ."

English spies were thick about the palace, and it was important that none of them should learn that the Prince was departing. The affair was cleverly arranged. Charles rose next morning before dawn, and slipped out a side gate, where Murray, with a few servants and extra horses, was waiting in a post-chaise. It had been previously announced that the two princes were going hunting that day at Cisterna; but Henry was asleep when Charles tip-toed out of the palace, for even Henry did not share the secret.

The little cavalcade drove out of Rome. It was very cold, and Charles said he would prefer to ride in order to keep warm. So he got out of the carriage and mounted one of the extra horses; and Murray, as though to humor him, mounted another. Soon after this, Murray purposely fell into a ditch and, during the confusion, Charles, pretending sheer high spirits, galloped ahead while the servants assisted the tutor to his feet. One servant, a faithful Norman, accompanied Charles. At the Frascati crossroads they drew rein and, when the carriage party arrived, Charles complained that he had fallen and hurt his foot. The Norman nodded gravely, confirming the story.

"You had better get in here," said Murray from the coach.

"No, I would rather ride. I'll go ahead to Cisterna and rest there. Pray tell my brother that I will join him later in the day."

All this, of course, was meant for the servants. The Norman, however, remained with Charles. The Prince then changed his coat, hat and wig, and these his servant carried to Albano, and later to Cisterna. Meanwhile, Charles had been joined by another retainer, one Graham, about whom we know only that he was privy to the escape. The two then rode hard through the snow to Massa, to Genoa, and thence by boat—slipping past the English fleet—to Savona and to Antibes.

Henry, at Albano, had learned the truth about his brother's destination and plans, and helped to keep up the deception by sending wild fowl to friends in Rome, as coming from Charles after a lucky hunt.

For five days and five nights the Prince traveled so hard that he did not have an hour's sleep nor a single change of linen. Such haste was probably unnecessary: but it was characeristic of Charles, who, after all, was only twenty-three! He traveled first as a Neopolitan courier, wearing a courier's badge. After reaching Tuscany, he traveled as a Spanish officer, Don Biagio, on a passport obtained through Cardinal Aquaviva. He arrived in Paris on February 10.

CHAPTER THREE

Defeat of Common Sense

HE went quietly to the home of Lord Semple, his father's agent, and remained a fortnight. There was much dark whispering and letter writing, and the examination of many lists and reports. Then Charles traveled to Gravelines, in order to accompany the grand expedition. Fifteen thousand men had been promised. Seven thousand were actually furnished. But Marshal Saxe was in command, and there was then no better military leader in the world.

The spies, however, had done their work; and England, forewarned, protested to France against the presence of Charles in that nation, arrested numerous Roman Catholics and active Jacobites, confiscated all accumulations of arms and ammunition, and ordered out the fleet.

The British fleet, under Sir John Norris, frightened away the French fleet, and a tempest, nicely timed, did the rest. The glorious expedition returned ingloriously.

But Charles Edward Louis Philip Casimir Stuart was not to be so easily discouraged. He lingered, as the Chevalier Douglas, in Gravelines. Here he lived in the greatest secrecy, attended by only one retainer, never even quitting his rooms, while he tried again and again to pull the strings which would set another adventure in motion.

It was not to be. Marshal Saxe was dispatched to Flanders. The army at Dunkirk was used elsewhere. Too often had the weather, the "Protestant winds," interfered with Stuart expeditions: Versailles was frightened, perhaps superstitious. The promising voices trailed off into a series of vague, disconnected mutterings, out of which the sanguine Prince got the impression (and maybe it was correct) that, if he set forth of his own accord and showed France what he could do, he might get some real assistance later. Thirty years afterwards, Benjamin Franklin received much the same assurances on behalf of the United States. But Franklin got men and munitions. Charles didn't.

This is rushing ahead of our story. After all attempts to renew the invasion had failed, Charles returned to Paris. He desired quiet and secrecy, so he took a house in Montmartre, which celebrated hill was at that time a sleepy suburb. Here he was virtually a prisoner, moping discontentedly, while the French court tried to make up its mind what, if anything, to do, and the Jacobites wrung despairing hands.

It is important to understand something of Prince Charles' thoughts at this period.

First, he was a Stuart, a type that is not bred any more. He believed that his family had been commissioned by God, Himself, to command a certain portion of God's territory on earth. Besides that, he believed that his father was *legally* entitled to the British throne.

Then, he was youthful. His twenty-fourth birthday anniversary came and went while he was living in that quiet little place in Montmartre. He was in wonderful health. He didn't see how he could fail. Why, all he planned to do was to conquer three kingdoms!

His father, tall and mournful, endlessly writing letters from his gloomy Roman palace, was not so optimistic. James had failed many times. But Charles was only beginning. Moreover, Charles had something his melancholy father lacked: he had Sobieski blood.

This we all know: that the things a person wants very much to believe he *will* believe, howsoever illogical they may be. Charles wanted to believe that France would help him and that the people of England and Scotland would be delighted to have him appear. He had been trained to believe this, just as he had been trained to believe in his special mission on earth as a descendant of Robert the Bruce and Allan the Stewart. The court of the Pretender, at Rome, ruled nothing save a few servants; but, excepting James himself, it was a strikingly optimistic court. And they had all told Charles that Scotland and England would welcome his coming: some of them said this because they were courtiers and made it a professional rule to tell princelings what they might be supposed to want most to hear; some of them were fanatics and believed it themselves. Charles believed it! He believed that it was only necessary for him to land in the Scottish Highlands, to unfurl his banner, and to explain the purpose of his visit: then, he supposed, the Scots would appear by thousands and offer him their swords; and that, as soon as he marched down into England, the people would hail him as their deliverer.

"I will go," he announced, "if I have only a single footman with me."

His father, who had common sense, objected. The Earl Marischal and others, similarly afflicted, told Charles that he was talking gibberish. Charles laughed. All that was needed, he thought, was nerve, and nerve he had aplenty. These old fellows were afraid. This letter writing and whispering, this counting of troops and watching for openings, was a silly business at best—a slow, bothersome business—always uncertain, often degrading. James had been whispering and writing letters for forty years; they were excellent letters, too, and serious whispers, but they wouldn't win a royal crown.

Barrymore, leader of the English Jacobites, was in the Tower of London, a prisoner. The Scottish Association agreed that nothing could be done at the time and Murray of Broughton was instructed to notify the eager young man in Montmartre not to appear. Somehow the letter went astray. Much later, Murray said he had done everything he could to prevent Charles from sailing; but, when he said this, Murray was trying to save his own neck at any cost, and it is quite possible, even probable, that he was lying.

Whatever the case, Charles was determined to go. Rutledge and Walsh, merchants of Nantes, fitted out for him the ships *Elizabeth* and *Doutelle*. He borrowed money, pawned his jewels, gathered around him a few desperate noblemen and adventurers, wrote to his father, and weighed anchor. France, he still believed, would help those who helped themselves, and he proposed to help himself—to three kingdoms.

"Let what will happen, the stroke is struck," he wrote in a letter to James, "and I have taken a firm resolution to conquer or to die, and to stand my ground as long as I have a man remaining with me."

This was on July the 13th, 1745.

Aboard the *Elizabeth*, the larger of the two craft, were 1,500 muskets and 1,800 broadsword blades. Aboard the *Doutelle* were the Prince and his staff. The Prince was not merely incognito now but actually in disguise; he was dressed as a young clergyman, a commoner, and it was given out that he had been born abroad of Scottish parents and was eager to see the Highlands for the first time, and to hear the Gaelic tongue; his companions addressed him as "Monsieur l'Abbe."

This was the army with which our hero purposed to conquer the British Isles: Sheridan, his tutor, already mentioned; the Rev. George Kelly, a non-juring priest who had been mixed up in the Atterbury plot,—one of the many unsuccessful schemes to restore the Stuarts—and had broken jail and skipped to the continent to save his skin; the Marquis of Tullibardine, oldest member of the house of Murray and therefore entitled to be Duke of Athole, but deprived of this title because of his participation in the uprising of 1715; Buchanan, a sort of messenger or aide-de-camp; Aeneas Macdonald, a well-connected Scot from Edinburgh; Sir John Macdonald, a gentleman of fortune, who held a captain's commission in the Spanish army; and one O'Sullivan and Sir Francis Strickland, courtiers.

It was not an impressive group. Sheridan, an Irishman, was aged and not military. Kelly was a minister of the Gospel, albeit a lively one. Tullibardine, who was more than sixty years old and looked at least eighty, suffered excruciatingly from rheumatism. Sir John Macdonald was seldom sober. Aeneas Macdonald was a banker and, as it later developed, a weakling and a traitor. O'Sullivan, Strickland and Buchanan had nothing to risk and everything to gain.

Now people who would invade Great Britain must bear in mind always her celebrated navy. Almost invariably there's a British war-ship in the offing. This time it was a sloop-of-war, the *Lion,* which, upon sighting these suspicious craft, moved out and opened fire. There was a spirited battle in which the *Doutelle,* a much smaller boat, took no part. The Prince, wildly excited, demanded that the *Doutelle* go to the aid of the *Elizabeth.* But Captain Walsh was not taking any chances with the life of a scion of the blood royal, so the *Doutelle* remained on one side, at a safe distance, and watched.

They fought all day, until both captains had been killed, along with many of the chief officers, sixty-four members of the *Elizabeth's* crew, and forty-four members of the crew of the *Lion;* and more than 250 in all had been wounded. Then the *Elizabeth* staggered back to France, and the *Lion* to England, and the little *Doutelle* was left alone.

This was four days out, and a bad beginning. All the arms had been lost, and they had cost a pretty penny and much trouble: Walsh had obtained them from the French Minister of War under a false statement that they were intended for use on his own plantations in Martinique. Charles was advised to turn back. But a Stuart, he thought, should never retreat. So the *Doutelle* sailed on for Scotland.

In France, the Earl Marischal was doubtless shaking his head and muttering, "Damned little fool. . . ." In Rome, a gaunt "King Here" strode up and down the dim corridors, worrying about his beloved Carluccio. . . . The Pope and the Cardinals prayed piously, but hardly with hope. Versailles was not quite certain what to say and what to do, so it did and said nothing. As for England, she did not even know that the Prince had sailed: England was never invaded with so little ostentation.

The battle had taken place off the Lizard. This extraordinary expedition now turned north, passed between England and Ireland and, on July the 23rd, landed on the bleak and lonely island of Eriska, one of the Hebrides, between the islands of Barra and South Ulst, off the West Coast of Scotland. The spot has since been known as Coilleagh a' Phrionnsa, the

Prince's Strand; but at the time it probably had no name at all. It was as remote from civilization as any part of central Africa. The day anchor was dropped, Tullibardine saw an eagle hovering over the ship and promptly took this to be a good omen. However, no eagle could diminish by one iota the ferocity of Scottish weather. A violent storm arose as though in greeting to this royal visitor, and a most appropriate greeting, too. Tullibardine went below with a severe attack of gout. The others landed to stretch their legs.

Fortunately they were able to find shelter from the storm. One Angus, a fisherman and a subject of the Macdonald of Clanranald, who owned this island, opened his hut to them, and they clustered around the hospitality of his peat fire. Charles at last was "seeing his people" at close range. Yet even he could scarcely have been enthusiastic about this hut. Picturesque though it was, it was also uncomfortable. There was no stove, no fireplace, and no chimney. The fire was built in the center of the floor (or where the floor would have been if there had *been* a floor) and the smoke got out any way it could. Angus didn't mind. But Prince Charles found it disconcerting, and he was obliged, from time to time, to stick his head out of the door (or rather out of the place where the door would have been if there had *been* a door) to breathe. This annoyed the host. "The de'il tak' the mon! Is he no' able t' keep still at all?" Charles smiled patriotically, and blinked. It would be a story to tell when he was the acknowledged suzerain of all this land.

The island of Eriska, remote from England, was in the heart of the district presumably devoted to the Stuart cause. Hereabouts were the Macleans, the Macleods, the Camerons, and the various Macdonald septs, or clan divisions; and not far away were the Grants, the Frasers, the Stewarts, the Chisholms, and other clans whose chiefs were listed as friendly to James. These Highland chiefs paid tribute to the reigning king in London only in the most casual manner, if at all. Tucked away in the black wilderness which had harbored their forefathers for uncountable generations, and which had kept them safe from the invasions of Romans, English and Lowland Scots, they still conducted themselves very much as they had done in the days of The Bruce and earlier. That is, they ruled their clansmen with an iron hand; and the clansmen, gigantic children, obeyed their chiefs in everything. James the Second, grandfather of Prince Charles, who had caused the original trouble, had been popular among the Highlanders, and they were still warm toward his family. There were other reasons, too.

Scotland, after many hundreds of years of bitter warfare with England, had given the bigger nation a line of handsome, dignified kings. But England, after a few generations, had deposed the Scottish kings, replacing them first with a chilly Dutchman and later with a couple of stupid Germans. The Scots were hurt: their national pride was involved. They would be badly governed in either case, but they preferred to be badly governed by fellow-countrymen.

In addition, the English government, by the shameful Act of Union, in 1703, had virtually purchased Scotland and was now inclined to make its bargain behave. There were still patriots in the hills, and in the Lowlands too, who remembered those wagonloads of gold—legitimate Scottish gold it was—sent down to Edinburgh to buy the consolidation votes. Ignoble Scottish noblemen had been bribed with Scottish money. Small wonder England wasn't popular! And there were other grievances: the treatment of the Scottish members of Parliament; the treatment of the Darien Company adventurers, and the treacherous, hypocritical attitude of King William's government in this connection; the appalling Glencoe massacre; the Malt Tax; and sundry attempts to curb the power of the clans and to stamp out the ancient clan system.

These things should have decided the clansmen of the Highlands in favor of Prince Charles. And, indeed, most of them probably wished him good luck. But when it came to risking their lands, their families, their titles, their estates, and their reputations, not to mention their lives—that was something different. Many of them had promised to fight if a French force were landed. But what could they do alone? The Highlanders were a small percentage of the population of Scotland, and Scotland had but one-sixth of the population of England and not one-twentieth of the wealth. They faced every conceivable disadvantage. They knew, as James and the Earl Marischal and the other wise gentlemen knew, that Charles had been nothing less than a madman when he insisted upon sailing for the West Coast.

He was so informed by the first person he interviewed in Scotland. This island of Eriska was part of the Macdonald of Clanranald's estate. His oldest son, Young Clanranald, shared the active leadership of the sept with his uncle, Alexander Macdonald of Boisdale. Boisdale was near-by. Prince Charles summoned him. Young Clanranald was absent at the time, but Alexander Macdonald promptly answered the summons.

The old laird told Prince Charles exactly what the Prince ought to have been prepared to hear. Not only did he refuse to summon his vassals to arms or advise his nephew to do so, but he said that he felt it to be his duty to warn other chieftains against any participation in this rash undertaking.

"Go home," he implored.

"I have come home," said Charles.

Charles, who changed his names and titles with the greatest ease, was now the Baron of Renfrew. He begged and pleaded in his best manner; and he must have been singularly appealing. But Boisdale was hard-headed and persisted in his refusal. Finally he rowed away, frowning gravely and shaking his head.

Still Charles would not give up. He sailed from Eriska and went to the mainland, dropping anchor in beautiful Lochnanaugh, a fjord surrounded by more of Clanranald's territory. From here he sent messengers to Sir Alexander Macdonald of Sleat and the Macleod of Macleod, commanding these chiefs to raise their men. He sent Aeneas Macdonald to summon his brother, the Macdonald of Kinloch-Moidart. He caused to be erected on the deck of the *Doutelle* a red-and-white striped awning supported by poles; and under this he spread a feast—shortbread, gingerbread, main bread, oat bread, wheat bread, partridge, venison, drake, capon, minced collops with butter, and other meats and delicacies, as well as liquid refreshments—brandy and claret, whiskey and usquabaugh, great beakers of ale and beer, and bottles of muscatel, malmsey, champagne, hippocras, canary, sack. . . . Then he issued further invitations.

Soon the waters of Lochnanaugh were cut by numerous small craft and if you had stood on the shore that summer's day, you might have perceived the blue bonnets and eagle feathers of many wild Scots moving about under the awning. The Macdonald of Kinloch-Moidart arrived, pledged himself and his clan, and was sent off to summon John Murray of Broughton, the Duke of Perth, and Donald of Lochiel, active chief of the Clan Cameron. Soon afterwards the Macdonald of Keppoch, the Macdonald of Scottus, Young Clanranald, the Macdonald of Glenaladale, and other personages came to pay their respects. They ate and drank, and discussed in whispers among themselves this turn of events.

Presently Young Clanranald was summoned below decks. This nobleman, a beefy-faced, indolent young fellow, was one of the most powerful clan leaders in the Highlands and was considered a pivot of the Great Clan Colla, children of Donald. No fiercer fighters existed. The Macdonalds were broken up into many septs under many leaders, but they were one in the matter of courage and martial spirit. It was of the utmost importance to Prince Charles, therefore, that Young Clanranald pledge allegiance and summon his clan.

The youth was gone about three hours. The other guests must have watched his face closely, when he returned to the deck and to the brandy. But they learned nothing, for Young Clanranald had not yet made up his mind.

Half an hour later, there appeared, according to one who was present, "a tall youth of a most agreeable aspect, in a plain black coat, with a plain shirt, not very clean, and a cambrick stock fixed with a plain silver buckle, a plain hatt with a canvas string haveing one end fixed to one of his coat buttons; he had black stockings and brass buckles in his shoes."

This person was introduced as a young clergyman visiting Scotland for the first time. He smiled, nodded, had a drink, and started to chat with one of the Highlanders, asking many questions about the kilt.

Soon he was deep in argument with his guests. One after another they refused to take any part in an uprising unsupported by foreign troops. It was folly, they said. They loved their rightful king, but they must not be expected to bring disgrace and disaster upon themselves and their clansmen merely for the purpose of making a gesture which could not possibly have any real effect. One after another they urged him to return to France, to obtain French assistance, and then to ask again for their own aid: he would learn, if he did this, that no prince had subjects more faithful and more willing to die in his cause. But to stay would not be courage, only suicide.

"I have come for a crown or a coffin," said Charles.

He was fighting a strange fight now, pitting his charm against the sagacity of these oaken, silent men. Prince Charles at this time was an uncommonly attractive young man, just six feet tall, built like the true athlete he was—"he had a body built for war," Lord Elcho wrote—broad-shouldered, narrow-hipped, long-legged, aristocratic of countenance, light-haired, blue-eyed. . . . He was talking to men in whom the ancient notions of chivalry were still strong. For these men, Prince Charles had an extraordinary appeal. His Quixotic mission, his high-spirited manner, his youth, and his cool courage, fascinated them.

He was aided, too, by the ancient tradition of hospitality, which is nowhere stronger than in the Highlands. There, in the old days, you might stab a man in the back; you might violate his wife, shoot his sons, drive out his daughters, burn his house and lay waste to his lands; yet nobody but his own kinsmen would think any the worse of you. But if he had thrown himself upon your hospitality and you did not receive and protect him and give him the best your house afforded in every way—then you were the lowest of the low. It was the violation of this tradition which made the crime of Macbeth so abhorrent. Killing a king was no breach of ethics in the ancient days in Caledonia: indeed, it was done by members of the best families. But killing a king who was also one's guest was an unspeakable barbarity.* The Prince had entered the Highlands, which was peculiarly the property of the clan chieftains, and had thrown himself upon their hospitality. They could realize that his coming had been folly, but they could not deny that he was, in a sense, their guest, even though uninvited; and the gentleman who hung back must always have this upon his conscience.

Nevertheless, they clung desperately to their reason, which they felt melting under this young man's smile. They were tempted sorely. One of them, a mere boy, a brother of the Macdonald of Kinloch-Moidart, watched and listened with wide eyes. Ranald Macdonald could not understand how any Highland gentleman could hold back when his rightful prince—and such a bonnie laddie too—was calling for assistance. Himself, he longed to draw claymore and fall upon all the Stuarts' foes.

Charles was almost discouraged but, when he observed this lad, he showed himself an adroit politician. Turning from the others, and addressing himself directly to Ranald, he exclaimed:

"*You*, at least, will not desert me?"

Ranald, who up to this time had taken no part in the conversation, cried passionately, "Not while I have a breath left in my body! Not if I'm the only man with you!"

That settled it. After such an outburst, the exuberance of the Highlanders could remain pent-up no longer but burst like an overstrained dam. Common sense was drowned. Clanranald pledged himself with all his men and all his influence, and the others followed his example.

But there were many personages yet to be won over. One

* We know nowadays, however, that Macbeth did not stab the King at night, in Macbeth's own castle. He met him fortuitously, on a hunting trip, outside the Macbeth lands, and killed him with a sword. The laird had excellent claims to the throne, too, and it was a legitimate enough murder, as murders went in those times. But Shakespeare, to whom this information was not available, followed the accepted legend, and so Macbeth has always been condemned.

was Sir Alexander Macdonald of Sleat, whose ancestors had been the Lords of the Isles, and who was himself one of the most powerful chiefs in Scotland and capable of calling more than 1,000 claymores into the field. Another was the Macleod of Macleod, chief of that numerous clan. Another was Simon, Lord Lovat, chief of the Frasers, an aged, villainous fellow, whom we shall meet later. Still another was Young Lochiel, to whom all the Camerons paid homage.

Sir Alexander not only refused to join the Prince but later even took the field against him, although, in all the original plotting, he had been set down as one of the most certain adherents of the Stuart cause. The Macleod, whose assistance had likewise been regarded as virtually certain, also refused to summon his clan.

Lord Lovat always played a double game, and was dickering now for a dukedom; he sent promises but no men; he wanted to see what the uprising amounted to before he committed himself.

Young Lochiel, perhaps the most important of all because of his influence over the other chieftains and the widespread respect in which he was held throughout Scotland, finally called upon the Prince at the little farmhouse at Borrodale, where Charles was now established with a bodyguard of Macdonald gentlemen. Lochiel's brother, the Cameron of Fassfern, had met the Prince and knew his charm, and he warned Donald not to go. "You won't be able to resist him," he told the chieftain. But Young Lochiel went, not for the purpose of listening to arguments but rather with the intention of persuading Charles to quit Scotland until a more propitious day for an uprising. He was determined, in any event, not to call out the Camerons.

Young Lochiel was a middle-aged, quiet man,* well-educated, amiable, fair-minded, rather more civilized and less war-

* The epithet, "Young," as it is used in the clan system, does not refer to age. It means oldest son of the chief, heir-apparent of the suzerainty, a sort of crown prince of a clan. Sometimes, of course, the heir *was* youthful, like the Young Clanranald of this period. But Young Lochiel was in his forties when Charles landed; his father was an exile in France, and a semi-invalid, and Donald was practically chief of the Camerons.

like than most of his compatriots in the hills, but no less a spirited gentleman and a man of honor. He could call out about 700 or 800 men from his own clan; but the prestige of his support was worth more than this. He had been one of the signers of the Association, five years earlier; but had pledged himself to support an uprising only if assisted by French troops.

For some hours Charles applied his blandishments in vain. Donald begged him to return to France and come back only with a force sufficient to guarantee the Highlanders at least a fighting chance of success.

At last Charles said, "In a few days, with the few friends that I have, I will erect the royal standard and proclaim to the people of Britain that Charles Stuart is come to claim the crown of his ancestors, to win it, or to perish in the attempt. Lochiel, whom my father has told me was our firmest friend, may stay at home and learn from the news papers the fate of his prince."

This was too much for a grandson of Sir Ewan. Out came the claymore. "*No!* I'll share your fate, and so shall every man over whom nature or fortune has given me any power!"

So romance again defeated common sense, and the good-looking young madman gained ground every day. The Macdonald of Glengarry was caught in an hour of comparative sobriety, and agreed, in writing, to call out his clan. He never took the field himself, and his oldest son, Young Glengarry, being in France at the time, was made a prisoner by the English when he started back; but the second son, Angus, and a kinsman, Lochgarry, commanded the men.

Out of nothing, therefore, Charles had made a fairly promising beginning. Much more, of course, remained to be done. Even if all the men pledged to him appeared, he would not have an army one-twentieth the size of the force he ought to have before venturing down into the Low Country. But at least he would not have to go south alone. And the followers he did have were fighters from their brogues to their bonnets.

It was agreed that the royal standard should be raised at Glenfinnan, not far from Borrodale, on the morning of Monday, August 19.* Charles wrote letters and proclamations galore, and messengers flew in all directions. The British government, suspecting that something was wrong because of the continued silence of their Paris spies, offered a reward of £30,000 to any person who captured or caused to be captured either the Young Pretender or the Old Pretender dead or alive.

Meantime, Charles was burning his bridges behind him. The *Doutelle*—his navy—sailed out of Lochnanaugh and went privateering. The fiery cross was carried by night over the hills, from glen to glen, summoning the clansmen to war. Women who were to weep later, bent over their sewing: they were making white cockades for the men, for a white rose was the Stuart emblem. Broadswords and Lochaber axes were sharpened. Target covers were tightened and polished. Smiths were kept busy at their anvils, and in dozens of tiny huts bearded men prepared for battle.

* There is some difference of opinion among authorities as to the exact date. I have accepted Blaikie's, as given in his "Itinerary," which is generally acknowledged to be most accurate.

CHAPTER FOUR

The Gathering of the Clans

IN the remote mists of pre-history (so tradition goes) there moved out of the region around Mesopotamia, the supposed cradle of the human race, a tribe of savage men and women. They drifted down to Egypt, and settled there for a time. Probably they were not very welcome, but the Egyptians apparently did not know how to get rid of them without causing trouble, so the reigning Pharaoh kept them quiet by giving in marriage to the chieftain of the tribe one of his own daughters, whose name was Scotus. The men of the tribe came to be known by the Egyptians, therefore, as Scots. In time they drifted away from Egypt, crossed northern Africa, and entered the Spanish peninsula. Still later, taking boats, they sailed to Ireland. Here some of them remained. Others, still feeling the wanderlust, crossed to the northern part of the island of Britain. There they settled at length, fighting anybody who came within reasonable fighting distance; or, when there was nobody else to fight, instituting grim little wars among themselves just to keep in practice.

The Scots were altogether unique. There had never been anything like them before; there has never been anything like them since. The only possible analogy is the Indian tribes of early America, persons the wild Scots (as they were called to distinguish them from the comparatively civilized Lowlanders) resembled in many respects. The rest of the world changed their customs and costumes, but the Highlanders remained the same. They still wore the kiltie, the ancient garb of their race. When the rest of the world passed on from feudalism, that system remained in full force in the Highlands. The rest of the world went to war only now and again, when the men were too bored to remain at home: the Highlanders kept on fighting as a matter of habit.

The Highlands of Scotland are lonely, even now. Splashed with rich, heavy browns and reds and deep greens, yet they are cold and dreary. Most of the year the mountain tops, at least, are covered with snow. Their sides are clothed with somber pine forests and with the curious heather—stiff, ankle-deep herbage, purple in summer and black, or a very dark brown, the rest of the year—which grows, irregularly massed, in the most unexpected places. All the countryside rolls; but the roll is restless and never amiable. It is not the roll of the pleasant English countryside. It is not the roll of Piedmont, with which Prince Charles was familiar. It is sullen, strong, and awesome.

Between the rolls, tucked away so adroitly that you do not see them until you are almost in their midst, are incredibly picturesque little ravines. Down the middle of each splashes a mountain stream—clear, bitterly cold, very earnest—it flashes high in silver splendor, then swings under crouching rocks, and emerges again glittering furiously. It worms its way in and out with rapid certainty. It pauses momentarily in a small, stern pool. Then it bursts out again in liquid fury, lashing itself into bright foam, tearing and ripping downward like a company of charging fanatics armed with bright swords. The roll of the ground is less sullen in these spots, though the springy moss is very thick, and dark almost to blackness; but even these sheltered nooks are cold and lonely.

The Highlands of Scotland brood always, seeming to nurse some ancient grudge against the race of men. They have no lighter moments. Even the lakes, in themselves pretty and shiny and small, become brow-knitted, glowering, when the hills hurl dark shadows across them and the clouds push past very low. These lakes, almost without exception, run east and west between the east-and-west hill ranges; and form alleyways down which the wet winds from the sea disport themselves so that, in the north and west of Scotland, it rains or snows most of the time. And always there is a mist which, if not directly about you, is writhing around the nearby hills and biding its time for an opportunity to obliterate the landscape from your sight. To this country came Charles Edward Stuart, who was born and reared in sunny Italy.

The time and the place, then, were set. Prince Charles was punctual, as always. He went to Glenfinnan with high hopes: he expected to see the valley alive with gayly dressed warriors and the glitter of steel: he expected a sea of blue bonnets, eagle feathers, and white cockades, and a loud rattle of scabbarded broadswords. When he stepped off the boat at the eastern end of Loch Eil and, accompanied by his bodyguard of Macdonalds, hurried to the rendezvous, he was already hearing the shouts of enthusiastic soldiers prepared to follow him wherever he went, to fight for him, and if necessary to die for him. He was already gazing proudly down upon a far-stretching mass of faces, and thrilling to the response of this "old and haughty nation proud in arms."

He found, instead only a deep, deserted glen, flanked by dark hills, peopled only by rocks and trees, and absolutely silent. No warriors were there, no banners, no lifted swords. Not even the song of a pease-weep assailed his expectant ears. Not even a red deer slipped away on his approach.

Glenfinnan is a desolate, depressing place, extraordinarily beautiful, but infinitely lonely. Loch Shiel, smooth as glass and blue as a baby's eyes, gleams with austere coldness, and the River Finnan leaps away over unresponsive rocks toward the sea. The hills roll down like the chest muscles of a giant: the clouds hang low: and Ben Bhreac, lifting a huge, white half-pineapple, sullenly blocks the west.

For the first time, Charles seems to have been almost discouraged, if not frightened. His own few companions, the scanty bodyguard, a group of scared, miserable peasants—these were the only persons with him now; and he was in a strange wild country, immeasurably different from any place he had ever before seen.

Two hours he waited. The loose crags hung precariously on the hillsides, as though poised to charge down upon him at any moment. The flawless lake glittered like unmeltable ice. The clouds slunk scowling past.

Two hours he waited, doubting, wondering. Then—blessed sound!—came the skirl of bagpipes. The Prince sprang to his feet. They had not deceived him! They were coming! His head went up again, his eyes flashed, and his hand gripped the hilt of his claymore as he listened to the marching song of the approaching Camerons.

Over the hills they came, seven hundred strong, moving in two columns with the pipers in front. Sporrans swinging, pistols clinking, Donald of Lochiel, surrounded by his kinsmen and principal gentlemen, advanced to pay homage to his Prince.

And Donald had more to offer than his own men. Already there were prisoners for, although the standard was not yet raised, first blood had been drawn. The previous day, the Prince was informed, two companies of Scots Royal had been seen marching from Fort Augustus, where the Governor had heard that there was some trouble in the heart of Lochaber, toward Fort William, less than twenty miles from Glenfinnan. A party of Keppoch Macdonalds, under Tiendrish, had opened fire upon them. The Highlanders were scarcely a dozen in number, but they were all crack deerstalkers and they knew the art of guerrilla warfare. Captain Scott and his fellow officers could not determine their numbers. His men were nervous, seeing nothing but smoke on the hills, hearing nothing but the bagpipes and the steady relentless crack of muskets. This was at the bridge over the Spean, about eight miles from Fort William.

Scott ordered a retreat. The Highlanders kept along with the column, remaining in the hills on either side, never exposing themselves, never missing a good chance to shoot. The pipers blew up bravely. The warriors shouted their war-cries. And in time, the regulars began to run.

Other Macdonalds, in small parties, came at the sound of the firing. The woods were filled with them. At the end of Loch Lochy the chief himself, stout Keppoch, marched up with some twenty men, and soon afterwards Young Lochiel, with still more men, appeared. The Hanoverian commander knew when he had enough and surrendered.

No Highlanders had been killed or wounded, and the regulars' loss was comparatively small. But the effect of this skirmish on the spirits of the men was marvelous.

So the Standard was raised. It must have been one of the strangest sights in the history of the world. This bleak, remote glen, so spectacular, so awful, swarming with tartan and bright steel; these medieval chieftains, tight-mouthed, grim-visaged; these frightened, staring peasants; the bewildered prisoners; the adventurers from the Continent; and this handsome, smiling Prince. . . .

Old Tullibardine, with much ceremony, unfurled the Stuart Standard.* The clansmen shouted madly—shouted strange, enthusiastic things in Gaelic—and threw their blue bonnets into the air until, as one witness put it, you could hardly see the sky. The Prince smiled that smile which had started a war. The Day had come.

Silence momentarily descended upon Glenfinnan when Tullibardine, supported on each side by a servant—for he was too feeble to stand alone—started to read from an impressive document. The clansmen listened intently, though not one out of fifty of them had the faintest idea of what it was all about, the proclamation being in English which they did not understand. Tullibardine made known to the whole world that James VIII of Scotland and III of England, King, Defender of the Faith, etc., was prepared to reassert his rights to the throne of his ancestors, to reëstablish his family in its legitimate glory, and to relieve his suffering people from the oppressive yoke

* There is some doubt as to the nature of this flag. Home says it was white, blue and red silk. Other writers describe it as bearing various legends—"Tandem Triumphans," "No Union," etc. But Keltie, Scott and others say it was without any motto, and there seems no evidence that there was woven in it a crown and a coffin. In his "Manual of Heraldry," Francis J. Grant, W.S., the Rothesay Herald, writes: "THE ROYAL BANNER, or, as it is more popularly and incorrectly called, the 'royal standard,' contains the four quarterings of the royal arms. No subject may fly this flag unless the king is personally present." The King was not present at Glenfinnan, but Charles, as Prince Regent, was his official representative. However, it is not likely that the banner Grant describes (which he does not say was the one used at Glenfinnan) is the same.

fastened upon them these many years by foreign tyrants. Tullibardine told the whole world (while the lackeys supported him) that once again the Scottish nation would enjoy its ancient rights; once again would the descendants of Robert the Bruce and Allan the Norman, rule perfectly over a perfect people, prosperous, peaceful, and happy, and proud in the possession of honor and freedom.

Then Tullibardine read an official commission of regency From Rome, James had appointed his older son, the Prince of Wales, to be Prince Regent of Scotland, England and Ireland All loyal subjects of the rightful King were enjoined to obey Charles as such: all others were warned to be prepared for the consequences of disobedience. Charles was also appointed commander-in-chief of all James' armies and navy. The whole army cheered and threw their bonnets into the air again when they had this interpreted to them; the navy was out privateering.

Charles himself now stepped forward and made a brief and pretty speech, modestly promising wonders. When he had finished, he smiled. Up went the bonnets again, the swords were raised, and lusty shouts rang through Glenfinnan until it seemed as though they would shake the crags from their place and bring the mountains tumbling down into the lake.

The Prince raised his hand, after a time, and there was silence. The Prince turned to one of the Hanoverian prisoner and, with that sense of the dramatically correct which he always possessed and rarely failed to exercise at an opportunity exclaimed:

"Go, sir, to your general! Say what you have seen, and add that I am coming to give him battle!"

It was exactly what the Highlanders loved most to hear They likened him to The Bruce because of it, and swore that they would follow a leader like that to the ends of the earth.

Still from the hills the bagpipes were sounding. The Macdonalds were coming. Keppoch brought three hundred. Glengarry the Younger and Lochgarry brought three hundred more The MacIan of Glencoe had one hundred and fifty, still thirst for revenge. A Macleod gentleman appeared with a few followers and formally renounced his allegiance to his chief who had refused to fight for Charles Stuart. One hundred Grants came from Glenmorriston. Appine and Ardsheil headed two hundred and fifty Stewarts. Clanranald and Kinloch-Moidart marched in with their warriors. It was a great day.

CHAPTER FIVE

Over the Rubicon

MEANWHILE there was consternation in the South News traveled slowly in those days; and so accustomed were the people to false reports of Stuart invasions that it now required a certain persistency of rumor to ge them frightened.

Frightened they became, however, when the news was confirmed that Prince Charles had landed on the West Coast and the fiery cross was being carried over the hills. London officia circles were much agitated. Edinburgh, upon which the invader would probably make his first real attack, was a scene o vast excitement. All sorts of stories were circulated: the Young Pretender had ten thousand men under him, twenty thousand fifty thousand, as many as you cared to name. He had cannon by the hundreds, and horses galore. He had French troops and Spanish troops, Russian troops, Scandinavians, Poles. Louis was back of him, and so was the Pope, and the Czar, and so too, o course, were the Devil and all his infernal associates and assistants. He was going to burn all the towns, cities and villages kill all the men, rape all the women, blow up the Protestant churches, and in short lay waste to fair Scotland, and afterwards turn England upside down.

So said some persons, who insisted that they were well informed. Others, quite as certain of their information, crie loudly that the Pretender had under him no more than scanty, miserable group of savages, that he had already bee defeated and made captive, or that he had not even dared t land. There was absolutely nothing to worry about, these persons said, afterwards taking the precaution to conceal the valuables.

The Jacobites came out in the open now and with glee drank healths to James and to Charles. Some of them got very drunk and told everybody about the wonderful things the Prince was going to do and the terrible things that would befall the House of Brunswick and all its adherents.

George the Second was visiting his beloved Herrenhausen, and the government was being managed, or mismanaged, by the puffy, pompous and altogether preposterous Duke of Newcastle, and by a body of bewildered personages known collectively as the Council of Regency. Much of the army was fighting on the Continent. The forces stationed in Scotland and immediately available consisted of Hamilton's and Gardiner's dragoons, the two greenest horse regiments in the service; three and a half battalions of infantry, two and a half of them newly raised; the Scots Royal, who were much more likely to fight for the Stuart than against him; and a few irregular companies recently formed to fill up gaps in the regiments in Flanders—in all, about 3,000 men.

These fellows were under the command of Sir John Cope, a middle-aged officer who had many powerful political friends and few enemies. Cope had been in Scotland less than a year at this time, and he knew more about bowing from the hips than about keeping the Highlanders in order. He was "easy, well-bred and affable," according to one who knew him, but was not overburdened with brains.

When he heard about the uprising, Cope was probably only annoyed by the thought that this business would take him away from his social duties for a while. He proposed to his superiors in London that he gather together all the available troops and march north with them, thus putting a prompt end to whatever troubles might be brewing. It was a soldierly resolution. It was also proof that Cope knew little or nothing about the Highlands.

However, in London, where even less was known about the Highlands, the plan sounded good; and Cope was authorized to carry it into effect. The dragoons were called in from forage, the foot soldiers were assembled, there was a great flapping of flags and beating of drums, and the army of the King marched north. They carried much baggage. They also carried some 1,000 additional muskets, in the hope that recruits would fall into line along the way.

The people of Edinburgh watched them go, smooth and scarlet, thrillingly aclank and bright with brass; and began to feel comfortable again. Any day now, they thought, would come the news of a great victory easily won, and soon afterwards Johnny Cope and his gallant men would be marching back in glory, the presumptuous Pretender captive in their midst.

But things went badly with Cope from the beginning. The residents of the countryside through which he passed, preferred their homes to the dangers of dubious battlefields, and there were no recruits at all. In addition, it was found very difficult to move such an army into the Highlands. Cope left Hamilton's dragoons to defend Edinburgh, and Gardiner's to defend the Fort at Stirling. At least, he did not try to take cavalry up into those hills! His purpose was to march straight to Fort Augustus, the second of three fortresses the government had stretched across northern Scotland to keep the clans in order; and from there to operate east or west as conditions suggested. He believed that by strengthening these forts he could make it impossible for the clansmen, howsoever active and bloodthirsty, to descend upon the lowlands of the South. It was a very simple plan: but then, Cope was a simple soldier.

At Crief he decided to send back most of the superfluous muskets and some other baggage. But he still had far too much. Once in the hills, he not only could not look for recruits but found a population distinctly antagonistic. They gave him false directions, stole his horses at night, delayed and insulted him in every manner possible. Cope was a worried and discouraged man when, stopping at a tiny inn at Dalnacaroch one evening, he encountered Captain Sweetenham, the officer Charles had sent south with a challenge. Sweetenham's story of the raising of the standard, of course, worried the good general still more. The captain had not seen a great number of men in arms; but he was certain that there were many, many more on their way to Glenfinnan; since wherever he had gone after quitting that remote valley, he had heard the skirl of the bagpipe and had seen evidences that the wild Scots were preparing for war.

The Highlanders were an unknown quality, a military "X." They spoke a different language, derived from a different source than English; they dressed differently, fought differently, marched and drilled and behaved differently; they responded to different emotions. A stranger could not estimate what they might do next, or how, or why. Blow air into an idiotic bag, produce therefrom a series of screeching sounds, howl something horrible in a strange tongue—and lo! the hills were alive with weirdly garbed warriors who battled for a medieval chief, and battled, too, with a medieval fury. Bristling with daggers, all stuck with feathers and badges, flowers and thistles and tassles and what-not, they wore also skirts of bright plaid, and usually no shoes or stockings; they were haughty, excitable, and ferocious; they carried round shields and, disdaining bayonets, fought with heavy, two-edged swords. Sir John Cope simply didn't know what to make of them. How many were there? He could not guess. When would they appear? from what direction? and what would they do when they did come? These were questions which might not be answered until it was too late. Cope sighed, poor man, and continued moving north.

Near Fort Augustus he came to the south side of the mountain called Corryarrack, which commands a strategic pass. The natives of Dalwhinnie told him that the rebels had already occupied Corryarrack from the north. Cope took one look at the long, back-and-forth series of steps which zigzagged up the south side, and realized that his army would be shot to pieces before any part of it reached the summit, if marksmen, however few, were stationed there. He was a fool, but not *that* much of a fool! Yet his orders were to march straight to Fort Augustus. He called a council of war; and all his fellow officers agreed with him that to attempt an ascent of Corryarrack would mean certain annihilation, provided the Highlanders were already there. Apparently it did not occur to any of them to check up on the reports by sending an advance guard to determine whether the Highlanders really were there (as a matter of fact, they weren't!), and the council decided to turn aside, moving northeast toward Inverness rather than on to the fort. This course would leave the Lowlands open to the Pretender's forces; but on the other hand, the clan chiefs, it was believed, would not take the chance of leaving their own estates at the mercy of an English army while they plundered in the South.

So Cope figured, and his officers agreed with him. The officers, it would seem, didn't know their business any better than did Cope. Still, it is difficult to see what else the poor general could have done, assuming that he could not ascend Corryarrack. With sufficient provisions he might have taken a stand south of Corryarrack and risked a battle, on their own ground, with the clans. But he lacked the provisions: the peasants had seen to *that!* So he marched to Inverness.

And now back to the Prince. After raising the standard (it was done on the very day Cope had received his orders from London and prepared to start his march), Charles and his tiny army moved slowly eastward, gathering strength as they went. John Murray of Broughton, that indefatigible schemer, had joined them, had been made Secretary of Scottish Affairs for the Prince Regent (a position he already held for James), and had proposed to Charles two daring schemes. One was to make a surprise attack on the castle of Inverary and capture the Duke of Argyle in his own home: Argyle was chief of the most numerous clan of them all, the Campbells, who with him at their head were certain to be lined up for the Hanoverian. Murray's other plan was more elaborate. He would circulate a false story of a grand conclave of clan chiefs in the wilds of Rannoch, getting this story to the ears of the government from the mouths of men who would certainly be believed. This, he calculated, would cause the government to attempt to surprise this imaginary conclave and kill the insurrection with one blow. The opposing military forces, being thus drawn off to one side, Charles would be enabled to attack Fort William and Fort Augustus and, after having made himself master of the Highlands by the capture of these important places, descend upon Edinburgh—while the government forces, presumably, would still be beating the bushes of Rannoch in search of him.

Neither plan was adopted, fortunately. Charles was too eager to come to grips with the Hanoverian forces in the open field of battle. He was not going to make the mistake Mar had made: he was not going to fritter away his time and the spirits of his men by small, silly skirmishes and unimportant marching and counter-marching. He was going to strike while their enthusiasm was hot—make directly for the enemy—fight, win, sweep down upon the Lowlands and upon Edinburgh—and then, before England had a chance to catch its breath, start his glorious march up to London.

The very wildness of this plan made it, paradoxically, as sound as any proposed to him, and much sounder than most. He had a nervous, fast-moving army, an army not well disciplined but full of warlike spirit and capable of enduring any hardships for the sake of a good fight. He must be dramatic. Move fast, strike hard, move on again: that was the system. Montrose had understood that, so had Dundee.

So he went eastward, stopping by night at the castles of various well-wishers, and keeping messengers on the go all the time. He still hoped to enlist the assistance of Lord Lovat, the Macleod, and Sir Alexander Macdonald of Sleat, besides that of lesser chiefs.

Charles wore the Highland dress now—the curious and very practical kilt. He walked with the men, talking with them. He astonished and delighted them by his knowledge of what they held most dear—stories of their ancient origin and the traditional heroism of their forefathers. He knew about the grand fighters of dim, mist-hidden days; and he knew who was whose cousin, and why this gentleman was called so-and-so in the Gaelic, and another gentleman something else. In the Highlands these are matters of tremendous importance.

When Charles heard that Cope was advancing toward

Corryarrack he sent a fast advance guard to take possession of the summit. Next morning, when he rose, he put on his brogues with the remark, "I won't take these off again until I've met Cope and defeated him."

But messengers came to inform him that the English general had come and seen and been conquered. Even before the advance guard had reached the summit of the mountain, Cope had held his council of war and had gone off with his army toward Inverness.

Charles was disappointed. He had wanted a real battle, promptly. But the men, who took this to mean that Cope was retreating before them already, were wildly excited. And Charles did not lose this excellent opportunity to stimulate their spirits still more. He called for brandy for the whole army, and each man took his dram. Charles raised his own glass:

"Here's to Sir John Cope, and may every general in the usurper's army prove himself as much our friend as he has done!"

And in fact, it was a great thing for the Prince—this side-stepping movement of Cope's. The English commander might fondly hope that the clansmen would not leave their own country unprotected in favor of the Lowlands; but if he had been a Scot raised in the service, and not a political appointee from London, he would have understood that while there was little to pillage and destroy in the Highlands, there was much below. He himself would not dare to remain in the North while the clansmen were in the South. A great victory had been won for the invader, though not a shot had been fired.

Charles himself wanted to pursue Cope—a course which was decided against at a hastily summoned council of war, and which would, indeed, have been unwise. Tullibardine (he was called the Duke of Athole by all true Jacobites, who did not recognize the government's attainder against him) was eager to return to his native heath and take possession of the castle of Blair Athole, which had been deserted by his younger brother, the actual Duke, in favor of the more salubrious neighborhood of London. On the other hand, Lord Lovat had sent a message urging the Prince to march to Inverness: and this doubtless had much to do with Charles' original desire to follow Cope, for the Prince was anxious to conciliate Lovat and gain his assistance.

Simon, Lord Lovat, was born in 1688, the oldest son of Thomas Fraser of Beaufort, and Sybilla, daughter of The Macleod, and was 77 years old when Prince Charles landed at Lochnanaugh. When he was thirteen he was jailed for his activities in behalf of the exiled King. He broke jail, and three years later was actively engaged under General Buchan in another abortive Stuart uprising. When the chief of the Clan Fraser, Hugh, Lord Lovat, died, Simon claimed the title and property, as the nearest male relative. Hugh's daughter, Amelia, disputed the claim, and she was supported by her uncle, the powerful Marquis of Athole. Young Simon might have lost his case if he had let it go to court. But he never trusted courts. He had methods of his own.

Amelia was about to be wedded to the oldest son of Lord Saltoun. The bridegroom-to-be and his father were ambushed while on their way to the ceremony; Simon led them to a gibbet, placed a noose around the neck of each, and forced them to sign away their claims to the heiress. Simon had decided to play safe by marrying her himself.

But the lady had been warned, and fled the Fraser country. Simon, annoyed, reasoned that perhaps the widowed mother would do as well. With a small body of men he invaded the dowager's home and carried her off to his own castle. Now the widow was at least middle-aged and probably not very handsome. This made no difference to Simon. She objected, and vehemently, to what he proposed. That didn't make any difference either. He had to hold a pistol to a priest, but they were married just the same.

Under Scottish law, the marriage was not legal unless and until it had been consummated. Simon had anticipated this. The priest was hustled away; Simon snicked out a dirk and cut the bride's stays; and with the assistance of henchmen ripped the clothes off her body and threw her on the bed. . . . The retainers remained in the room while the marriage was consummated: they were witnesses in case of any future legal action. And in the next chamber the loudest bagpipes were played furiously, to drown the lady's squeals.

That was going a bit too far, even for those days. A warrant was issued for Simon's arrest, and he was cited to appear before the High Court of Justiciary in Edinburgh. When he refused to do so (he never did care for courts) they issued letters of fire and sword against him. A company of the King's soldiers, accompanied by a considerable body of Athole's avenging clansmen, moved into the Fraser country. Simon skipped to France.

The Stuart needed all the noblemen he could get, and did not dare to inquire too closely into their reputations. At St. Germains, Simon ingratiated himself into the favor of King Louis the Fourteenth and of Mary of Modena, she who had held the baby Prince that night in Lambeth. Heaven alone knows what he told them! Anyway, they gave him money and the rank of Major-General, and sent him back to look over the Highlands with an eye to the possibility of raising the clans for still another attempt to place a Stuart on the throne.

The warrant was still out against him, the marriage had been annulled and, in those days, rape was punishable by death. Nevertheless, Simon swaggered into Edinburgh, very grand in the clothes the King of France had bought for him. He called upon the Duke of Queensbury, Anne's Royal Commissioner in Scotland, and told the Duke all the secrets of St. Germains. Of course he did this for a price: he wanted his lands and title back, and the indictments quashed.

Even then he had the audacity to return to St. Germains to make his report. But they had heard about that talk with Queensbury, and they were waiting for Simon not with open arms but with a set of chains. Another Stuart plan had been upset; once more the French court and the exiled family were forced to start all over again. On August 4, 1704, Simon was thrown into prison.

When he had first gone to St. Germains, in order the more effectively to ingratiate himself into that court's inner circles, he had been converted to the Roman Catholic faith. He would have become a Hindoo if that would have gained any power for him. Now, in jail, he went so far as to take holy orders! Three years' imprisonment and he was out again, a respected and apparently respectable member of the Society of Jesus. He was made a curé at St. Omer.

Then came the 'Fifteenth, when Mar once more led out the clans. Simon forgot his vows, tossed aside his habit, and hurried over to London. If it had seemed to him that Mar was headed for victory, Simon would undoubtedly have espoused the Stuart cause again. But his real interest was to be always on the side of the hangman and the keeper of the money chest. There were whispers behind locked doors in London; and, on the eve of the battle of Sheriffmuir, the Fraser clansmen received orders from Simon to lay down their arms and return to their native heath. The Frasers, almost to a man, loved the Stuarts; and they had been called to the field by the Mackenzie of Fraserdale, who had been married to Amelia and was acting as chief of the clan. But they still esteemed Simon their true leader by blood, despite what might be written on impressive parchment, besealed and bestamped and beribboned in the law courts of the South; and so, when he ordered them back, they went.

That desertion probably cost Mar the battle, for the Frasers were a strong clan and Sheriffmuir was a close fight. Simon had saved a dynasty; and he was rewarded, according to previous arrangement, by the restoration of his lands and title, the command of a Highland regiment, and considerable gold besides.

The son of Mackenzie of Fraserdale later brought two suits to recover the title and estate. Simon won the first and compromised the second. It is likely that Mackenzie was glad enough to compromise, for Simon was not a pleasant neighbor if he happened to bear a grudge. Scott writes: "If a man of substance offended Lovat, or, which is the same thing, if he possessed a troublesome claim against him, and was determined to enforce it, one would have thought that all the plagues of Egypt had been denounced against the obnoxious individual. His house was burnt, his flocks driven off, his cattle houghed; and if the perpetrators of such outrages were secured, the jail at Inverness was never strong enough to detain them till punishment." Scott adds significantly, "With persons of low rank, less ceremony was used."

Simon was married twice more—once to the daughter of the Laird of Grant, by whom he had two sons and two daughters; and later to a Campbell lady, closely related to the house of Argyle, whom he treated with fiendish cruelty until she left him.

And now he wanted to be a Duke. The government would not oblige him; so he turned again to the exiled Stuart. James should have had better sense than to deal with such a traitor. But Lovat was eloquent. He convinced the King Across the Water, promising much.

Yet when Charles landed the old villain was doubtful. It was still his policy to be on the winning side at all costs; and although Prince Charles promised a Dukedom, the young man's backing was none too impressive. So Simon vacillated. Instead of refusing to play with either side, he played with both at the same time, helping neither. He wrote to Murray of Broughton that he was always loyal to the Stuarts and would soon take the field under the white banner; with the same pen he wrote to Duncan Forbes, the Lord Advocate, that he was always loyal to the House of Hanover and would soon take the field against "that mad and unaccountable gentleman," as he called Prince Charles.

Lovat was a power in the Highlands, and understood better than any other man of his time the peculiarities of the Highland character. His influence was great. So when Charles, moving out of Glenfinnan, pressed Simon for assistance, the wily Lord tried to gain time by requesting Charles to march into

LORD LOVAT COUNTING THE CLANS
From the Painting by Hogarth

Inverness—planning, it may be, to seize the young Prince and gain for himself that £30,000 reward. But Charles decided to take the advice of his officers and descend promptly upon the Lowlands.

After he had crossed Corryarrack, he sent a party of Camerons to surprise Cluny Macpherson of Cluny at his own castle and take him captive. The chief was evidently no unwilling prisoner. He had been corresponding with Cope and presumably was preparing to raise his men for the government; but, after a few days in the company of Charles, he was won over to the Stuart cause, and thereafter the Macphersons fought for the white rose.

Duke William of Athole having fled to London, Charles took Blair Castle easily enough, and the aged Tullibardine, after thirty years' exile, was restored to his lands. He immediately started to raise his vassals for the Prince. This same day John Roy Stewart joined the Prince; and George the Second, by the Grace of God King, Defender of the Faith, etc., landed in London, after a record-breaking trip from Hanover, to take over the affairs of government himself.

Hope was high in the North. The Prince dined at Blair Castle, was joined by Mercer of Aldie and Lord Nairn and, marching into Perth without resistance, formally proclaimed his father King of Great Britain and Ireland and himself Prince Regent thereof. In Perth, too, he received assurances of assistance from both Spain and France, and these he used to good effect, promising and promising and promising, whenever discouragement reared its head among his leaders. He remained in Perth six days, reviewing his troops and enlisting new recruits.

By far the most important of these recruits were James Drummond, Duke of Perth, a Roman Catholic, and Lord George Murray, younger son of the Duke of Athole. These men were made Lieutenants-General, the Prince himself being commander-in-chief. To the end, however, there was jealousy between them.

The Duke of Perth (the title had been conferred by James

and was not recognized by the government at London) was thirty-two years old, high-born, high-spirited too, and dearly beloved by his many followers. He was six feet tall, but slender, weak, pale, fair. Bred in France, he never could talk English well. He was generally amiable, but not experienced in military affairs and none too wise in council.

Quite a different sort of person was Lord George Murray, perhaps the only real genius of them all. Lord George was strikingly similar in character to that young Virginian surveyor, George Washington. He was the sixth child of the same parents who bore the Marquis of Tullibardine. He was a stern man, a fighter, a born general; but no courtier, and not at all the sort of person likely to tell Charles the things Charles preferred to hear. Bluntness of expression and a distaste for fanciness were characteristic of most of the leaders of this uprising; but in none were they so pronounced as in Lord George Murray. He had not been too well educated: younger sons weren't in those days. A hot-headed youth, he had been one of the first to enlist under the Stuart banner when the Earl of Mar had declared for James and sent out the fiery cross. After this insurrection, Lord George disappeared. He lingered somewhere in the Highlands, waiting for another chance to draw sword for his rightful King. That chance came when the small force of Spaniards landed on the West Coast and Lord Seaforth led out a few warriors to reinforce them. Lord George was in the thick of it at Glenshiel—that indefinite, indecisive skirmish which terminated the feeble attempt of 1717. He escaped, wounded, to the Continent.

What he did there is not clear. He is accredited with having distinguished himself in the Sardinian army, but his biographer, Winifred Duke, has been unable to find any proof of this, and other historians are strangely vague about it. At any rate, in 1725, through the good offices of his brother, the Duke, he was pardoned and returned to Scotland. The oldest brother, Tullibardine, remained on the Continent, attainted.

When Prince Charles came over, Lord George was, to all appearances, a Whig and a supporter, if a lukewarm one, of the Hanoverian régime. He had, however, always held aloof from politics. He was married, fifty years old, and had four children, the oldest only sixteen. His brother, the actual Duke, at the first stirrings of trouble, had appointed him Sheriff-Deputy of the county; and, in this capacity, Lord George had waited upon Cope just before the English general had started north. This interview was to be brought against his lordship many and many a time afterwards.

Charles must have had some special reason for wanting this man's services. He wrote Lord George a letter: what was in it we do not know, but it decided the man, who bade farewell to his wife and children and departed to join his Prince. His appointment as Lieutenant-General is a mystery. He was not a person of brilliantly high rank, he was a younger son; he had, to be sure, already fought for the Stuart restoration, but this much might have been said for dozens of other men who doubtless sought the same appointment. At any rate, Lord George knew his business. He was impatient and quick-tempered, and never very polite. But he was an all-around soldier, who could map out a clever plan of battle, fight in the thick of it himself, and never lose sight of the prosaic details concerning food and ammunition. And the men trusted him. Chevalier Johnstone, who was there all the time, wrote that "had Prince Charles slept during the whole of the expedition, and allowed Lord George to act for him, according to his own judgment, there is every reason for supposing that he would have found the crown of Great Britain on his head when he awoke."

But Charles was amazingly busy. He wanted to be off and away: the necessity of organizing his army irritated him. When he had come to Perth a single coin danced in his purse; but he raised money easily enough from the city and from surrounding municipalities and, in addition, managed to raise a convenient supply of arms and ammunition. Drilling the clansmen was more difficult. They were excellent shots, had plenty of courage, could march all night and all day without complaint, and were wonders with the broadsword and the long Highland dirk; but wild mountaineers that they were, they had difficulty falling in with orthodox military ideas.

They seemed the slower to Charles because of his impatience. To a linen draper who applied to him for a passport to return to London, the Prince said, signing the paper, ". . . and tell your friends there they will see me within two months." One night the Jacobite ladies of Perth staged a ball in his honor: he stayed for one dance and then excused himself, explaining that he wished to make an inspection tour of his camp. It was probably true. Many a clansman might have opened his eyes in the middle of the night to see his Prince stalking back and forth, here and there, counting this, estimating that, while his Irish companions implored him to get some sleep if only for his health's sake.

He was in Perth eight days. Then came a message that caused the hurried calling of another council of war. Cope was forcing his hand.

CHAPTER SIX

The Defense of Edinburgh

DESERTERS from Cope's army—Highlanders of the Scots Royal who wanted to rejoin their rightful clans—were constantly straggling into the Prince's camp. They kept Charles well informed as to the movements of the English general. It was probably from some of these fellows that the Prince learned that Cope had sent a captain down to Leith for the purpose of dispatching ships to Aberdeen. This could mean only that Cope was planning to march thence, and from there to sail to Leith, which was the port of Edinburgh,* hoping, no doubt, to get to the capital before the Highlanders.

Quick action was necessary. Somebody proposed, in council, that the army march north from Perth and try to cut off Cope on his way from Inverness to Aberdeen. This was a foolish plan, and was abandoned in favor of a much better one: to march directly to Edinburgh and take that city, thereby preventing Cope from disembarking at Leith.

They crossed the Forth at the ford of Frew, where the water, at that season, was uncommonly low. The Prince himself was the first to plunge into the stream; up to his hips, he waded to the southern shore, and there waited, congratulating the officers as the various groups following him reached dry land.

Now they were definitely in the Lowlands. They could be sure of easy foraging and a sufficient supply of money; but they were in enemy country, and in case of an attack would not have the advantage the mountains gave them.

Gardiner's dragoons had talked of disputing this ford but,

* Leith is now a part of Edinburgh city, but in 1745 it was still a separate burgh.

at the approach of the Highlanders, had retreated to Falkirk. Hamilton's dragoons were still at Leith. All the rest of the organized enemy in Scotland was with Cope.

Charles moved around Stirling, and over the battlefield of Bannockburn, where Robert the Bruce had won the most glorious victory of Scottish history. Charles, however, had little opportunity to meditate upon this for, as he was passing, the cannon of Stirling castle spoke out with a boom, and the earth not twenty yards from him was churned up by the balls. The Prince was unhurt. One of his guardsmen, wildly indignant, fired a horse pistol in the direction of the castle.

That night he slept at Callander House, where his host, the Earl of Kilmarnock, a more or less impoverished nobleman, informed him that the dragoons were at Linlithgow. Charles retired, but stayed in bed only a short time. He then rose, put himself at the head of some 500 men kept in arms for the purpose, and made a secret night march to the palace of his forefathers. But the dragoons had been warned, and Charles returned with claymore unblooded.

Of course the steady and rapid advance was reported, with embellishments, in Edinburgh, which ancient and honorable city was now engaged in being preposterous. It happened that the Prevost of Edinburgh, one Archibald Stewart, was at least a Tory and possibly a Jacobite at heart. The administration, in power for four or five years, was of like sympathies. Election day was coming. When the news of Prince Charles' approach was reported in the city, Sir John Cope and his redcoats were thought sufficient protection. But when Cope's side-stepping movement became known, and the good people of Edinburgh learned that the wild Scots were sweeping down upon them, there was raised a cry of defiance.

It was, in fact, chiefly a political cry. The Whigs thought to embarrass the administration by clamoring for a defense. Should Edinburgh, proud Auld Reekie, submit to the first discredited princeling who sought to attack it with a handful of jabbering savages? No! A thousand times no! Proud old Edinburgh should defend itself, and *would* defend itself (cheers) no matter how many the thousands that marched against it, no matter how frightful the forces of Mariolatry!

It sounded well. And it had its effect. Archie Stewart made gestures—though as few as possible—and Edinburgh began to take steps to defend itself.

The defense was like trying to strengthen a pasteboard shack in anticipation of a whirlwind. Edinburgh had been a warlike city in its day. But it had became a city of merchants—merchants who could talk well enough, and add and subtract, but who were certainly not trained to cope with fighters like the Highlanders. Moreover, although it was a walled city, the walls were weak. They stretched around three sides of the old city, the north being defended by the North Loch and the rock on which the Castle stood. For the rest, the walls were more like high, thick, garden walls, not built, except in a few places, with turrets and ramparts and towers, not equipped with curtains and loopholes and machicolations, and for the most part not strong enough for the mounting of cannon. In many places, too, there were tall houses just outside the city proper but very close to the wall: by occupying these houses, an attacking force could readily sweep the wall with musket fire.

As to soldiers, there were, of the regulars, only the garrison of the Castle, which could not be spared, and the two green dragoon regiments. There were also the City Guards—a little over 100 men, who, according to Henderson, were mostly "superannuated soldiers, or else broken Watermen, Chairmen, or gentlemen's servants, most of whom keep lewd Houses and are notorious Pimps." Then there were the Trained Bands, about 1,000 residents who were equipped with rusty muskets. These militiamen never had entertained any thought of being called upon to fight. Theirs was really a social organization. They had no discipline. Indeed, they only put on their uniforms and got together once a year, on the King's birthday, which they were wont to celebrate by getting drunk together; and the only time they ever fired their antiquated weapons was on this day, too, when a few of the bolder spirits would brace the butts against window sills, close their eyes, and turn their heads, as they tremblingly pulled the triggers—a wise precaution, since the ancient weapons were likely to explode in their hands.

This defending army being deemed insufficient for the emergency, the citizens of Edinburgh asked for and were granted a King's patent to raise a regiment of 1,000 volunteers. Recruiting officers worked hard, but only a little more than 200 men presented themselves. However, some 400 others formed themselves into a second volunteer regiment, to serve without pay. These were supplied with muskets from the city magazine, located in the Castle.

The preparations did not stop there, for Edinburgh was in earnest. Dr. M'Laurin, professor of mathematics at Edinburgh University, who was supposed to be an expert on the Vauban system of fortification, was given charge of strengthening the walls. He had no little difficulty keeping the exuberant volunteers at work, so frequently were they distracted by stump speakers.

One thousand stand of arms were brought down from London. Arrangements were made to fetch Hamilton's dragoons from Leith. Eighteen pieces of cannon were taken from ships in the harbor and placed at strategic points along the wall.

To defend or not to defend the city was the big question. The Jacobites, reasonably certain of their position for the first time in many years, only occasionally objected to the preparations. The persons who really worried were those who believed that any show of resistance would mean severe punishments, and confiscations, when the Pretender *did* take the city. The others, generally, tried to talk themselves into believing that this would not happen.

Altogether it was a very silly business. General Guest, in command of the Castle, was more than eighty years old and ought to have known better when he suggested that the volunteers and the dragoons move out to dispute at Corstophine the Prince's progress toward the city. But this, too, sounded good; and it was agreed that whenever the fire bells were rung in signal, the Edinburgh Regiment should assemble in the Grassmarket, shoulder muskets, and sally forth. At eleven o'clock in the morning, on Sunday, September fifteenth, the bells were accordingly rung. There was much excitement. People came pouring out of the churches. The dragoons, up from Leith, clashed their sabers together and shouted to encourage the volunteers. The volunteers thwacked one another on the back and told each other they were the bravest lads in the world. The officers hurried back and forth, shouting orders, bumping into one another, looking very stern.

But by now the wives and mothers and daughters had commenced to act as wives and mothers and daughters are not supposed to act in time of war. They were weeping, begging their men not to risk their valuable lives in a battle with those big, rough Highlanders. They were pointing out that the Edinburgh regiment volunteers had signed up with the understanding that they were to be used in defense of their fair city—not with the understanding that they should be sent out into the open to fight an ordinary batle, as if they were nothing but professional soldiers.

Their words fell on willing ears; their arguments were most sympathetically received. The volunteers began to have doubts. When the command for marching finally came, many of them slipped quietly away. The rest started down the Bow, through the Grassmarket, to the West Port. But by the time the gate was reached less than fifty of them were left! The rest had discreetly decided to let the others hold back Charlie; one by one, two by two, and in little groups, they had dropped out in doorways and alleyways and closes along the way.

So the dragoons—the important, beautifully dressed dragoons—trotted out alone. They sniffed at this display of lay cowardice. Still, what could one expect from mere shopkeepers? This was an emergency, and real soldiers were needed for it. The people of Edinburgh would soon learn that dragoons alone, unsupported by civilian foot, were quite capable of putting down this trifling riot.

However, they were soon joined by Gardiner's dragoons

and, the next day, by a few hundred of the City Guards and of the newly formed and very shaky Edinburgh Regiment. At Colt's Bridge, an excellent place for a few men to hold many in check, they formed a crescent. Commanding them was Colonel Gardiner, very old, very fierce, wrapped in a huge blue cloak and with a handkerchief below his hat and tied under his chin. Were it not for Colonel Gardiner, we could laugh without any reservation at that which followed this brave display. But he, at least, was a gentleman and a soldier.

The Colonel sent out a small party to reconnoiter. This patrol galloped over the bridge, a bit nervously and, not far ahead, came upon a few members of Charlie's army, a similar patrol. The Highlanders fired their pistols, rather over than at the dragoons, and wheeled to go back with the information that the enemy were coming.

That information, however, was incorrect before they could start. The enemy by that time, were not *coming* but *going*. Those few pistols, playfully discharged, had frightened them half out of their senses. They wheeled about without firing a shot themselves, and dashed madly back to the bridge.

"*The rebels are here!*"

Ah, the brave, brave soldiers! The gallant dragoons! Once again the cavalry showed their superiority over the foot soldiers, for they were able to get back to Edinburgh ever so much sooner. Colonel Gardiner to the contrary notwithstanding (and the Colonel did everything he could to hold them), the dragoons turned like one man. Pop-eyed, red-faced, positively panic-stricken, they tore across the fields that are now the modern part of Edinburgh; while the fond citizens, who had been waiting to learn the result of the battle, watched them with dismay.

The foot soldiers eventually stopped, exhausted. But the dragoons, luckier, were able to keep their horses going. On they dashed. Nothing could stop these fellows! Not till they got to Leith did they draw rein. Even there, before they had ventured to dismount, some waggish person cried, "*Here come the rebels!*"—and they were off again. They rode like fiends from the nethermost Hell. They rode to Mussleburgh, where at last, courage seeping back into their bosoms, they dismounted and made some pretense at encampment. Poor Colonel Gardiner! Here was Pinkie House, his very home. The old soldier, too disgusted to say a word, went to bed.

But the Colonel must have felt even more miserable the next morning, when he went out on the moor to find that his soldiers had gone again. During the night one of their number had fallen into a coal hole: this fellow had yelled for help, and such a yell was enough to set the dragoons going. To horse again! Not until Dunbar, this time, did they draw rein. Colonel Gardiner had no trouble following them; for the soldiers, really believing that the wild Scots were pursuing them, had cast away their weapons, and the ground along their route was strewn with carabines, swords, and pistols.

This little skirmish came to be known as the "Canter of Coltbridge."

By now the good people of Edinburgh, who for several days had been watching the weathercocks and praying that Cope would have another of those "Protestant winds" at his back on the voyage from Aberdeen, were themselves wholly panic-stricken. The most violent Whigs no longer talked resistance, and the mouthings of the politicians were at last drowned by the wail of frightened shopkeepers and clerks. If the noble and beautifully dressed dragoons could be frightened at the mere sight of these Highlanders (although the greater part of the dragoons had not even *seen* the enemy), what in the name of Heaven could the residents of Edinburgh expect to do? Prevost Stewart, beset on the streets, was induced to call a public meeting for discussion of the question, to defend or not to defend. In the middle of this meeting, somebody handed the clerk a letter. The clerk looked at the seal and turned pale. He whispered to Prevost Stewart, and the Prevost, already under suspicion of being a Jacobite and not inclined to make matters worse now, refused to remain if the letter were read. He quit the meeting; but he was soon induced to return, and the clerk read the letter.

Charles informed them briefly that he was Prince Regent of the Nation and expected to be received as such. ". . . and we promise to preserve the rights and liberties of the city, and the particular property of every one of His Majesty's subjects. *But if any opposition be made to us, we cannot answer for the consequences.* . . . being firmly resolved at any rate to enter the city; and in that case, *if any of the inhabitants are found in arms against us, they must not be expected to be treated as prisoners of war.* . . ."

The Italics were the clerk's. They had their effect, too. It is hardly possible that Prince Charles meant what he wrote in this letter (if he even wrote it, for we are not certain of its authenticity), for mercy was a fault of his. But the citizens of Edinburgh did not know this. And when it came to a vote, only two persons expressed themselves as favoring defiance.

It was therefore decided to send deputies to the Young Pretender, requesting a fuller explanation of what he meant when he wrote that he expected to be received as befitted a Prince Regent. This, at least, would serve to occupy a little time.

The amateur soldiers were perhaps the most nervous of all. Muskets in their hands, and in their ears that phrase about "any of the inhabitants found in arms against us," they stood in groups in the streets, whispering, wondering, biting their lips. . . . Then along came a man (nobody recognized him, and it was never learned who he was) riding a gray horse and shouting that the Highlanders were at the city gates, sixteen thousand strong! That put an end to all hesitation. Four companies of the Edinburgh regiment raced right up to the castle and handed their muskets back for storage in the city magazine.

Of course, the Highlanders were not at the city gates, nor were they sixteen thousand strong. Less than two thousand in all, they were encamped at Gray's Mills, about two miles southwest of the city; and it was there the Edinburgh deputies sought out the Prince.

Poor Edinburgh! it simply couldn't make up its mind! Scarcely had the deputies departed when there came an encouraging note from Sir John Cope, begging the citizens to hold off the rebels and assuring them that he was approaching with all possible speed and hoped to arrive the day after receipt of this very letter.

Only a show of defense was needed now, only a pretense. If the rebels could be kept off for another twenty-four hours, perhaps the brave general would be there to chase them away forever. It was proposed to ring the alarm bell again, return to the castle and ask for the muskets back, and, in general, to put up a great display of military ardor in order to give Charles pause.

Then somebody remarked that if the alarm bells were rung, this fact would certainly be reported in the Highland camp, and the deputies would be hanged. If only those deputies hadn't been so prompt! Anyway, General Guest, in the castle, refused to let the would-be soldiers have their weapons back, on the ground that they didn't know how to handle them; and Edinburgh had to do as best it could with the other volunteers and with the City Guards and the Trained Bands.

Soon the deputies came back. The Young Pretender had informed them that he would not brook delay. "Give me the city by two o'clock in the morning," he had said, in effect, "or I'll come and take it anyway."

It was now about ten o'clock at night. More talk, more worried whispering. Then it was decided to send the deputies back to the Highland camp and beg for an extension of time until nine o'clock in the morning. By pretending that they needed more leisure for deliberation on this matter, the city's elders might yet delay until the coming of Cope. So the deputies climbed back into their hackney-coach and returned to Gray's Mills.

This time Charles would not even admit them into his presence. He must have known, or at least suspected, that Cope was very near and that the Edinburghers were only trying to tread water until that life-preserver was thrown to them. Charles had, meanwhile, commissioned Young Lochiel, O'Sullivan, Murray of Broughton, Stuart of Ardshiel, and a few others, to capture the capital. They were to do so as quietly as possible and, if they could, without bloodshed.

Young Lochiel was in command of this party. Besides the gentlemen mentioned, and a few more, there were with him some 900 Highlanders, mostly Camerons. They advanced over the moor to a point not far from the old Netherbow Gate which divides the High street from the Cannongate. Here they paused, while the leaders conferred. It was a difficult assignment. To take the city would be easy enough. But to take it before dawn and without bloodshed was another matter. A dozen plans were discussed, weighed, and rejected. Four of the clansmen carried a barrel of gunpowder, and this could be used to blow open a gate. The houses in St. Mary's Wynd could be stormed and taken easily, and from these one could almost step over to the wall. The hospital could be attained through the College church. But all these plans involved the risk of fighting, and it was of great importance that the Prince, for his popularity's sake, enter this ancient capital with no preliminary splashings of gore.

Finally Lochiel sent a follower to the gate. This fellow, wrapped in a huge cloak and with a riding hat pulled low, posed as the servant of a dragoon officer and demanded admittance. The guards refused to open for him, and chased him away with threats of musket fire: and the Highlanders crouching in the shadows on either side of the gate, were foiled.

Yet the presence of this body apparently was not suspected inside the city. There were sentries at the gate but none along the walls, and Edinburgh, worn out with nervous alarms, slept a dreamless sleep. It was one of those nights when the moon wanders from behind clouds to open sky and from open sky behind clouds again with a tantalizing air of indifference and of leisure; at one moment they were bathed in silver, at the next they were scarcely able to see the men beside them.

Already the dawn was smearing itself lazily across the sky. And no plan having presented itself—at least, no plan they were certain the Prince would later approve—the leaders had just decided to retire to camp for further instructions, when the city keys were virtually dropped right into their laps.

The deputies, unsuccessful ambassadors of delay, had returned, made their report, and dismissed their hackney-coach. The driver of the coach, who lived down in the Cannongate, wanted to go home and go to bed. The warders of the gate knew him, and opened the leaves for him to go out.

This was enough for the Highlanders. In an instant the place was a blaze of bright swords, and the air rang with war-cries. The coach driver was paralyzed with amazement. So were the guardsmen at the gate.

It was all over in a twinkling. A few residents, hearing wild yells, looked out of their windows and saw the weird figures of Highlanders running back and forth, disarming the startled gatemen, making for the guardhouse, posting sentries, moving very rapidly and certainly through the vague, gray light of the dawn. But for the most part the town slept peacefully, all unaware that it was captured by the enemy. The City Guards, assembled within the guardhouse, were intimidated, disarmed and made prisoners with ludicrous ease. The sentries at the various gates were replaced with Highlanders as quietly and as naturally as though this were a military exercise carefully rehearsed in advance by both parties. Not a shot was fired.

They say that a good citizen of Edinburgh, out for an early constitutional that morning, gasped in amazement when he saw a wild Scot, in all the barbaric grandeur of the kilts, standing watch where a City Guardsman had been stationed the previous night.

"Why—why, you don't belong to the regiment that was here last night!"

The Highlander shook his head, grinning.

"They've been relieved," he said.

CHAPTER SEVEN

They March to Battle

AT ABOUT 10 o'clock that morning, the main army moved out of Gray's Mills and, in order to avoid exposure to the castle guns, took the long way round to Duddingstone, and there pitched camp. Prince Charles, surrounded by an official guard and a few noblemen and clan chiefs, came down from out of the shadow of the great rock they called Arthur's Seat, and entered the King's Park.

Whigs and Jacobites alike came out of the city to greet him: for even though he might be a devil with horns, they were curious to see this lad, and curiosity is a stronger emotion than fear.

Charles wore a white short-coat, the white tartan of his royal family; a blue sash covered with gold lace came up over his left shoulder; his blue velvet bonnet was trimmed with gold lace and fronted with a nodding white rose; and he wore red velvet breeches, and military boots to the knees. Pistols hung from his belt, and at his side was an Andrea Ferrara claymore with red padding showing through the bars of the silver basket-hilt. On his breast glittered the Star of St. Andrew.

Whigs and Jacobites described him differently. Yet even the Whigs were obliged to admit that here was an uncommonly attractive young man. His tanned face, a beautiful oval; his violet eyes, small mouth, and pointed chin; his barely discernible blond eyebrows; the hesitant freckles on his nose; the light brown hair combed over the front of his wig;—they all praised these. But both remarked the melancholy cast of his countenance. It may be that the sight of this ancient palace, where his ancestors had ruled and held brilliant court and suffered, had awed and saddened the boy. It may be that the realization of what he was doing and had already done, descending upon him in full force for the first time, rendered him thoughtfully still. Or perhaps the sadness was only hereditary, for the Stuarts were always sad, even Charles II, who was called the Merry Monarch.

Certainly Charles' royal blood showed on this occasion. The shouts of adulation brought from him just enough of a smile to baffle those who would have liked to describe him as cold, but not enough to leave him open to a charge of being a mere swashbuckler pleased at the furore he had created and glowing in the light of his popularity. He let the eager ones crowd around him to kiss his hand, and he was just properly gracious. But he did not appear to be overpleased, or excited, because of this demonstration; for he was absolutely princely and, having been born to this sort of thing, accepted it with a becoming grace and no fluster. It is not the least recommendation for Royalty that it remains calm and dignified in the midst of all excitement and, while never seeming to be actually bored, or wholly uninterested, yet always conveys the suggestion that it is somehow more than human and not subject to those fits and furies of mixed emotions which from time to time agitate the most stolid of the common herd.

When the people crowded around Charles too closely for comfort, he called for his horse—a bay gelding which the Duke of Perth had given him. They said afterwards that if he had ridden through Edinburgh, or any other city, in rags, alone, unheralded, unrecognized, he yet would have attracted attention because of the way he sat in the saddle.

On one side of him was Lord Elcho, son of the Earl of Weymis. On the other side was tall, pale Perth, who was explaining to the Prince that the route they were taking was the Duke's Walk, so named because Charles' grandfather, then Duke of York and Royal Commissioner in Scotland, was wont to stroll here at the close of day; and that now, by night, it was a lovers' lane and, by early morning, a popular meeting-place for those gentlemen who had differences of opinion of the sort that only pistols or swords could set aright.

Charles nodded, politely but absently, and gazed down over the palace of Holyrood. He rode, said Henderson, who was present, "through repeated Acclamations, which he received with a continued tho' an irregular smile." When he entered the palace and soon afterwards reappeared at one of the windows, the crowd went wild.

But Charles was too busy for much balcony posing. There were many matters to which he must attend. First came the official proclamations. These were read at the old Market Cross in the High street behind St. Gile's. On the east side of the cross was hung a huge Persian rug. The Lyon Heralds and Pursuivants were out in full regalia, with their trumpeters. Around them the Highlanders formed a large circle, five or six deep. The author of the Woodhouselee Manuscript reports that they carried "guns of diferent syses . . . some without locks, and some matchlocks, some had swords over ther showlder instead of guns, one or two had pitchforks, and some bits of sythes upon poles with a cleek, some old Lochaber axes. . . ." Hardly a well-equipped outfit! And yet these were the cream of Charles' army, the men Young Lochiel had personally selected for the peculiar assignment of capturing a capital without noise.

Behind the Highlanders was massed the populace. Every square inch of pavement was occupied by somebody's boot, and the doorways and windows were packed with the throng.

David Beatt, a bankrupt writing master, read the proclamations to Roderick Chalmers, Herald, who repeated them in "ane awdable strong voice."

The first was the one that the warriors and the people of Perth had already heard—James' declaration of his intention to retake his kingdoms, and his promises to the subjects thereof. In it, full religious liberty was granted, and James assured his people that his first act would be to call a free and full Parliament for the righting of old wrongs. The Malt Tax was condemned, and so was the Act of Union, for it was declared that Scotland and England ought to be, and would be, independent kingdoms, recognizing a single monarch but governed by separate Parliaments and subject to separate laws.

The next was the Commission of Regency. Then came the announcement of a reward of £30,000 sterling for the person of the Elector of Hanover, the usurper of the Stuart throne—namely, George the Second. The Prince had not wanted to make this offer. When he learned at Kinlochart that King George had offered £30,000 for him, the Prince was shocked: he could scarcely believe it for, whatever the differences between them, they were both princes of the blood-royal and it was fitting that they agree in certain matters of conduct. For one prince deliberately to injure the dignity of another, was a thing more horrible than Charles could at first believe. Charles might lead thousands of men to hopeless, meaningless slaughter, devastate farmlands, set brother against brother and father against son—but he would never treat an honest enemy like a malefactor. He might be ambitious, but he was no hypocrite. Moreover, the thing was not sporting; and although the King of England wasn't the least bit English, this young exile, who had never been in England, was.

Filled with disgust, it was Charles' first impulse to ignore the manifesto as something beneath him. But his Highland advisors were not so squeamish. They told him that there was only one answer to make: if the usurper insisted upon treating the Prince as an outlaw, the Prince must adopt the same attitude toward the usurper. It was some time before Charles could be persuaded to do this. Once he offered to compromise by issuing a sort of burlesque proclamation, setting £30 as the reward he would be willing to pay for the capture of the usurper, but eventually he raised this to £30,000. The proclamation was accordingly issued (in part) in the following terms:

". . . we were not a little surprised to find that the Elector of Hanover, had not only contrary to the moderation of Christian Princes, but even to humanity itself, given encouragement to Parracide by setting £30,000 upon the Head of our Royal Father, or our own, and so make us fall a Sacrifice to the Hands of bloody and cruel men, as our Great-Grandfather, King Charles I, of Glorious Memory, had done near a Century ago. . . ."

King George's offer was, in fact, an "encouragement to Parracide." Frequently enough, Charles had pistols snapped in his face. He led a dangerous life.

And the reference to Charles I was shrewd; for if Englishmen blushed when they remembered the murder of that monarch, Scotsmen blushed the hotter, recalling with shame that it was their own countrymen who had violated the law of hospitality and sold the King to his enemies. Scotsmen were therefore most earnestly attached to the memory of the First Charles. Indeed, it was because of this feeling that his parents had named our hero Charles.

When all the announcing was finished, bonnets were thrown into the air, hands were clapped, and throats were strained with cheering. Recruiting sergeants rolled their drums and invited citizens to enroll under the white banner at the very eve of a battle—an invitation which was accepted by few. White cockades were distributed; and hundreds of persons, carried away by enthusiasm, became Jacobites—for a few hours.

While all this was going on, Prince Charles was a very busy and a very serious young man. In truth, the melancholy countenance which the residents of Edinburgh had remarked, was not uncommon with him. Up to this time he had been obliged to be exuberant, in appearance at least; it was important that he display high spirit on all occasions, for there were doubtful, worried persons watching him day and night, and any indication that he was losing heart would have been injurious, if not actually fatal, to his cause. So he played one part, while he frequently felt another: he was like a man in a den of wild beasts, who must depend on sheer nerve, and who, if he shows a second's slip of confidence, may be torn to pieces.

He had written to his father, to his brother, to Versailles, pleading for assistance. He had organized, planned and plotted, written to vacillating noblemen in an effort to make up their minds for them, and acted the interlocutor at the curious councils he was accustomed to call. With a trained army, officered by trained gentlemen, this would have been an undertaking of the boldest and most desperate description. With a council of grim, jealous, Highland chieftains, each a suzerain among his own people, each impatient of contradiction and accustomed to absolute and instant obedience, it was doubly so. Perhaps the strain was telling on Charles that afternoon in Holyrood.

If such was the case he dissembled skillfully. That night he received. It was a brilliant affair, such an affair as the people of Edinburgh—except those who had gone to court in London—had not seen in generations. The rabble was delighted, gaping with open mouths and straining eyes. Chairmen and porters and link boys hustled about in the glare of torches outside the doors. Yellow candlelight lay blandly across the courtyard pavement. Grand ladies, resplendently gowned, and gentlemen who were stiff with sartorial perfection, strode in to meet this extraordinary boy. The sound of violins was heard, then the sound of bagpipes—for Charles called for Lowland music now, and now for Highland music, wisely alternately the melodies and the dances. Weather-browned men whispered darkly in dark corners, officials bobbed busily about, white perukes rose and fell rhythmically before beauties, and the flounces of Valenciennes and thick rose-point half collapsed against the floor and then drew out like rising perfume as the ladies curtsied in return; and through it all stalked those handsome, haughty, Highland chiefs, bristling with beautiful weapons, brogued and befeathered, with polychromatic capes ballooning bravely behind them as they walked.

The Prince himself charmed every one beyond expression. Had he been possessed merely of exquisite manners, a fine figure and a handsome face, the encomiums might not have been so numerous and so frenzied; for in those days good manners were not uncommon and beauty was taken for granted. But Charles had, additionally, a boyish shyness which was irresistible, especially with the women. Yet he was no ladies' man! Perhaps that is why they adored him. "His speech was shy, but very intelligible," writes Henderson; and Lord Elcho says that "he had not been much used to Women's Company, and was always embarrassed while he was with them."

Yet this same shy boy was still thinking about his army, for in the army lay all his hopes. There was so much to be done. . . . His real desire was to rush down into England, march through Lancastershire, recruiting as he went, and scare the German from the throne before his Highlanders had even reached the capital. Everything depended upon speed! In London it would be supposed that he must have a huge force behind him or he would not dare to do this: the government would be thrown into confusion, and the fight would be half won before it was started. But there was still much to be done. He had demanded of the Edinburgh city magistrates 1,000 tents, 2,000 targets, 6,000 pairs of shoes, and 6,000 canteens. Would these be ready in time? The Castle still held out against him, the strongest castle in the world. Glasgow must be made to pay tribute. Many, many more recruits must be brought in. Stirling Castle must be taken, and if possible Dumbarton. It was important, too, that the seaport towns be kept in friendly hands, in order that French ships might land men and money without trouble, once they had slipped past the men-o'-war. And there was much necessary correspondence, and the not-yet-familiar routine of maintaining an undisciplined army.

But first of all there was Sir John Cope. Flatter him as they might, the young women of old Edinburgh could not get Charles' mind away from that camp in Duddingstone and the approaching battle with the English.

Cope was kindlier with Charles' patience than the Highland chiefs. The Prince entered Edinburgh on September 17, 1745. The previous day, Cope had disembarked his men at Dunbar, having decided against Leith when he learned of the proximity of the Highlanders. On the 19th, Cope started his march toward the capital.

Delay at this juncture might have been fatal. As before, everything depended upon the morale of the Highlanders. Untried in battle, unaccustomed to the Lowlands, superstitious about cannon (they called it "The Mother of the Musket" and imputed to it all sorts of marvelous powers), these clansmen were capable of putting up a magnificent fight if only they were led into action while they were still enthusiastic by somebody they loved and respected.

The little army was growing larger now. Maclachlan of Maclachlan had joined with 150 men; Lord Nairne had brought in several hundreds more from Athole; the recruiting sergeants had managed to get a few Edinburghers to join the two hundred-odd men serving under Perth's banner. There might have been more soon. But Cope was coming and, on the 19th, leaving only a small palace guard, Charles placed himself at the head of his men and drew sword. Then he unstrapped the scabbard and threw it into the roadway, saying:

"We will return with victory or not at all! See here is my sword—I have thrown away the scabbard!"

There was a great cheering and the bonnets went up again; then the pipes blew up and the clansmen marched out of Duddingstone. They left Friggat Burn behind them and took the pleasant way to Musselburgh, where they crossed the Tweed by that ancient bridge you may still see there. The Romans had built that bridge; and stout Wallace had trod it; and Robert the Bruce, and the Black Douglas, and all the Stuart Kings of the old times had crossed it, going to war or returning from war; and lovely Queen Mary had cantered over it; and Cromwell had thundered across it on his charger. As for Prince Charles, he crossed the bridge on foot. He had refused a coach, refused even a horse. Instead, he walked at the head of the men or, surrounded by staff officers, strode through the stubble fields by the side of the road. He was gay; and he waved his hand to the chieftains, and smiled at the pretty girls who came out to watch the army pass.

You must not suppose that he walked a mile or so for effect, and then called for a carriage. One of the things it is pleasant to report about this young man is his ability to endure fatigue. The hardy mountaineers with whom he was associated thought nothing of tramping thirty-five or forty miles a day over the roughest sort of countryside; and Prince Charles never lagged behind.

The men, too, were gay that afternoon. The nearness of

fight filled them with happiness. The pipes were playing, and some of the Highlanders were singing:

"Oh, who'd na ficht for Charlie?
"Oh, who'd na draw the sword—"

They went swinging up Edge-Buckling Brae, passed around Walleyford and over Fawside Hill, took the post road at Douphiston, ascended Birsley Brae and, about half-a-mile west of Tranent, came suddenly upon the enemy.

The men raised a shout, drew their claymores, unslung their targets, and would have rushed down upon the enemy without further ado had not the gentlemen, their officers, restrained them.

Cope's officers, when they were leaving Dunbar, had boasted that the Highlanders would not even put up a defense of Edinburgh. Whether or not Cope himself believed this, we do not know; but he took no chances. His men were well arranged for battle, marching due west with the right flank toward the sea and the left flank inland. Cope had evidently not supposed, at least, that the Highlanders would take the high road instead of the smooth low road that ran alongside the sea. The high road was shorter, but Cope could not understand how an army could carry its baggage and artillery over it. He could not believe, of course, that the Highlanders had no baggage, and that their artillery consisted of one preposterous little mortar which wouldn't work. So when the clansmen appeared shouting, on the brow of the hill, there was a considerable dashing here and there of messengers below, and the foot regiments were wheeled, the dragoons shifted, the cannon dragged forward. Cope took a stance: it was about all he could do for the hour.

And yet, the Highlanders would have been rash to attack then. Wiser heads advised an examination of the ground between the Prince's men and the English. Ker of Graden, an aide-de-camp, volunteered to reconnoiter: he rode down the hillside, stopped at a wall, drew off some stones, led his horse through the opening, mounted again, nodded, made notes, and in due time rode slowly back to report. All this, you must understand, was done in a shower of bullets from the English camp. Ker of Graden, however, was not touched, and his coolness had a good effect on the clansmen. He reported that the ground between the armies was marshy, spotted with dangerous holes, intersected by enclosures, and cut at the bottom by a broad, deep, ditch alongside of which ran a thick hedge. To charge down such a hill would be foolishness. Besides, it was getting dark. So they decided to camp for the night. Lord Nairne was dispatched with 500 men to a point where they could block Cope if the English general tried to slip off to Edinburgh.

The night was chilly. There was no moon, and no stars. The Englishmen, on the plain below, had lighted great fires which pressed harshly through the gloom, round and yellow and geometrically spaced: but a mist crawled in from the sea, and there was a faint, tiny-specked drizzle of rain, so that the campfires became blurred like lights seen through glazed glass. Prince Charles wrapped himself in a plaid, wished his officers good night, and curled up to sleep on a pile of straw in the middle of a field of cut peas.

Suppose you were a sentinel in this camp, watching the glare of those perfectly spaced campfires—wondering about the battle to come. Here was a fifteenth century host about to attack an eighteenth century army. The difference was enormous. The wild Scots were medieval. They belonged to the days before standing armies existed, the days when every man was a soldier who responded, not when his King called him out but rather when the baron to whom he paid tribute did so; the baron was responsible to the King. These sleepers around you, like the men of the Middle Ages, knew little or nothing about the cause for which they bore arms. They knew only that they had been summoned by their respective lords, and that they were to have other men pointed out to them for killing. They knew that they must fight in such a manner that their ancestors would feel no obligation to blush for them. They had seen the fiery cross whirl past their doors: they had heard the pipes sounding the ancestral rallying songs: and they had strapped on their claymores, gravely kissed their wives, and walked out to the castles of their various chieftains to report.

But down where the fires glowed the case was different. Those were hired soldiers, men who had embraced fighting as a profession, who received pay for it, and were trained and drilled until they had come to behave as nearly like machines as it was possible to make men behave. They, too, had little idea of what the quarrel was about. Soldiers don't usually. But they had agreed to do battle when called upon; and now they were ready to live up to the terms of their contract. They would be shot if they didn't. It was a choice between certain death and possible escape—not a difficult choice for any man to make.

This difference is of the highest importance to our story.

You must pause to note, also, while you are doing sentry duty, that these armies differed not only in spirit but in material things as well. The men below, around the fires, and the men who slept near you on the wet ground, were alike in that each had two arms, two legs, a head, etc. Otherwise they were different. The Englishmen had muskets, and had been taught to fire them in a certain manner. They were not asked to take any sort of aim, but merely to level their weapons in the general direction of the enemy, turn their heads in order to guard against a flare-back from the touchhole, fire, reload as rapidly as possible, fire again in the same manner, and then fall to with the bayonet. This had been drilled and drilled into them. They had been informed that the enemy, in each case, would do thus and so, and that they must meet this by doing exactly so and thus. It was all they knew, all they were expected to know. The English army, like its general, was absolutely conventional.

But not these men who slept around you! They had tribal spirit in common, but their weapons were a bewildering assortment—matchlocks, firelocks, swords, daggers, Lochaber axes, Jedburgh axes, even a few clubs and ancient crossbows; and one whole company of Macgregors was armed with scythe blades on poles. These men still used targets—round wooden shields over which leather was stretched tightly, and which were ornamented, usually, with big bosses, knobs and brass nails, and highly polished and cut in foliaceous designs. Moreover, although those who had muskets were excellent huntsmen, they had never learned to feel dependent upon this weapon but trusted more to their good claymores. The claymore was a long, heavy, two-edged broadsword, basket-hilted, pointed, and often cut with deep blood-gutters so that it might be withdrawn quickly from a human body. In the days of knightly combat it was, no doubt, highly effective: indeed, it was nothing more than a slightly abbreviated falchion. But would it be of any use against bayonets and cannon? Can you imagine an army with long bows and single-shot rifles attacking a force fully equipped with Springfields, machine guns, and hand grenades?

There on the hill that night you might well have had great fear for the slumbering Highlanders, looking down as you were on that trim camp where the fires were so exactly spaced. . . .

But there would not have been many hours for this sort of meditation. While the clansmen were dreamlessly slumbering, their weapons by their sides, one of their number, Robert Anderson, an East Lothian gentleman, son of Anderson of Whitburgh, was awake and wondering whether or not the Prince would be interested to know about something that he knew. This Anderson, after some excogitation, awakened his friend Lord George Murray and informed him of a path by means of which the soldiers could encircle the bog and without once being exposed, get between the Saxon and the sea. The spot was high ground, too, and all dry. Anderson had hunted over this territory many times, he told Lord George, and he was certain he could find the path despite the darkness and fog.

The Lieutenant-General did not hesitate. Within a few minutes Prince Charles, sitting on his pile of straw and wrapped in his plaid, was listening to Anderson, and like Murray was realizing that the suggestion was good. It was therefore decided to start the march promptly, and to make the high ground before dawn. The officers hurried in and out among the figures on the ground, shaking shoulders and hissing softly into upturned ears. The men rose, fully armed. One advantage of the Highland kilties was apparent now: it was not necessary for the wearers to buckle, button, trim, load, dress and arrange: they were ready as they stood.

They fell into line—two columns of three abreast—and marched away in perfect silence, careful not to let their weapons click or to expose the brightness of uncovered steel. A messenger was sent to fetch Lord Nairne and his men.

They came to a ditch. Prince Charles, on foot at the head of the Macdonalds, tried to jump it but fell short by inches and was covered with mud. He laughed, forgetting for the moment the need for silence. "Does any other man think he can make that ditch?" But it would hardly be polite to succeed where one's Prince had failed; and the Highlanders declined to try, instead lifting their kilties around them and wading through, wetting only their legs and brogues.

But they had been heard. Perhaps the Prince's laugh had given them away. There came a voice, calling, in English, "Who goes there?" The Highlanders gave no answer but stood motionless. Some shots were fired nearby, and then they heard receding hoofbeats on the soft, wet earth. A wee ribbon of smoke, in which there was the smell of gunpowder, drifted past their faces. Evidently a couple of cavalrymen, outposts, who had given the alarm. But it did not matter. For the clansmen were safe now, and it had not been part of their plan to launch a surprise attack: their only concern had been to get around the bog without being surprised. Let Cope know where they were! He would learn soon enough anyway!

They climbed a rocky hill, and the morass was behind them. It was dawn, but the fog obscured the enemy. Robert Anderson, however, informed them that they had reached a spot almost directly opposite to the one they had previously occupied. Not far away, down a slope, were the redcoats they could not see.

"Keep the men awake," was the order, but it was superfluous, for the men had no thought of sleep. The clans were wheeled into position. The Macdonalds were given the post of honor, the right wing, which had been theirs since Bannockburn. In the center were the wild Macgregors and the comparatively civilized warriors of the Duke of Perth. The left consisted of the Camerons and the Stewarts. Perth had command of the right, Lord George Murray of the left. In the second line were the Athole men and the vassals of Menzies of Struan. The Prince commanded this line, which was fifty yards behind the first. He had, of course, wanted to place himself at the very van, but the chiefs would not tolerate such rashness. They pointed out that if the Prince were killed their own necks were as good as noosed, their properties confiscated, and their families and friends insulted, scattered, hunted down, killed. So the Prince reluctantly and unpicturesquely consented to lead the second line.

They made their last prayers, unbonneting and raising their faces towards the sky. Targets were then unslung, swords unsheathed, and plaids tightened in place or cast off entirely. The order was given to advance, and they started down the hill.

"Mr. Cope shall not escape us this time," cried Prince Charles.

CHAPTER EIGHT

They Make Great Slaughter

THIS was a sloping cornfield, broad, level, and bare. The harvest had only recently been taken in, and the clansmen pushed through a thick stubble, their brogues rush-rushing against the stalk stumps. A breeze came in from the sea, and the mist curled away, writhing. The enemy was revealed.

Gentlemen of the Highland army afterwards admitted that their hearts sank when they saw the Englishmen, in serried ranks—every button, every bandolier, every cartridge box in the right place; the straight, unbroken row of Brown Besses and bright bayonets; and the black mouths of the cannon.

Cope's relative position was unchanged. He had simply made a right-about-face and now was facing east, just the opposite direction from which he had started, and with his back to Edinburgh. The cannon were in the center, with a dragoon guard and a foot guard, and manned by seamen brought up from Dunbar. Hamilton's dragoons were on the left, Gardiner's on the right. Bankton, Colonel Gardiner's mansion, was in the rear. The left extended toward the sea, while the right was protected by that same morass which on the previous night had stretched between the two armies.

At the sight of the enemy, the Highlandmen quickened their pace. Except for the rush-rushing sound, they were silent. They were described by one in Cope's army as looking like a hedge, when the mist first began to lift.

A ship stood motionless in the sea, its rail lined with staring sailors. On the heights and on the roofs of all the surrounding houses, the peasants watched.

The left wing had received too soon the order to advance,

or perhaps the right wing had not received it soon enough. At any rate, the army moved forward obliquely; and the left was about opposite the center of Cope's forces and doomed to charge directly into the dreaded cannon. Lord George Murray perceived, when the fog lifted, that a section of firm ground was left unoccupied on the left tip, and he was frantically trying to induce the Camerons to sidle into this for fear the dragoons would take advantage of it in a flanking movement. The Camerons moved into the position as they went forward, but this left a space between them and the Macgregors.

In truth, there was little plan or order. The clansmen instinctively formed into phalanxes, each chief at the front, his kinsmen, chieftains and principal gentlemen immediately behind him, with the soldiers, less well armed, coming up in the rear.

The men would walk no longer. They broke into a trot, which soon became a sprint. Those in front bent low, holding their targets above their heads to serve much the same purpose as modern trench helmets. The men began to yell at the top of their lungs—horrible war-cries hundreds of years old, in Gaelic. Bearded, half naked, sporrans swinging, swords held high, they dashed like madmen into the fray.

The sailors who manned the cannon took one look—and fled without firing a shot. The commander of the cavalry guard, Lieutenant Colonel Whitney, brought his dragoons forward and touched off some of the cannon himself: but he soon found that he was commanding men who had not changed since the canter of Colt's bridge. The onrushing Camerons fired a scattered volley, several redcoats were struck, the commander himself was wounded in the wrist; and then the Highlanders saw again the tails of Gardiner's horses. The foot guard, thrown into confusion by this precipitous retreat, fired one volley. As well try to stop a cyclone! The Camerons came in, screaming, with great leaps. They passed the cannon, cutting and slashing to right and left. Bayonets did not stop them: they would drop on one knee, throw off the opposing point with the target, and rise, thrusting or cutting with their claymores. The ancient scaling axes pulled dragoons from their horses, while other Highlanders dived underneath the animals, slashing open their bellies with sword and dirk. The *Skene dhu,* the ancient Highland *misericorde,* did deadly work. Some of the clansmen grasped it in the left hand, and carried the claymore in the right, so that they were able to deal out death on both sides at once.

Nearer the center, the Macgregors under Glencairnaig were sprinting into glory with the Camerons and the Stewarts. The Macgregors under young Malcolm of Craigtree were separated from the others because of the oblique movement of the Camerons: and, too, they were the poorest armed men in the Prince's army, depending almost entirely on scythe blades and clubs. They were met with a withering volley. Craigtree fell, five bullets in his body. But he braced himself on one elbow, and while the blood poured out of his wounds he cursed his men: "I'm not dead! Go on! Go on! The man who stops will hear from me!" So the Macgregors went on, and made great slaughter among the English.

The Macdonalds, on the right, were almost cheated of their tussle. The very sight of this clan approaching, with hellish ferocity, shrieking, brandishing their broadswords, was too much for Hamilton's dragoons. Once again Highland eyes were treated to a sight of the tails of English horses: the dragoons did not even pause to fire a shot. The foot soldiers here also broke and ran, wishing, doubtless, that they, too, had horses.

All this, which takes many words to tell, *actually happened in less than five minutes!* There was a charge, a clash of weapons, then a panic. The second line of the Highland army, which was only fifty yards behind the first, and which charged as rapidly, found not a single redcoat on his feet when it swept up to the place of battle.

The clansmen could not be restrained, but flew after the panic-stricken enemy like the savages they were. The deadly claymore rose and fell, bloodier at every stroke. It was a heavy weapon and, in the hands of powerful men, it clipped off the legs of horses and the arms of men as neatly as though they were twigs of trees. One redcoat faced a Macgregor whose claymore was uplifted: the poor fellow threw an arm over his head to ward off the blow, but the claymore bit through the arm, severing it, and sank an inch into the skull beneath. There was a profusion of blood. Heads were sliced off with single strokes. Bodies were slashed open from shoulder to hips. Brains were laid bare.

Colonel Gardiner, overcome with humiliation when he saw his men retreating again, did all that a soldier and a gentleman could do. He tried to bring up what horsemen he had left; and when this failed, and he saw a few companies of infantry striving to make a stand, he dismounted, placed himself at their head and fought with vigor until an axe blow from behind stretched him upon the field.

A great number of the foot soldiers dashed blindly back toward Preston Park, which was walled and seemed to offer some sort of refuge. The crush at the gate, however, prevented most of them from entering that way and, when the poor fellows attempted to climb the wall, the Highlanders fell upon them unmercifully. More than 400 were killed before the chieftains could call off their followers. About 700 others gladly surrendered.

Some 200 men escaped, but had Charles possessed a few squadrons of cavalry, even these men would have been captured or killed. As it was, the clansmen, on foot, went sprinting in every direction in pursuit of the Saxons, who cast their weapons from them in order to run the faster.

One Highlander, armed with pistol and sword, chased a group of ten Englishmen. "Stop!" he cried. They stopped in their tracks, dropping their muskets, trembling, not even daring to turn their heads. The victor marched the entire group back to the field.

The Earl of Traquair's chaplain, unarmed, came upon half a dozen soldiers at Peebles, and called upon them to surrender. So terrified were they that they were about to obey when a Whiggish farmer, waving a pitchfork, urged them to run—and they did that instead.

Colquhoun Grant killed a dragoon, mounted the dead man's horse, and chased a whole company of cavalry all the way to Edinburgh. The gates were opened for these cravens, but Grant was so close behind them that he, too, got inside the gates before they were closed. He chased the men up the High street, but they reached the safety of the castle too soon for him. Then he found himself alone and faced by a hostile populace. He merely grinned, dismounted, and went into a draper's shop and ordered a fine new tartan to be made up for him in time for the triumphant return of the Prince. He rode back to the Netherbow Gate. There was a movement in the crowd to stop him, to swarm over him. But he did not budge. "*Open that gate!*" The huge shoulders, the brawny arms, the long and bloody broadsword, the stern face, were too much for the Edinburghers; Colquhoun Grant rode out untouched.

Prince Charles was soon in the center of things at the field, directing the work of quieting the clansmen—the most difficult job of that bloody day. He wore a coarse tartan, a scarlet waistcoat trimmed with gold lace, a blue bonnet, and boots which were splashed with mud to his knees. He was troubled about the wounded: if he took them to the churches there would be a hue and cry about sacrilege ordered by a Catholic; if he used private homes it would be complained that he was violating property rights. He was considering a plan to send them all to Holyroodhouse, throwing open his own apartments for them if necessary.

But it was difficult to decide on anything, or to do anything. The clansmen, once they had been restrained from slaughtering what Saxons were left, thought only of plunder. They stripped the bodies of the English dead, leaving them bare on the muddy field. They looted the baggage, and this afforded them vast delight. For the first time in their lives they tasted chocolate and other delicacies. The officers' extra wigs were a revelation also, as were the clothes, the razors, and, in fact, almost everything that was turned over. There were brandies, too, and some fine wines. The wild Scots helped themselves, after the ancient custom. Soon the field was filled with jabbering savages wearing bright bandoliers over their tartans, powdered perukes on their heads, and silk and satin knee breeches—another novelty—under their kilts. One fellow found a mirror, and presently he had a crowd around him, for this was marvelous. Another found a gold watch, and because of the ticking supposed it to be some sort of an animal: the next day, when it had run down, he sold it for a few pennies, later chuckling over his shrewdness at having obtained any price at all for a dead beast!

Meanwhile, Cope was making a frantic attempt to rally his cavalry, a mile or so from the field; but they were hopelessly unnerved, and he was swept along with them. They went full-speed to Lauder and Coldstream and, not feeling safe even there, to Berwick, where Lord Mark Kerr greeted their commander sarcastically. "I think you're the only general in Europe who ever brought the first tidings of his own defeat."

But Cope, at least, did not follow the usual practice of generals and report that he had been vastly outnumbered and had deemed it prudent to order a short retreat, and that this purely strategic movement had been conducted in good order. He wrote bluntly that ". . . our troops gave way . . . and we lost the day." He laid most of the blame on the dragoons, whose example of cowardice struck terror to the hearts of the foot soldiers.

The dragoons deserve most of the blame. Nevertheless, the infantry are not to be excused. Certain broad-minded authors, determined to see both sides at all costs, have attempted to apologize for these foot soldiers. The French say that all women are beautiful: and it is a fond English history-writing tradition that all British soldiers are brave. Perhaps, however, all British soldiers are not brave in a uniform degree; and such occasions as Prestonpans are to be explained with the statement that the men happened to be *least brave* then. Bad generalship, green horses, a dubious defensive position, and the unfamiliar and terrible attack of the wild Scots, explain much, but not all. "None of the soldiers attempted to load their pieces again," Lord George Murray wrote afterwards, "and not one bayonet was stained with blood." And the Chevalier Johnstone, who was also present at the battle, wrote that "the cowardice of the English surpassed all imagination."

The conduct of Colonel Gardiner was a gratifying exception. What remained of him—for he had been badly hacked—was carried to his own house nearby, where he died a few hours later without having recovered consciousness. He had been a grand soldier, and at all times picturesque. As a youth, and in early middle-age, he had been a notorious rake. But while waiting at an assignation place one night for a married woman, he saw a vision of Christ on the Cross, imploring him to lead a holy life: from that night he had been a religious fanatic. A poet said of him, "Joseph Gardiner was afraid to sin, but never afraid to fight."

He was not the only wounded man taken to Bankton. Charles finally decided to remove all the wounded there. He was still having difficulty getting the dead buried. The Highlandmen, for all their barefootedness and ignorance, considered such a task beneath their dignity. They were warriors, not laborers. A true clansman was not supposed to work, but only to fight and drink. Eventually it was necessary to have the burial labor performed by peasants. The dead all went into one huge grave; but this was the next day.

Henderson, a Whig, draws a colorful picture of Prince Charles laughing and joking on the field after the battle, while the groans of the dying rose all around him. But Home, who was also a Whig, says that Charles stayed on the field until nearly midnight, taking care of the wounded and seeing to the comfort of the prisoners. And remember, Charles had not enjoyed more than an hour or so of sleep in the past forty hours.

In fact, although he naturally rejoiced in a victory so spectacular and so decisive, he was downcast at the sight of so much blood and suffering. He was a tender-hearted lad. That night he wrote to his father: "If I had obtained this victory over foreigners my joy would have been complete: but as it is over Englishmen, it has thrown a damp upon me that I little imagined. . . ." He gave out strict orders that there should be no official celebration, since the victory had been won at the expense of so many English lives—the lives of honest but misguided subjects of King James.

The Prince finally retired to Pinkie House. It had been a glorious day. He was entitled to his sleep. Nor could he be kept awake by the groans of the wounded men, the shouts of the drunken Scots, and the awful wails of the women who stumbled through the rain and the mist, over the muddy, bloody field, seeking among the naked corpses for their loved ones.

CHAPTER NINE

The Dash for London

WHAT was the best way to reap the benefits of this victory? The very night of the battle there was a discussion on the advisability of marching straight to Berwick and frightening the English into submission; but the more cautious advisors did not believe that the army was yet large enough to keep up communication with the North, and this must be done, they argued, if they were to hope for French assistance.

Charles, that night, sent a proclamation to Edinburgh instructing the Presbyterian clergymen to continue their services as usual the next day, which was Sunday; but the clergy, either from fear or subtlety, refused to do so.

Charles returned to the city with some show; but his command that there should be no official celebration, remained. He dispatched a messenger to the Court of France, giving a glowing account of the battle and begging for troops, and another messenger was sent down into England to warn the Jacobites there to be ready to rally around the Stuart standard.

Holyrood became a brilliant court, with a formal levee every morning, a council of war, public dinners, balls and receptions. Recruits were coming in faster now—Lord Olgivy brought 600 men, Farquharson of Montaltrie brought 30, Gordon of Glenbucket came with 400 Grants and Farquharsons, Lord Pitsligo had 132 horsemen and 248 foot soldiers under him when he appeared, and the Earl of Kilmarnock, The Mackinnon, Viscount Dundee and others, each appeared with a small body of warriors. The army at Duddingstone was drilled and drilled. Two companies of cavalry were organized, under Lord Elcho and Arthur Elphinstone, who was soon to become Lord

Balmerino; and Kilmarnock was given command of the newly raised horse grenadiers. Money was received, and levies of shoes, tents, canteens, etc., collected. The Highlanders objected to sleeping in tents: they consented to do so only as a favor to the Prince, who was eager to have his army seem a bit more orthodox. A treaty was made between the French Minister of War and Charles' agent in Paris, by which Louis the Fifteenth bound himself to assist the Prince in defending such provinces as had submitted to him. Charles was now master of Scotland. There was no English army in that nation; the militia was unable to rise; and the only regulars left in arms were the small garrisons at the Stirling and Edinburgh castles, and at the four fortresses of the Highlands.

It all looked well. The world had been amazed. The victory sounded impressive both in France and in London. In London, to be sure, they could scarcely believe it. Walpole wrote to a friend, "But sure, banditti can never conquer a kingdom!"

Yet there were troubles, even then. Underneath the brilliant court were things to worry Charles. For example, so much still hung on the promises of French politicians. . . . Much also depended upon harmony in his council, and this was never remarkable. The council, which met in the palace every morning at 10 o'clock, consisted of the Duke of Perth, Murray of Broughton, Lord George Murray, Young Lochiel, Lord Ogilvy, Lord Nairne, Lord Elcho, the Macdonald of Keppoch, Young Clanranald, the Macdonald of Locgarry, the Stewart of Ardshiel, Sir Thomas Sheridan, the Gordon of Glenbucket, and O'Sullivan, who was quartermaster-general of the army. A few, notably the Irishmen and Murray of Broughton, believed or professed to believe, that a prince of the blood royal could do no wrong. The others did not feel that way about it. Murray of Broughton was maneuvering to get Charles' fullest confidence, and his chief obstable was the plain-spoken Lord George Murray. So Broughton began to make up little stories about Lord George, and to circulate these. . . . It was said that the lieutenant general was really a traitor, a man who had joined the cause for no other reason than to betray it. Nothing could have been less true. Charles had no more ardent and faithful servant. But Charles did not like to be told to his face that he was sometimes wrong and Lord George, from the beginning, was the spokesman for that two-thirds of the council which had a mind of its own. Bad feeling was engendered between the Scots and the Irishmen. The Scots were supplying the real brawn for the uprising: they were taking the chances: they had staked everything on this enterprise, and felt they should have some say in the manner in which it was conducted. The Irishmen had staked little or nothing. Most of them were penniless adventurers anyway, and many held commissions either in the French or Spanish services so that, in case they fell into the hands of the British government, they could not be hanged. Murray of Broughton, although playing his own little game all the time, sided generally with the Irishmen. He also sided with the Duke of Perth, a favorite of Charles. Murray encouraged the jealousy between Perth and Lord George, with a view of effecting his lordship's downfall.

All Scotland was Charles'; but the possession was none too secure. The Lowlands did not seem to get enthusiastic for the Stuart cause. The recruits were mostly coming from the Highlands. Lowland gentlemen joined, but not many Lowland commoners.

Moreover, even the Highlands were none too certain. The Lord of the Isles and of Sleat, stubborn Sir Alexander Macdonald, was still refusing to enlist under the Stuart banner, and so was the Macleod of Macleod. Lord Lovat continued to procrastinate: Simon was trying to arrange matters so that he could have charge of an army to remain in the Highlands, ostensibly to serve Charles' purposes there, but actually to be of service to whichever side appeared to be destined for victory. With these three chiefs pledging him their men, Charles' army would have been doubled; and he still hoped to get them.

The fact that the clergymen, excepting the Rev. Mr. Macvicar of the West Church, who was protected by the guns of the Castle, refused steadfastly to preach on Sundays, was also discouraging. Then, too, it was difficult to conduct business in the capital because the bankers at the first alarm had transported all their specie up into the Castle and now, in spite of Charles' promises, they refused to bring it down for circulation. The Castle itself still held out against the Prince. General Preston, who had succeeded General Guest in command, could afford to remain defiant, for he had plenty of provisions. Charles established a blockade. That did little good. General Preston sent down word that he would open fire upon the town unless the blockade were removed. Charles could not believe that any modern commander could wantonly destroy property and endanger life in this fashion, so he kept his men on guard. But the Cannon of the Castle spoke, a couple of houses were blown to pieces, and Charles hastily removed the blockade.

In Rome, James continued to write graceful letters. He wrote one to King Louis, informing him that his younger son, Henry, Charles' only brother, was soon to be sent to Paris. Henry, with British spies thick about the palace, was reported to be confined to his bedchamber with smallpox: and, while the reports were circulated, he slipped out of the city as quietly as Charles had done more than a year before. He might have gone to Madrid as admiral of the fleet the Spanish government was about to assemble for a descent upon Ireland, or he might have gone to Paris to take nominal command of an army of 10,000 men King Louis was to assemble at and near Dunkirk for an invasion of England. He chose Paris—unfortunately, as it happened. He was well received by Louis, and for six months he reviewed troops and said his prayers. The Duc de Richelieu was in actual command of the army of invasion, and Henry was not highly esteemed. "You may perhaps gain the Kingdom of Heaven by your prayers, but never the Kingdom of Great Britain," Richelieu remarked one day when Henry held up a council of war because of attendance at a mass. Henry did all he could, but it wasn't much, for the lad was not cut out for this sort of work. He sent off boats with money and arms, privately financed; but most of these were stopped by British privateers or men-o'-war. Some few vessels anchored at Montrose not long after the first battle, bringing about 10,000 stand of arms, some money, and a sort of unofficial observer from the Court of France. The exact status of the Marquis D'Eguilles was never altogether clear. Charles received him with great pomp as an official ambassador, but it soon became apparent that D'Eguilles was sent chiefly or wholly to watch and report. France, like Lord Lovat, was procrastinating.

Meanwhile the British government was not idle. George the Second was back on the job. Parliament voted him confidence and plenty of money for the raising of men. The militia was summoned in both Scotland and England; General Wade, at Newcastle, was reinforced; the Duke of Cumberland, the King's younger son, was given command of another army in England; commissions were distributed in the Highlands so that the loyal clans, such as they were, could assemble under Lord Loudon; Colonel John Campbell, heir to the chiefship, hurried up to Argyle and raised his clan for the service of the German; regiment after regiment was hastily called in from Flanders; and 6,000 Dutch soldiers were brought over as mercenaries. . . . "I wish they were all Dutch, that I might not have the pain of shedding English blood," Charles wrote to his father.

Charles had hundreds of prisoners on his hands. The British government, which persisted in treating his invasion as a popular uprising rather than as a legitimate civil war, refused to arrange a cartel for their transfer. Some of them were induced to join the Prince's army, though most of these deserted at the first opportunity. The others he was obliged to release on their paroles that they should not bear arms against him—paroles which many of them promptly broke. Charles was urged to keep the principal officers taken at Prestonpans, as hostages, in case any of his own officers fell into the hands of the British; but this he refused to do, for he would never, under any circumstances, take their lives in cold blood, anyway, he declared and it was beneath his dignity to threaten something he never meant to do.

And now the time had come for some further action in the field. The Highlanders, with nothing to do in camp, were restless; after the battle, as was their custom, many of them had deserted, honestly supposing that the war was over. The private contributions were not coming in as fast as they had been immediately after the battle; and the public levies were not aiding Charles' popularity. Evidently France was not quite ready to move yet. Nor was Spain doing anything more about the invasion of Ireland. So Charles proposed to his council that the army, numbering now close to 6,000 men, move against London without further delay.

This was a proposal in keeping with his high spirits and confidence. But most of the Highland chiefs disapproved it and, as usual, Lord George Murray was their spokesman. The chiefs urged Charles to remain in Scotland, to take the castles of Edinburgh and Stirling and the forts of the north; to continue to receive reinforcements; and to wait for the arrival of the French assistance he was always promising them. General Wade, at Newcastle, already had a superior army: if they marched against Wade, the chiefs said, their chances of success were poor, but if they forced Wade to come to Scotland after them they could pick their position and fight at a much greater advantage. A defeat in England would lead to fatal confusion; whereas a defeat in Scotland might be remedied by a prearranged rendezvous promptly sought. Not only that, but the chiefs had no desire to subdue England. They had already restored a Stuart to the throne of Scotland, and they were willing to fight to keep him there; but they failed to see why they should fight another nation's battles. If the Jacobites of England really desired King James instead of King George, let them say so, and let them do something about it.

Charles insisted that the Jacobites in England would rise in large numbers and enlist under the white banner. They only awaited his coming, he said. The chiefs were not so sure of that.

Lord George Murray finally suggested a compromise. The army should march for England, but cross the border on the west, not on the east, where Wade was. If Wade wanted to intercept them, he would then be obliged to do so in hilly country—the sort of country in which the Highlanders would have the advantage—and only after a fatiguing series of marches.

If Wade did this, they could stop and meet him with good chances of success, or they could easily slip past him. If they slipped past him, he would be afraid to march up into Scotland and leave England at the mercy of the wild Scots—just as Cope, after his side-stepping at Corryarrack, had been afraid to do anything but hasten south again.

To be sure, Cumberland was assembling an even greater army further south. But that was a bridge they could cross when they came to it.

This plan was accepted by Charles, who was determined to get into England by any route.

So on the first day of November, about six weeks after the battle of Prestonpans, the army started south in two columns. Ker of Graden led a cavalry feint to give the impression that the army was about to descend upon Newcastle. The whole business was skillfully arranged: Wade knew that the Highlanders were about to invade England, but he did not know by which of the three main routes they were coming. Charles marched at the head of the clans, a target over his shoulder, a claymore by his side. "In dirty lanes and deep snow he took his chance with the common men," wrote Maxwell of Kirkconnell, "and seldom could be prevailed upon to get on horseback to pass a river." His carriage he turned over to Lord Pitsligo, who was very old and a semi-invalid.

They crossed the Eske on the 8th of November, and then they were in England. The clansmen were superstitious about it—the more so because Young Lochiel, in drawing his claymore for a dramatic crossing of the border, accidentally cut his hand. The clansmen had been deserting ever since the start south; there were about 1,000 fewer of them when the Eske was crossed.

On the tenth they sat down before Carlisle. The city refused to surrender, and like Edinburgh earlier, made many boasts to keep up its courage. A siege was commenced, under the Duke of Perth, although it was Lord George Murray who had made the plans.

Then came an alarm that Wade was marching across country. Charles called his men away from the siege and assembled them at Brampton, where the ground was mountainous. But Wade, who found the snow too deep for him, struggled only part of the way west and then struggled back again. Charles sent half his army back to boastful Carlisle and, on the evening of the 14th, the white flag was hoisted in that city.

The garrison and the commandant, Colonel Durand, were disarmed and dismissed on their parole not to bear arms against Charles for twelve months, and the city was well treated.

But Charles had appointed Murray of Broughton and the Duke of Perth to make arrangements for the capitulation and Lord George Murray was not to be ignored like that. Lord George, in a fit of indignation, wrote his resignation as Lieutenant-General, offering, however, to serve as a common soldier without pay as long as the Prince desired.

Charles answered childishly. "I think yr advice ever since you join'd me at Perth has had another guess weight with me than what any General Officer cou'd claim as such. I am therefore extremely surprized you shou'd throw up yr commission for a reason which I believe was never heard of before. . . . I accept of yr demission as Lieutenant General, and yr future services as a Volunteer."

Then Charles mounted a fine white charger, and preceded by no less than 100 pipers, formally entered Carlisle.

But the matter was not permitted to rest there. Murray of Broughton might congratulate himself that he had at last obtained what he wanted. But there were men of cool sense in this army, and they knew that Lord George was the military genius of their midst, the man for the job. They would not stand for the acceptance of his resignation. They waxed outspoken. And the Duke of Perth, who was never mean, despite his dislike of Lord George personally, settled a delicate matter by resigning his own commission as Lieutenant-General and requesting of the Prince that Lord George be given sole command. This was done, fortunately.

But the business left more hard feeling than ever. Prince Charles was incurably suspicious of Lord George. Broughton kept muttering that his lordship had been in conference with Cope before joining the Stuart army; and this remained in the mind of the Prince. Lord George, too, had tried to get a second audience for the delegates from Edinburgh before that city had surrendered; and this, too, although probably prompted by nothing more than misplaced politeness, made Charles suspicious. The big objection to Lord George, however, was the fact that when he thought Charles incorrect he said so. The Stuarts weren't accustomed to being told they were wrong. In fact, the Stuarts could not believe they ever *were* wrong. In the old days, Scotland had kept them somewhat in their place: when a king presumed too much, the feudal barons killed him, or exiled him, or at least made it perfectly clear to him that he could go no further. But when the Stuarts moved into St. James, and became Kings of England and Ireland, as well as of Scotland, they found humbler subjects. The seventeenth century idea of kingship spoiled them. The example set by Versailles, the divine-right theory, went to their heads. And Charles still thought that a Stuart could do no wrong.

Nevertheless, Lord George was a good general. Even Charles could not deny this. The march into England was a little masterpiece of military art. The army slipped dexterously past Wade, leaving that old gentleman in a swirl of bewildering reports. Now it was to slip past Cumberland's army, at the time commanded by Sir John Ligonier. This army numbered about 10,000, more than double the size of that of the Prince.

Before the invaders moved south, they held another council. Should they return to Scotland? march east and attack Wade? wait in Carlisle and see what happened? or go on for London?

Lord George and the other Highland gentlemen thought it dangerous to go on to London when England, thus far, had not contributed a single recruit. But Charles still cherished that pretty dream about the population throwing itself on its knees in front of him the minute he appeared. Charles was obliged to admit that something had gone wrong so far. But in Lancaster, notoriously a Jacobite stronghold, things would be different. Charles pointed out that when he appeared in person at Manchester, the Jacobites would have no further excuse for not offering their services. The chiefs were doubtful; but they did not want to seem cowards, and they agreed to go on with the understanding that if the Jacobites did *not* appear in reasonably large numbers, the army would turn back while turning back was still possible.

So on the 21st they started for Penrith. The people there were not sympathetic. Up and down the army, at least among the gentlemen—the only ones who knew what it was all about—ran the murmur that all England was going to be lukewarm, if not definitely hostile, and that the army was going to be caught between two other armies and London.

On the day they reached Penrith, the 22nd, the King of France sent the first official reinforcement—Lord John Drummond, himself a Scot, who landed with about 800 men at Montrose. These men, although in French pay, were all Scots and Irishmen. But they were still technically French; and because of this the Dutchmen at Newcastle were forbidden to bear arms against them, under a previous treaty between Louis and the Netherlands. However King George had anticipated this. The Dutchmen were ordered back; but 6,000 Hessian troopers had previously been ordered over, and what had been gained to Charles was almost immediately lost.

Lord Drummond and his men marched to Perth, where other reinforcements for the Stuart army had already gathered. Notable among these were 800 Frasers. Lord Lovat had at last ventured to call out his clansmen for the cause; but he was afraid still, and instead of leading them out in person, he had commanded his oldest son, the Master of Lovat, to lead them forth, hoping in this way to have a scapegoat in case Charles' expedition failed.

This army at Perth was sufficient to hold in check the still smaller, and more uncertain, army under Lord Loudon, around Inverness. But it was of no immediate value to Charles in his dash for London, being much too far away.

The Highlanders marched to Kendal, then to Lancaster, then to Preston. Because in the great Civil War the Duke of

Hamilton had penetrated into England no further than Preston, and because, in 1715, Brigadier MacIntosh, too, had marched just that far south, there was a superstition in the Highland army that Scots could go no further. Lord George Murray knew this, and moved promptly to counteract it. He marched a good portion of the army over Ribble bridge, about a mile south of Preston. The spell was thus broken.

But although the clansmen might be happy, the gentlemen in charge of them were not. A few cheers had gone up when Charles had marched into Preston, and at Manchester there was genuine excitement. But the recruits were few. Altogether, less than 300 men enlisted and, excepting a few gentlemen, they were of the lowest sort—worthless, penniless, felons and hangers-on, who enlisted because they had nothing else to do, or because they hoped for loot, or because they wanted to be sure of regular meals.

On December 1, they pushed on to Macclesfield. Here they heard that Cumberland, with his 10,000 regulars, was at Lichfield. That put them in a dangerous position. Lord George made another neat and effective feint: he marched a column to Congleton, on the road to Newcastle-under-Lyme and Lichfield, while the main body hurried south to Derby. Cumberland, supposing that the entire Highland army was about to attack him, grinned grimly, fell back to Stone, and took up an excellent position. He waited. But he waited in vain. For Lord George had turned left, marched his long-legged clansmen through Leek and Ashburne, and rejointed his Prince at Derby.

Without maps, this maneuver is difficult to understand. In effect, the maneuvering was this:

A small army had started south. A greater one, confused because of the feints of its opponent, had fumbled for the smaller one, had missed it, and had remained, gasping, bewildered, at Newcastle. Another army, much larger and commanded by a younger and more energetic man, had tried to intercept the Highlanders. And the Highlanders, side-stepping like a good open-field football runner, had caused it to tackle too soon, had straight-armed it, and had gone sprinting down the field toward the goal.

There were, however, still more players in the way. The Prince was at least one day's march ahead of Cumberland now, thanks to the strategy of Lord George, and several days' march ahead of Wade. But German George had started to gather about him still another army. George, you must understand, had plenty of spunk! He might lack dignity, even decency, but he did not lack courage. On Finchley Common was assembled a motley host of some 30,000 volunteers. Almost six times the size of the Prince's army, this host nevertheless would probably have been put to rout by the Highlanders, its size, its loose-jointedness, and its exaggerated fears of the ferocity of the clansmen, all contributing to make it a doubtful protection for London.

The distance to London was but 127 miles and for the mountaineers that was no great distance at all. The clansmen had already exceeded the usual estimates of military experts by their speed on the march. They could easily do so again.

London was near panic. Only a trick prevented a run on the Bank of England. King George, himself at all times fearless, had placed his family and the royal art treasures on his private yacht, ready for a dash out to sea. Jacobites were drinking to the health of King James (it was all most of them ever did for James). Roman Catholics were delighted, Whigs were frightened.

It was not merely the approach of four or five thousand Highlanders which scared London like this. The thing that caused the panic was the threat of an invasion by the French or the Spaniards, or both; for although neither France nor Spain had really moved, or even meant to move, Englishmen could not believe that Prince Charles and his men would be so mad as to invade their country unless they had excellent assistance from another quarter. What was coming next? Nobody knew.

Even at Derby they did not know. The Highlanders, who had been eager for a fight these several months past, were sharpening their claymores, and every smithy in Derby was working overtime. The clansmen were speculating on what this, to them, almost fabulous city of London would prove to be like. They sang their songs, and danced their reels, and quarrelled over matters of hereditary precedence at the sharpening stones. They were ready, more than ready.

But the gentlemen were doubtful. In council, that morning of December 5, the Highland chiefs were telling Prince Charles that he must retreat.

As usual, Lord George undertook to do the telling. It was a task any other man would have been glad to avoid. Lord George talked common sense as opposed to chivalry and blind ambition. There were two armies behind them, one within a day's march; and one army in front. The countryside, even Manchester, had proved itself to be lukewarm, sometimes openly hostile to the Stuart cause. Recruits had been negligible. There was almost no money coming in. Five or six times their number, at least, were closing in on them, and unless they acted promptly to get out of this accidental trap, they would never get out at all. Once broken, in a strange country, the Highland army could never be reassembled. The chiefs had promised Charles that they would follow him into England in order to determine whether or not the English people wanted him. It was apparent now that the English people either did not want him or did not want him badly enough to lay down their lives for him. But the people of Scotland, Lord George said, *did* want their rightful Prince. In Scotland, the army would have some encouragement, and some support. There would be a feeling, unfortunate in the long run perhaps, but immediately desirable, that England was trying to crush her sister kingdom; and such a feeling would doubtless draw to arms many a man who was not sufficiently interested in the Stuart cause, as such, to risk his life for it. On the other hand, in England there was no doubt a feeling that this was a national affair—that the Scottish nation was up to its old tricks, and that all the Highlanders sought was excitement and plunder. With such a feeling current, how could they hope to get coöperation from the English?

Furthermore, in Scotland they could make themselves masters of Stirling and Edinburgh castles at their leisure, and still have time left with which to march out and meet an invading army. Also they could join their tardy reinforcements, the Frasers, the French troops, and the others, at Perth, and thus almost double their numbers. They would have prestige behind them, and something like an even chance in front of them.

When Lord George was finished the Prince flew into a rage, cursing them all, calling them traitors and cowards. Was he, or was he not, Prince Regent of Scotland, England and Ireland? Were they his subjects, or his masters? *They* give *him* orders! Did they realize that they were addressing Charles Edward Louis Philip Casimir Stuart? Or were they mad entirely? Or perhaps not mad, but merely frightened?

This, under the circumstances, must have been very hard to endure. But the chiefs were silent.

Charles changed his tactics abruptly. He stepped down among these grim, haughty mountain nobles, and appealed to each personally. Had Lochiel forgotten the deeds of Sir Ewan? Was Clanranald going to bring shame on the proud fighting name of the Clan Colla? And Ardshiel, did he purpose to watch Stewarts retreat before a Saxon enemy? Charles appealed to them, as he had appealed to them in the first place—not as a Prince but only as a brave and gallant young man, a handsome and high-spirited young man, who needed help and who had thrown himself upon the hospitality of men whose fidelity the veriest knave had never dared to question. Would they stand by and see the son of their King deserted in his hour of need? Had all the heart gone out of them, and were they mere cravens, considering only the material wants of the hour and the danger of the day?

This was yet harder to bear. But the chiefs were silent. Once before, when they should have known better, they had succumbed to Charles' charm. They were calloused against it now. And the Prince, in a rage again, dismissed the council.

All that day he had the chiefs in conference, one by one, trying to win them over to his side. He simply could not believe that they would be willing to turn back. Why, here was London hardly more than a hundred miles away!

London meant a lot to Charles. But it did not mean much to the chiefs. The thing was too obvious now. Even though they roundly defeated the host in Finchley Common, and took possession of the capital, Cumberland would be upon them almost before they could catch their breaths, and Wade was making all possible speed to join Cumberland from the north. Defeated, what mercy could they expect in England? How could they hope to escape? How, too, would their mothers and daughters, sisters and sons and aged fathers—how would they fare? What would happen to the ancient castles and the far estates? What would happen to the proud names?

All that day Charles argued with them, threatened them, implored them. . . . But when the council met again that night, the chiefs were still determined to retreat. And it was so ordered.

CHAPTER TEN

More Fighting

THE next morning, very early, they started back. Should they have done so? It is a fascinating theme for speculation. Now we know what they didn't know: that a large force of irregular volunteers was advancing to join them from Wales; that Lord Barrymore was out of the Tower, and with some other Jacobites had raised £10,000 for the Prince and was preparing to move out of London to greet him; that the population of the capital was panic-stricken; and that the army assembling on Finchley Common, for all its size, was composed chiefly of the riffraff of the city, was without discipline, and would probably scatter at the first volley.

In short, we know now that the Prince might have taken London, had he been able to persuade the Highlanders to follow him. At least, Lord Mahon and other reputable historians so aver.

Even then, however, his defeat would have been almost certain. The combined armies of Wade and Cumberland would certainly have attacked the Highlanders very soon after the capture of London and before they could have reassembled in a proper position. Retreat would have been definitely cut off. And the populace, although frightened, would still have been for the most part antagonistic to the Prince and would have done whatever it could behind his back to injure his chances of success.

In short, Charles probably could have captured the capital, but he could not have retained it; and when he had lost it he would have lost everything, his life included.

All this the clansmen did not know. They were in high spirits, their claymores sharp, their appetites for blood sharpened too. They went swinging along the country road out of Derby, fondly supposing—for it was not yet dawn—that they were on their way to the English capital, really believing that they would have a fight soon, and never doubting that they would win. The pipes blew up, and the men were singing *The Carles Wi' the Breeks,* and *Hey Tuttie, Tattie,* and *The Bonny Earl o' Moray,* and

"Hey, now the day dawis,
"The jolly cock crawis,
"Now shrouds the shawis
"Through nature anone;
"The thrissel cock cryis,
"O'er lovers wha lyis,
"Now skaill is the skyis;
"The night is near gone."

But they were not so happy when the dawn *did* come, and the fog lifted, for up and down the marching columns the clansmen began to recognize landmarks they had observed the day they had swung down into Derby. So they began to understand that they were in retreat. The singing died, the pipes were silenced, and there rose from the ranks a loud muttering which swelled to a howl of anger.

It was not good to retreat. They did not dare to disobey their chiefs; but they were no longer the eager soldiers of the march south. They fell in with the spirit of their Prince, and did not seem to care any longer what happened to them. Coming south they had been careful not to loot; going north they did not exercise this care, and it required all the efforts of the gentlemen to prevent outrages. They took their food where they found it, and sometimes they took more than food. They no longer had any heart for the cause of the white rose, now that they had been, as they supposed, disgraced.

Nor did Charles do anything to give them cheer and hope. Instead, the Prince behaved like a spoiled child, and no longer walked with the men and talked with them, but rode alone, on horseback or in a carriage with closed windows, snapping angrily at the chieftains and gentlemen who carried messages to him, glowering, muttering. . . . He rode in the van, while Lord George Murray followed, a day's march behind; his lordship had volunteered to command the rear, the post of honor because it was the post of danger, on the understanding that the artillery and baggage would all be kept in the van, so that he and his men would be free to maneuver as they thought best.

In spite of all this, the army was not really disorderly, and the men never got out of hand. As the difficulties increased, indeed, their discipline became better. For if the trip south had been hard, the trip back north was harder still. The roads were atrocious, and made even worse by small bodies of newly raised militia and groups of peasants who ripped them up and felled trees across them in order to harrass the Highlandmen. Cumberland had been neatly evaded, and left two days march in the rear; but Cumberland used all his cavalry in quick pursuit, and might be expected to attack soon. The situation was serious.

They marched up through Leek, Macclesfield, Manchester, Wiggan and Preston. The countryfolk, enheartened to observe that a retreat was in progress, pestered them continuously, swarming around them like flies on the back and flanks of a tired horse. The Duke of Perth was given a small body of cavalry and sent ahead to summon the reinforcements south: if the men at Perth met the northbound Highlanders at or near the border it might be possible to hold Carlisle and attack Berwick. But the Duke and his men were not permitted to advance far; the militia, greatly outnumbering them, forced them to retreat, and they rejoined the Prince at Penrith. Charles, meanwhile, had decided to turn on Cumberland and give battle. After the council at Derby, the chiefs had no say in any decision, Charles having announced his determination to run everything himself in the future, without consulting them. However, when Charles learned about Perth's return, he ordered the army to continue north toward Kendal, by way of Shap.

Perth's failure, and the hostility of the English people,

made Charles more peevish than ever. He had been accustomed to rise at dawn, or even earlier, but now he was up late every morning, and every morning the army was kept waiting for him. In spite of his promise to Lord George, the artillery and baggage were permitted to lag, and the care of them was added to the other work his lordship was now obliged to do. And Cumberland kept hurrying along in the rear.

It was a dark night, and the moon, in its second quarter, was visible only at irregular intervals, when Cumberland came upon the rear of the Highland army. Lord George and his men were at Clifton; the Prince's part of the army was a full day's march ahead.

Lord George moved out on the moor to reconnoiter. One of his parties captured two men, an officer in a green uniform, and a liveried person who turned out to be one of Cumberland's own footmen. From these fellows they learned that the Duke himself was in command of 4,000 men only a few miles away. It might have been an exaggeration. But on the other hand, it might have been true. Certainly there was a considerable body of horse gathering across the moor—at least as many men as Lord George had available, and possibly more. If Lord George retreated now he would be obliged to march his men along a narrow road bordered by high banks, where they would be exposed to fire on both sides and where a rout would be absolutely fatal. Even if he should retreat in fairly good order upon the Prince's part of the army, the Highlanders there, whose spirits were bad enough anyway, might be thrown into panic. On the other hand, here on Clifton moor Lord George had an excellent position, where, if he could only hold it, he might check the English advance for a time. There were ditches and enclosures on both sides of the narrow lane.

So his lordship sent to the van for reinforcements, and then tried an old military trick. He caused the banners to be unfurled and carried forward into the various ditches; then he caused them to be rolled up again, carried back, unfurled, and carried forward again and again. In this manner he created doubt in the English ranks as to the number of men who were waiting.

About 500 of the horsemen across the moor, not able to see very clearly what was taking place, and not having any Highland prisoners to wring the information from, dismounted and moved cautiously forward.

The Macdonalds of Glengarry, under Ker of Graden, were kept on the right, a position from which they might be enabled to flank the English; but they were given strict instructions not to cross the lane. Lord Pitsligo's horse were sent forward to egg the enemy into attack. The Macphersons, under Cluny, and the Stewarts, under Ardshiel, had the left and center.

So matters stood when Colonel Roy Stewart, who had carried forward the request for reinforcements, returned with the Prince's order to retreat!

Obviously the Prince had no conception, from where he was, of the gravity of the situation. Lord George led Colonel Stewart out on Clifton Moor and explained. Any soldier could understand. The two men agreed to "forget" the command.

Now Lord Pitsligo's horse, who had evidently learned a lesson from the Saxon dragoons, received a couple of musket shots and retreated in haste. The foot soldiers, however, stood firm.

The English dismounted hussars and dragoons crept forward and occupied a ditch within pistol shot of the Highlanders. This was done while the clouds blanketed the moon, and the Highland officers knew nothing of it until they were greeted with a terrific volley.

Lord George tells us that at the time he was talking with Cluny Macpherson, who looked up, startled, when the air was suddenly all angry whizzes.

"What the Devil is this?"

Lord George drew his sword and unslung his target. There was only one thing to do now. He went racing across the moor, yelling, "Claymores! Claymores!" Cluny Macpherson went after him. And all the others went after them. All the others, that is, except the Glengarry men, who, fortunately, obeyed orders and remained where they were.

They fell upon the English with delight. Some they killed, but most of the Saxons scrambled out of the ditch and started back across the moor. And the Glengarry enfilade split the air. Indeed, Lord George's plan had been the more effective because of that slight English advance. The only trouble was, that the Macphersons and Stewarts did not dare to pursue, for fear the Macdonalds would not be able to tell them from the English and would pour their deadly fire into every group they saw.

The English lost forty or fifty men, the Highlanders only a few. Ker of Graden did wonderful work keeping the Macdonalds in place. He was, according to Lord George, "an excellent officer, and was riding through the fields at the time of fire, as if it had been a review." * The Lieutenant-General himself lost his hat and wig, and had a great deal of paint knocked off the target Gordon of Glenbucket had lent him.

The Highlanders lingered for several hours on the moor, as though to say, bully-fashion, "Come on back, if you want to fight!" But the English had seen enough for one night, and indeed, for some time. The skirmish—it was too small to dignify with the name of battle—was of the greatest importance. It probably saved the Highland army from destruction, and it taught Cumberland to respect the clansmen, so that the English Duke, during the rest of the retreat, did not press his enemy too closely again.

Charles did not like to abandon Carlisle. It was suggested to him that the fortifications be torn down, so that the town could easily be retaken later. But instead of that, Charles left more than 300 men there as a garrison. He might as well have tied their arms behind them, put halters around their necks, and delivered them over to Cumberland as a little gift of war. It is not certain that Charles alone was to blame for this extraordinarily stupid act, but it is probable that he was. For he was giving all the orders now, and taking few suggestions from anybody except Sheridan, Murray of Broughton, and the other bootlickers.

This pitiful garrison consisted chiefly of the men of the so-called Manchester Regiment, who volunteered to remain, be-

* Henry Ker of Graden appears to have been what we would call today a "fightin' fool." He is the same who examined the ground at Prestonpans before the Highland change of position, when he rode calmly, even slowly, through a hail of bullets. At Culloden, too, he was remarked for his cool bravery. He was one of the Prince's aides-de-camp.

lieving, according to Captain Morgan, one of their members, that "it would be better to be hanged in England than starved in Scotland." They were easily captured two days afterwards.

The Highlanders went back across the Eske. This was the Prince's twenty-fifth birthday anniversary. They went up the west coast to Glasgow, which had been opposed to the Stuart cause from the beginning and had raised about 600 volunteers, who at the time were guarding the fords at Frew for the purpose of preventing Charles from again attacking the capital or retreating back into the hills from whence he had come. Charles was coldly received in this city. He extracted from it some £10,000, and remained about ten days, wearing his fanciest French clothes and putting up his greatest show of power, but failing to impress the inhabitants. Here he reviewed his entire army in one place at one time: it had previously been his custom to review the army only in broken groups, in order to give no one an opportunity of estimating its size.

On January 3, 1746, he started east for Stirling. The Glasgow troops at Stirling retreated to Edinburgh, where they joined the members of the reassembled Edinburgh Regiment. For the Scottish capital was again all pride and preparation. On January 13, the State officers, who had disappeared before the coming of the Highlanders, returned with much pomp and marched in triumphal procession while the music bells of St. Gile's rang gaily and the garrison in the castle fired a round of cannon in salute.

The first night on the way to Stirling, Charles stopped at Kilsyth. The second night he stopped at Sir Hugh Patterson's house in Bannockburn. Sir Hugh was an ardent Jacobite. So was his niece, Miss Clementina Walkinshaw, who had been named after Charles' mother and who fell in love with Charles himself the moment she saw him. Of Miss Clementina we shall hear more later. She was at this time twenty years old and, judging from her portraits, attractive without being conventionally pretty—a thin, passionate girl, with a sensitive face.

The citizens of Stirling, even more foolish than the citizens of Edinburgh had been—because their walls were weaker and they themselves fewer in number—made a great show of defending their city. A few cannon shots brought them to reason, and they surrendered in a hurry.

But the castle was not so easily captured. The Prince demanded that it be surrendered to him. General Blackney invited him to come up and take it. So the Prince opened a siege He had the gates of the city closed, locking his army inside, as though to show the world that he would not engage in any other undertaking until he had captured this castle.

It was too brave a boast. Charles was obliged to give thought to what was going on in Edinburgh. The volunteers there had been joined by several regular regiments, including Hamilton's and Ligonier's (formerly Gardiner's) dragoons. This force was trifling, but it was soon increased by a considerable group from Wade's army and, about the same time that Charles was opening siege on Stirling Castle, the main body of Wade's and Cumberland's combined armies was brought up. There were then about 8,500 soldiers in Edinburgh. Cumberland himself had been obliged to return to court, and General Hawley, a blustering old veteran who had fought at Sheriffmuir, was in command.

Hawley thought Cope had been a pusillanimous fool. What was needed, Hawley said, was a *soldier,* a real *fighter!*—not a dandy in uniform who thought of his commission, when he thought of it at all, as he would think of an especially pretty snuffbox or some new and expensive periwig. What these rebels needed, Hawley said, was a line of bayonets and afterwards a lot of rope. He started to get things ready for his victory as soon as ever he arrived in Edinburgh, when he supervised the construction of no less than ten gallows for the benefit of any rebels who might be left after the battle to come.

The reinforcements from Perth had joined the Prince at Stirling, and the Highland army now numbered about 9,000. Hawley, with slightly less than this number, was expecting 5,000 Hessians. But Hawley saw no reason for waiting until he had superior forces. Once the gibbets were up, he commanded the drums to be sounded and the banners unfurled, and set out to lift the siege of Stirling. Charles, at this time, was one day in Stirling directing the progress of that siege, and the next day at Bannockburn enjoying the hospitality of Sir Hugh Patterson and the company of Sir Hugh's charming niece. Lord George Murray, with his own five battalions of foot and Pitsligo's and Elcho's horse, marched out to check the English; but at Linlithgow, when he learned how many they were (he had evidently been misinformed, previously, of their numbers) he retreated to Falkirk, and later joined the Prince at Bannockburn.

Hawley took his time. He hoped that the rebels would stand and face him, but he hardly expected them to do so. They had, to be sure, faced Cope. But they were going to meet a *real* soldier this time. The right wing at Sheriffmuir, in which Hawley had fought, had been victorious against the Highland left wing, and Hawley judged all of these fellows by the ones he had met at that battle. Besides, Cobham's dragoons and the Argyleshire militia (the Clan Campbell) had joined him on the march, and he now considered himself invincible. He camped at Falkirk.

Now near Falkirk stands Callander House, the seat of the Earl of Kilmarnock—that thin, handsome aristocrat who had lost much in the Stuart cause in 1715, and who had turned out under Bonnie Prince Charlie, as a cavalry commander, because his wife had urged him to do so and because, being practically penniless anyway, he couldn't lose much except his life. General Hawley was invited to breakfast at Callander House on January 17. He knew that the Earl was "out" under the white rose, but he had also heard that the Countess was both good-looking and clever; so he accepted.

The countess (she had been Lady Ann Livingstone, daughter of James, Earl of Linlithgow and Callander) was, of course, a Jacobite. Practically all the women in Scotland, and most of the women in London, were Jacobites: they could not resist the romance of the thing.

Countess Kilmarnock, then, wanted to do her bit for the Bonnie Prince. Whether or not she had secret information of Charles' plans, we do not know. But she set herself to entertain

Hawley so very well that the general would forget his camp for a time. He was breakfasted in grand style, with much wine, and a profession of flattering speeches from a lady who was (you could tell it to look at her) really intelligent and discriminating—a lady who would know a real man when she saw one. Hawley beamed. He told about building those gibbets for the rebels. He explained that this little campaign meant nothing to *him*. He was almost ashamed, he told his hostess, to be crushing this petty uprising. The rabble had defeated Cope, to be sure, but what was Cope, he asked her, but a bobbing, smirking dandy who didn't know any more about commanding a *real* army than he knew about flying like a bird?

Somebody came in to inform the general of a report that the rebels were advancing. Hawley didn't believe it. Why were they troubling him with idiotic rumors like that? Anybody with any sense in his head would know that the rebels not only would not *dare* to advance but probably wouldn't even *stand their ground!* And oddly enough, the hostess agreed with this conviction. So Hawley had another drink, and the messenger went away.

Breakfast lasted a long time. In fact, before they realized it, it was time for luncheon. Wouldn't the general stay for luncheon? The general would. Delighted to. He took another drink, unbuttoned his coat and vest, stretched his legs, and told his charming hostess that a Highlander would run every time a *real* soldier faced him.

After luncheon another messenger came. The rebels had crossed the Carron at the steps of Dunnipace and were making for the top of Falkirk Moor! This was no rumor: they had been seen through a telescope. At the camp they could not move against these fellows without orders from their commander. Wouldn't the general please come immediately?

The general went. And *how* he went! The clear, calm day had recently become clouded, and just as Hawley started out of Callander House the rain began to fall. But he didn't stop for his hat. He didn't stop to button his coat. He didn't even stop to say farewell to his charming hostess; he went away as fast as ever he could go, jabbing spurs into his horse and cursing magnificently.

Seen like this, he becomes somewhat impressive again. In the dining-room, purring under the blandishments of the countess, he had been only foolish. But on the field he became picturesque.

Arriving in the camp, he bellowed orders to right and left, and sent aides-de-camp flying in all directions. For the top of the moor! The dragoons first: let them take it and hold it until the infantry got there, and the cannon.

The cannon never got there at all. Clear days are rare in Scotland, and the day previous to this, and many days previous to that, had been typically rainy; so that Maggie Wood's Lane, the narrow road which led from the camp to the top of the moor, was a mass of mud. In this the ten pieces of cannon stuck firmly. It might have been accidental, or it might have been because the carriers, who had been pressed into service, were all Stuart sympathizers. Anyway, the cannon were mired.

Hawley was afraid he would find himself in the same position in which Cope had been at Prestonpans—facing the enemy from lower ground and open to a furious downhill charge. This was the reason why he ordered the prompt advance up Maggie Wood's Lane. But he had not reconnoitered: had he known anything about the lay of the land atop the moor, he would never have sent the cavalry ahead. The effect of Countess Kilmarnock's work was beginning to be apparent.

The dragoons galloped on, splashing, cursing, waving their carabines and their sabers, and telling one another (after the dragoon tradition) what they were going to do to the rebels. The foot soldiers followed in double-quick time, fixing their bayonets to the ends of their Brown Besses as they went.

Let us return to the Highlanders. It was probably Charles' idea to advance against Hawley when Hawley least expected it. The Prince always believed that a good attack was the best defense. Lord George Murray had been assigned to draw up a plan of battle, and this he had done with his accustomed brilliance. That morning the Highlanders had performed all sorts of strange maneuvers, accurately calculated to keep the English guessing. Indeed, they seem to have kept the wild Scots themselves guessing. The wind was strong from the southwest, and the wind was no mean factor on the battlefield in the days before smokeless powder and percussion caps. So Charles started for Hawley's right. At the same time he sent Lord John Drummond with most of the cavalry, toward the left: this group, which would be worth little on the rocky ground at the top of the moor, made a great display of banners. Still another body of some 1,200 men under the Duke of Perth, he sent back to Stirling to continue the siege of the castle; and this group, too, was loud with pipes and bright with battle standards. Plean Moor, which the army had occupied, almost in sight of the English encampment at Falkirk, was now deserted. But Charles left his own great standard floating over his tent there.

Thus the English officers at Falkirk did not know whether the Highlandmen were trying to flank them on the right, or on the left, or were trying to encircle them entirely and win toward Edinburgh, or were retreating, or were standing still, or were doing none of these things but merely drilling their troops. Nor could the English officers move, even if they had known what to do, so long as their commander was enjoying the curiously warm hospitality of Callander House and refusing to be disturbed there.

The Prince left his cannon behind. He had the majority of his men with him, the wind at their backs, and was going for the top of Falkirk Moor. The moor is all farmland now: but in those days it was an irregular, desolate, rocky place which rose to a sort of flat peak. The ground was altogether unsuited for cavalry. There was no vegetation except heather. Down the Falkirk side ran a ravine, which grew deeper and wider as it neared the town.

Now it was a race for the top of the moor. Although Hawley had sent his cavalry ahead, and although he had originally been much closer to the moor, the Prince had the advantage of a good start and the Highlanders won the desired position before the horsemen arrived.

The Macdonalds were to have come up first, so as to be wheeled into their hereditary position on the right wing. The impetuous Macgregors, however, rushed ahead and took a place on the extreme right—but fortunately this incident led to no feud between the clans. The children of Donald still occupied most of the post of honor. Next to them were the Stewarts, the Camerons, the Frasers, and the Macphersons. In the second line were the Athole men, the Ogilvies, the Gordons, the Farquharsons, Cromarty's men, and the French Scots and Irish. The Prince stood just behind the second line on a slight eminence still called Charlie's Hill. As at Prestonpans, he had wanted to lead the first line, but again the chiefs had restrained him.

The ravine (called a "dean" in Scotland) began at about the Highland center, and ran past the left of the Highland line. The English were slightly to the north, so that about two-thirds of them were separated from about half the Prince's men by this ravine. The dragoons, however, had comparatively clear ground in front of them, being above the ravine and facing the Macdonalds and the Macgregors.

The clans raised a howl of delight when they saw the foe—a howl that was almost drowned in the shriek of the wind which blew the cold, heavy rain down into the faces of the Saxons. It was four o'clock in the afternoon, but almost as dark as midnight.

Hawley thought, "surely these savages will never stand up before a cavalry charge?"—and he commanded the horse to move forward. The dragoons were none too eager. They waved their sabers with doubtful enthusiasm, and started slowly across the moor. The Macdonalds, opposite them, were marching forward at this time also, but when they saw the dragoons really coming (after several false starts) they leveled their muskets and waited. In front was Lord George Murray, his claymore raised: the Macdonalds were not to fire until that claymore was dropped.

The dragoons gained speed, waved their sabers a whit more exuberantly, and shouted as they spurred their beasts. The Macdonalds waited, obediently; not a man of them moved. But when the dragoons were less than 100 feet away, Lord George dropped his sword. There was a terrific roar, and the air was filled with smoke.

The smoke blew across the English lines, for the wind was in that direction. When it cleared, the Macdonalds screamed with delight. Ligonier's and Hamilton's dragoons, the heroes of Colt's Bridge and of Prestonpans, had turned tail and were galloping back down the hill for all they were worth, trampling over their own infantry supporters, and yelling, "Run! We'll all be massacred!" Cobham's, a regiment which had seen considerable service in Flanders, turned at a right angle and went galloping down the ravine: this took it practically the whole length of the Highland line, and the Stewarts and Camerons had a wonderful time pouring lead into it.

At Prestonpans, you will recall, Lieutenant-Colonel Whitney had been almost alone as a brave man and an honest soldier. At Falkirk, too, he behaved well. He rallied what few horsemen he could get around him after that first terrible volley, and with this little group went dashing into the Highlanders, scattering them to right and left. But where the claymore and musket were useless, the long Lochaber axe and the short and very sharp *skene dhu* were invaluable. The Scotsmen could, and did, fight equally well standing, kneeling, or flat on their backs. When they could not bring down a dragoon by ripping open his horse's belly they could often pull him down by means of his long and fancy coat and, in hand-and-hand combat, rolling on the ground, the Highlanders almost invariably had the better of it. So that the bravest of the dragoons were killed, and Whitney followed his former colonel to the grave.

Lord George Murray was yelling commands that the Macdonalds and Macgregors should not advance but should load where they were and prepare for a second volley. But there was no stopping them once they had got a taste of blood. They raced down the slopes, loading their muskets as they ran, firing them, throwing them away, and then driving into the redcoat ranks with drawn claymores.* Hawley's infantry broke and ran.

But the right wing had met only about one-third of the English army. The other two-thirds, across the ravine, was opposed by only half the Highland army; and for this reason the Stewarts, Camerons, Macphersons and Frasers were exposed to a diagonal flank fire. Reloading after their volley into the fleeing cavalrymen, they were for the moment at a disadvantage and fell back in some confusion.

This made a gap between the two wings. Those near the gap, on the left, could not see the Macdonalds at all—the smoke, the rain, and the darkness hiding almost everything—and supposed they had been defeated; so these men started to run away. Thus the right wing was chasing the English left wing; the Highland center was a mass of bewildered men who shouted to one another, trying to determine whether to stand, to advance, or to run while they could; and the Highland left was staggered by the fire from three steady English regiments. Those three regiments stood their ground; and they were joined, soon afterwards, by two brigades of Cobham's horse, who had reassembled and climbed back up the ravine. The Prince saw, from his eminence, that on one side the battle was won, while on the other side it was in doubt. He was one of the few persons in a position to realize this; and he acted quickly, ordering up the reserves and running toward the confused center himself, where he cheered the men, begged them to pick

* This was an invariable custom of theirs. The field after a Highland charge was always strewn with muskets. The clansmen argued that if they defeated the enemy their claymores would serve to do the final damage and they could return for the muskets later; whereas if they were themselves defeated, muskets in their hands would only impede their running. They never used bayonets. Yet it was the Highlanders and their peculiarly wild attack which first inspired the sort of bayonet we know today. Previous to the battle of Killicrankie, bayonets were screwed into the barrels of the muskets: soldiers receiving an attack were supposed to fire one or two volleys, and then screw in their bayonets. But at Killicrankie, the clansmen who fought under Bonnie Dundee, because of their long legs and their fiery enthusiasm, were in upon the English before they had an opportunity to fix their bayonets. The result was a spectacular slaughter of the Saxons, and later the invention of a bayonet which would not interfere with the discharge of the musket and could be affixed before the actual fighting commenced.

up their muskets, and assured them, with all truth, that the day was as good as won already.

The Camerons, the Stewarts and others rallied readily. With any sort of support, those three unbroken English regiments might have given Hawley a chance to redeem himself. But most of their companions were running for their lives and, with the Highland reserves coming up, the redcoats retreated in good order, falling back toward Falkirk. There Hawley endeavored to rally the whole army. Failing in this, he abandoned the mired cannon, the baggage, and everything else, and continued the retreat through the village and toward Linlithgow. He got out of the village barely in time: Lord John Drummond came in on the east side, while Lord George Murray led in the Macdonalds in the center, and Donald of Lochiel brought in the Camerons from the right. Stray groups of Saxons fell into the hands of the clansmen and, for the most part, were well treated. But the Glasgow Regiment was given no quarter, for these fellows were not even Englishmen but rank Lowlanders.

Hawley tried to fire his camp before he quit it, but the heavy downpour of rain soon put out the flames and allowed the villagers and the clansmen good looting.

That was the Battle of Falkirk. Prince Charles lost about forty men killed, Hawley about ten times that number (there are no official figures). Moreover, Hawley's losses included an exceptionally large proportion of high officers. Many Englishmen were taken prisoners. The Prince only lost one man as a prisoner. That was a brother of the Macdonald of Keppoch, who killed a horseman and mounted the fellow's charger himself. But this horse, familiar with his regimental customs, knew just when it was time to run away; and the Highlander suddenly found himself being carried off in the retreat. So anxious were the others to get away from the claymores that for a time they did not notice the enemy in their midst; and he, for his part, wrapped himself in a military cloak and prayed they would not notice his bare legs and plaid hose until he had a chance to drop out of the troop. But they discovered him, and instead of thinking it was funny, and letting him go, or instead of treating him as a legitimate prisoner of war, they hanged him without trial.

CHAPTER ELEVEN

The Giant in Armor

AFTER all, the fighting in a battle amounts to very little. Good generalship in advance and on the field is at least half, and a proper follow-through is a good part of the remainder. In the case of Falkirk, the Highland attack had been admirably planned but indifferently executed—the rain, the darkness, the peculiar lay of the land, and the impetuosity of the Macdonalds and Macgregors, being responsible for the confusion.

But the follow-through was even worse. A small party was sent to harass the English stragglers: that was no more than military custom. But no real attempt was made to clinch the victory. In the first place, the Highlanders for some time were not really certain that they had won. They could not believe, for several hours, that men could be so cowardly as the dragoons and the English left wing had been. They suspected a trap. Then too, the clansmen, as soon as there were no redcoats left to fight, fell to at their old sport of plundering the baggage and robbing the dead; Chambers knew an aged man who described the scene after the battle by saying that the naked bodies of the dead Englishmen on the hillside looked like so many sheep.

Still, Charles might have assembled his men and clinched the victory, even the following day, for the English were thoroughly scared and would probably have bolted at the first sign of a tartan. Some of the leaders proposed another descent upon England, arguing that they could be knocking at the gates of London within a few days after the arrival there of the news of the battle and before the government had caught its official breath. Other leaders wanted to pursue Hawley to Edinburgh and complete the job begun at Falkirk, incidentally retaking the capital. Still others insisted that the siege must be continued; for it would be a strange army, they said, which after commencing a siege, marched out and defeated another army sent to lift the siege, and then apparently forgot the fortress they had started to capture and went tumbling off after the defeated foe. Well, perhaps it would have looked strange . . . but the purpose of war is to win, not to wonder what people will think. Nowadays we know that the Prince should have pursued Hawley. But the Prince was stubborn. He returned to the cannonade at Stirling, and continued this futilely, while the Duke of Cumberland hurried north to take command at Edinburgh and to receive reinforcements.

This being done, Charles was in as bad a position as he had been at any time since the beginning of the campaign. He must have Stirling Castle in order effectively to open a passage to the North, but unless he took the castle very soon he would not have a chance to take it at all. For Cumberland meant business and was hard at work drilling his men. The clansmen, too, were deserting by hundreds, after their custom, with the spoils. And precious few supplies were coming in. The Prince had won two major engagements and one minor engagement, and had not at any time suffered a serious loss. He had repeatedly outgeneraled the enemy. His troops were filled with ardor for his cause, while the English soldiers were frightened or disheartened. Nevertheless, the Prince was in a serious position.

He had about given up hope, by this time, of ever receiving word that the promised French expedition had arrived. The French court helped him with a few ships, some gold, some cannon, the Irish and Scottish regiments in the French service, and a handful of so-called military experts as advisors. But this was worse than nothing at all, because it served only to hold out hope for more. As Scott puts it, the treatment France accorded the Prince was like that of a man who stands over a starving friend and gives him a crumb now and then, just enough to sustain life but never enough to enable him to get to his feet and go forth to seek his own food.

There were some privately financed ships, too, sent over largely through the efforts of Charles' younger brother. But many of these, as well as many of the official French vessels, fell into the hands of English men-o'-war or privateers.

It would seem that the Prince by this time had decided he could win even without the help of France—although he continued publicly to express confidence that the great expedition with which Versailles was teasing his brother, really would be landed soon on the coast of England or Scotland. But Charles believed now that these Highlanders were invincible, that any of them was worth at least four ordinary soldiers and that, so long as he had them at his back, he was prepared to meet any army at all.

The chiefs knew better; and they worried as the bootless siege continued.

For the siege was a miserable business. The Highlanders, in the first place, were not accustomed to that sort of work: they wanted action all the time, personal fighting, not this popping at unseen enemies with loud-banging cannon, and being popped at in return. Grant, the chief of artillery, had submitted a plan of attack which, it was generally conceded, would have been successful had it been carried through; but the plan called for the destruction of part of the city of Stirling, and this the too-merciful Prince would not permit. So M. Mirabelle de Gordon, a Chevalier of the Order of St. Louis, sent over by France to assist in just such matters, was given charge of the siege; and he made a mess of it. Some contemporary writers say this was because he was not properly supported; others say that it was because he was simply stupid; still others because he was drunk all day every day, and didn't know what he was doing. At any rate, his attacks did not seriously annoy the garrison, and meanwhile the Prince was losing valuable time, and losing also a dozen or so of his best men every day because of the poor lay-out of the trenches. M. Mirabelle was dubbed Mr. Admirable, in derision.

The Prince, during this time, was occasionally at Stirling, but more often he was at Bannockburn, where he got along famously with Sir Hugh Patterson's niece. To be sure, Charles was not a man to be neglecting military duties to philander with a girl of twenty who happened to be infatuated with him. It is doubtful whether anything serious occurred between these two at the time—except a promise on her part to go to him at the end of the campaign, if he still wanted her, no matter where he was or in what circumstances. It is pleasant to record the oath. Any story-teller, even though he happens to be an historian, likes to have at least a dash of love interest in his tale.

Cumberland was drilling his troops, provisioning them, pumping spirit into them, at Edinburgh. Any day now he might start forward to do what Hawley had not been able to do. Lord George Murray was instructed to draw up a plan of battle. He did this, and the Prince approved. It only remained to wait for the English to come, and to hope, in the meanwhile, that M. Mirabelle's siege operations would somehow produce an effect upon the castle.

But Lord George himself was thinking otherwise, and so were all the Highland chiefs. Since Derby, Charles had not called a real council of war; and the chiefs were troubled. When the Stuarts had been kings in Scotland the nobles had kept them in their place and the Scots had not changed during this time; or at any rate, the Highlanders had not. They still believed that a king should be respected as a gentleman, as a person of superior blood, but not as a leader unless he proved himself in that capacity. The Irishmen and Frenchmen around Prince Charles "yessed" him in everything he did. But the Scots told him frankly when they believed him to be wrong; and when he snapped back at them, as at Derby, they nevertheless continued to make their objections. It was so now, at the siege of Stirling Castle. The chiefs believed that they should retreat to the Highlands and linger there for the winter, to descend again with reinforcements in the Spring.

They had been talking this plan over, while Charles had been fondly believing himself commander-in-chief of a victorious army. On January the 6th, they presented him with a memorial, written and signed by Lord George Murray, in which it was proposed "that his Royal Highness shou'd from time to time call a Council of War . . . and that all Operations for the carrying on the War shou'd be agreed on, by the majority of those in his Royal Highness' presence, and once that a Measure is taken, it is not to be changed except by the advice of those, or most of them, who were present when it was agreed on. . . . That upon any sudden Emergency such as in a Battle, Skirmish, or in a Siege, a Discretionary power must be allowed to those who command. This is the Method of all Armys. . . ." The memorial makes the indiscreet observation that "had not a Council determined the Retreat from Derby, what a Catastrophy must have followed in two or three Days!" A council of war would have saved time at Lancaster, and would have prevented the leaving of a garrison at Carlisle, the memorial continues, closing with the reminder that "this is an Army of Volunteers, and not Mercenarys."

In other words, Prince Charles was informed that if he had listened to their advice previously he would not have made the mistakes he did make, and that unless he listened to their advice in the future it was likely that they would not give him any chance to make further mistakes.

The Prince, considering how furious the receipt of this memorial must have rendered him, replied with moderation.

"When I came into Scotland I knew well enough what I was to expect from my ennemies, but I little foresaw what I meet with from my Friends. I came vested with all the Authority the King could give me, one chief part of which is the Command of the Armies, and now I am required to give this up to fifteen or sixteen Persons . . . and nothing is left for me but the honour of being present at their debates. . . . I am often hit in the teeth that this is an Army of Volunteers, and consequently very different from one composed of Mercenarys. What one wou'd naturally expect from an Army whose chief Officers consist of Gentlemen of rank and fortune, is more zeal, more resolution and more good manners than in those that fight merely for pay: but it can be no Army at all where there is no General, or which is the same thing no Obedience or deference paid to him. Every one knew before he engaged in the cause, what he was to expect in case it miscarried, and should have staid at home if he cou'd not face Death in any shape: but can I myself hope for better usage? At least I am the only Person upon whose head a Price has been already set, and therefore I cannot indeed threaten at every other word to throw down my Arms and make my Peace with the Government."

He expresses amazement that he should be accused of folly in leaving the garrison at Carlisle, and reminds Lord George (to whom this answer was personally directed) that his Lordship raised no objection to the plan at the time and even offered to remain at Carlisle himself with his Athole men. He concludes, ". . . and I shall only tell you that my Authority may be taken from me by violence, but I shall never resign it like an Idiot." *

Now there can be no doubt that the Prince was often high-handed in his method of dealing with these touchy mountain nobles. But on this occasion, Charles seemed to have been more right than wrong. We cannot know the whole inside story, but from this distance his is the stronger side of the argument. The chiefs had taken their chance. They should have stuck by it. To advise their Prince was one thing: to insist upon a council of war—in which, as Charles pointed out, they would have the control—was quite another. In time of peace it would have been different. But in time of war a dictator is requisite and group decisions are almost invariably unfortunate. For there can be no compromise in war, which has one purpose and which should not be turned from that purpose for reasons of democracy, policy, humanity or any other thing. Indubitably, Lord George was the better general. But the Prince's policy of assuming a bold front at all times, of taking the line of the most resistance, of defending by attacking and always doing the unexpected, was essentially sound in this peculiar conflict;

* This letter was not written by Charles, who was never able to spell so well. The Prince's handwriting was bad, his grammar was astounding, his punctuation haphazard and inconsistent; but his spelling was nothing short of atrocious. Probably he dictated this particular letter to Sheridan or to Hay.

and although he went too far at Derby and was quite properly checked, the action of the chiefs in demanding a council and chiding the Prince for his mistakes, can hardly be called discreet or even sensible, much less polite.

However, they were not silenced. They could be as stubborn as their prince. On January 30, after the Battle of Falkirk and after Lord George had submitted his plan for the next battle, the chiefs presented another memorial, or petition, to the Prince. In this they remarked the large number of desertions from the Highland army and the increasing strength of the enemy at Edinburgh. "For these reasons, we are humbly of the opinion, that there is no way to extricate your Royal Highness and those who remain with you, out of the most imminent danger, but by retiring immediately to the Highlands, where we can be usefully employed the remainder of the winter, by taking and mastering the forts of the North." In the Spring, the chiefs added, they had no doubt they could get together 10,000 Highlanders "to follow your Royal Highness wherever you think proper."

This was handed to John Hay of Restalrig, private secretary of the Prince, who refused to deliver it to Charles until the Prince got out of bed. The petition was therefore held up for several hours. When Charles arose, Hay presented it to him. The Prince read it, Hay said later, and seemed to go mad with grief and rage: he banged his head against the wall until he was dizzy, and cried, "Good God! have I lived to see this!"

Nevertheless, again his answer was, all things considered, very moderate. "Is it possible that a Victory and a Defeat shou'd produce the same effects, and that the Conquerors should flie from an engagement, whilst the Conquer'd are seeking it?" he asked. "Shou'd we make the retreat you propose, how much more will that raise the spirits of our Ennemys and sink those of our own People? Can we imagin, that where we go the Ennemy will not follow, and at last oblige us to a Battel which we now decline?" The French and the Spaniards, he insisted, would certainly not continue to help men who retreated after a victory. And what would become of "our Lowland friends?" What encouragement would such a move be to those in Scotland and England who were yet wavering between loyalty to their rightful king and devotion to their more recent monarch?

But the time for argument was past. The chiefs had not spoken until their minds had been made up; and they were not men to be changed by entreaty. In the quietest manner possible it was made clear to Prince Charles that if he didn't want to go to the Highlands with them he could remain in the Lowlands without them: at least, Charles interpreted it this way, and he was probably correct. So he ordered the retreat.

At first it was more like a rout. "Their was no where 1,000 men together," Lord Elcho wrote afterwards; and they crossed the Forth at the fords of Frew "in great Confusion, leaving Carts & Cannon upon the road behind." The Church of St. Ninians was blown up by an accident; of course, the Stuart enemies said this was an example of Popish vengeance, but the fact was that Highlanders lost a considerable quantity of good gunpowder besides several soldiers, because of it. Commands were miscarried. There was no advance guard, and no rear guard.

Part of the army assembled at Crieff, part at Perth. It was decided, when some manner of order had been restored, to split into two groups, Lord George Murray and Lord John Drummond with the horse and the so-called Lowland regiments (which, however, were composed almost entirely of Highlandmen) going by the coast road, Montrose and Aberdeen, to Inverness; and the Prince, leading the clans, to go by the high road to the same place. In order to give the Farquharsons and Lord Ogilvy's men a chance to visit their homes, these two regiments were marched up the center, through Coupar-Angus, Glen Clova and Glen Muick to Speyside.

Prince Charles was within eight miles of Inverness when he stopped at Moy House, seat of The MacIntosh. The chief himself was a captain in one of the loyal regiments commanded by Lord Loudon, at that time barricaded in Inverness; but Lady

MacIntosh was a staunch Jacobite and set herself about raising all the clansmen she could for the service of the Prince.

That night—it was the 16th of February—Lord Loudon conceived a plan to surprise the Prince. He marched 2,000 men toward Moy House in the dead of night, having received information that the Prince was there with only thirty guardsmen. The dowager Lady MacIntosh, who lived in Inverness, got wind of this, and sent Lachlan MacIntosh, a lad of fifteen, to Moy House to give the alarm. Lachlan could not get past the silently marching men; but he took a short cut in the darkness and beat them to the castle. Lady MacIntosh summoned one Fraser, a blacksmith (the blacksmith was a most important person in any clan), and instructed him to take four companions and go out by the road to reconnoiter. When these five fellows came upon Lord Loudon's army, they saw no reason for disturbing the Prince at all. They hid in the bushes by the side of the road and fired gaily into the vanguard. Then Fraser sprang to his feet shouting various war-cries, in Gaelic, and summoning members of this clan and of that clan, while his companions ran here and there, reloading and firing as fast as they could, and themselves whooping war-cries at the top of their lungs. Lord Loudon's men were themselves Highlanders and of course understood the Gaelic. They were unable to see these fellows in the darkness, and supposed that they had stumbled upon the whole of the Young Pretender's army. So they retreated in confusion and the Prince was not disturbed.

The next day Gordon of Glenbucket surprised and captured the barracks at Ruthven; but Lord Loudon, when Charles had assembled all his men and started toward Inverness, slipped across the Moray Firth to the Black Isle. His Lordship wanted to get around the Prince and down to where he could join Cumberland. Garrisons were stationed at Elgin and at Nairn to prevent this. Lord Cromarty was sent against Loudon with several of the clans, and when he failed to find the slippery leader, the Duke of Perth who succeeded him had better luck, finally dispersing the army of the North in Sunderland on

March 20. Charles was so pleased with this that he sent the news of it to France—still hoping, it would seem, to inspire assistance.

But the list of the military operations of the Highlanders at this time is long and—unless you happen to be interested in military tactics and familiar with the countryside—not thrilling. They were for the most part cleverly conceived and energetically executed. Inverness Castle was captured, and so was Fort Augustus; but Fort Williams, beseiged under the direction of the blundering M. Mirabelle, remained as stout as Stirling. Lord George Murray and Cluny Macpherson slipped neatly down into Perthshire one dark night, surprised thirty government posts simultaneously, and took them all without losing a man. Promptly after this the same two leaders besieged Blair Castle, Lord George's own family seat, but without success, being obliged to withdraw when the Prince of Hesse approached with his mercenaries.*

These were only a few of the activities with which the Prince kept his men busy that winter. But they were futile. For this display of military pyrotechnics was sputtering out already, up there in the hills; whereas England, a Goliath upon whose helmet the rocks of David rattled like hailstones but without effect, was just beginning to stretch its muscles for a real effort.

"It's about time we ended this thing," said England.

So she picked a commander fit for the work to be done, and gave him unlimited authority and the support of the whole navy. The Duke of Cumberland was the second son of George the Second. He was just about Prince Charles' age;

* These Hessian mercenaries, later, were highly unpopular in America, where they were used against the colonial revolutionists. But in Scotland they were well liked. There were 6,000 of them—tall, blond, handsome fellows—under Prince Frederick himself. They were clean, well behaved, amiable chaps, who introduced into Scotland the "black raparee" snuff which later became so popular. Their commander was not eager to be helping to put down an uprising like this: he seems to have had little regard for a war in which the enemy prisoners were treated like spies and traitors. Cumberland he treated with great politeness; but one guesses that His Serene Highness had little real regard for that young man. Anyway, the Hessians were never brought into action but were kept as a sort of reserve force.

but there the resemblance stopped. Charles was all fire and enthusiasm, all chivalry and mercy and high purpose. Cumberland was phlegmatic, hard, merciless, a square-faced fellow with features set like stone, and icy eyes, who had been reared in the Prussian school of militarism and never bothered about questions of ethics, precedent, honor, or even common decency. He symbolized the giant perfectly. He gathered all his forces about him at leisure, like a warrior putting on his armor and buckling tight his falchion belt. He located the enemy, smiled a slow ominous smile, and began to clank in that direction, step after heavy step, like some ponderous mechanical monster. His plan was simplicity itself. There was an end to this island: he would push the rebels as far as they cared to go and then crush them, leaving nothing. He was no Cope, this young Royal Duke, and no Hawley. He was rather a symbol of the terrible end to come—the end that was foredoomed from Glenfinnan.

He first stationed garrisons here and there to prevent the Highlanders from slipping down to the Lowlands again: he thus bottled them up in the northern part of the island. Then he moved to Perth, to Montrose, to Aberdeen, with the main part of his army, numbering close to 9,000. Always he took his time. Already his advance guards were having minor skirmishes with the Highland outposts—skirmishes from which the Highlanders usually carried off the honors. That did not trouble Cumberland. The real battle was yet to come. Cumberland was instructing his men in different defense tactics. He taught them that they must not lunge for the man in front, with their bayonets, but rather for the man on the right: if every man in the line did that, each would protect his neighbor by killing that neighbor's immediately assailant. It was good advice. And Cumberland drilled and drilled it into the redcoats while he waited for the Spring thaw that would open the way for him to continue his advance north.

He started out of Aberdeen on April 8th, and on April 12th crossed the Spey with a loss of only one soldier and three camp women, who were washed away and drowned. Lord

John Drummond was defending the fords of the Spey with 2,600 men and, outnumbered four to one, he retired without disputing Cumberland's passage. Drummond, a brother of the Duke of Perth, has since been bitterly criticized for this. But it does not appear that he was blamed for it at the time. Keltie defends him, asserting that although the Spey, when swollen, might easily have been held by an inferior force, it was, at this time, extraordinarily low, and that Cumberland was able to cover the few difficult zigzag fords with his artillery. At any rate, the redcoats crossed the river and moved into Elgin and then into Nairn. The giant was clanking nearer.

Prince Charles was at Culloden House, near Inverness on the edge of Drumossie Moor. The clans were almost everywhere else. Poor fellows! they had run short of food: Murray of Broughton was seriously ill, and John Hay was attending to the commisariat, and attending to it very badly. Foraging parties were scattered here, there and elsewhere. On April 15th, when Cumberland was within nine miles of Culloden House, a desperate attempt was being made there to bring the clansmen together. Lord Cromarty was still up in Sunderland, stamping out the stray embers of Loudon's army; Cluny Macpherson had not returned from Badenoch; Barrisdale, Glengyle and Mackinnon, and most of the Frasers, were scraping the hills and valleys for whatever morsels of food they could find. Officially there were about 8,000 men in this ever-shifting army, but less than 5,000 said "Here" when the muster roll was called, and these were half-starved and half-frozen.

What to do? There was a council—the second since Derby—and various schemes were proposed. Some were for fighting it out and having it over with, one way or the other. Some favored crossing the Nairn and making a stand there, where the hills and the rock country would be to their advantage and would work against the Saxon cavalry and artillery. Then a night march was proposed, either by Charles or by Lord George Murray—at any rate, they both approved it heartily. This day was the Duke of Cumberland's birthday. Beyond doubt, the redcoats would be given special rations, consisting largely of beer, and would be sleeping heavily just before dawn. American Indians used to attack just before dawn; and the old Scottish Highlanders used the same system.

But could the men stand it? could they walk nine miles on such a night, in their condition? They could try. As well to do that as to stand and wait for the tornado. They were awakened, grouped into columns, and the terrible march began.

Just as there are many things about Lord George Murray to remind us of General George Washington, and many things about the Prince's last army encampment to remind one of Valley Forge, so there are many things about the beginning of this night march to remind one of the crossing of the Delaware and the attack on the celebrating Hessians at Trenton. The chief difference, however, is all-important: the battle of Trenton was a victory for the attacking force.

Nine miles seems little enough, even in Scotland, even to a non-mountaineer. But in the icy winds of that night, in the sticky mud, with stomachs that were shrieking for a crust of bread and throats that had not known the sting of spirits for days, it was a terrible task indeed. Lord George led the first column, and these were the strongest; time and again, some fifty times in all, they were obliged to stop and wait for the others to overtake them. Everywhere the clansmen were slipping into black, crumbled heaps of tartan, not able to twitch a muscle. Everywhere the men were falling, as though a ghostly enemy with silent muskets was firing into their midst. They would stumble once too often: their knees would bend involuntarily, the legs would become suddenly like wet paper, and they would drop into the mud without a sound.

Orders had gone up and down the lines—it was our old friend Ker of Graden who carried them—that no muskets were to be used, but claymores, dirks and battle-axes. The men were to cut tent ropes and thrust wherever they saw a lump on the canvas. They were to shriek all the time.

It would have been a horrible scene. But by the time Lord George and the vanguard had reached a point near the English camp, the dawn was already in the sky and the rest of the army was still stumbling through the mud far behind. There could be no attack. Nor did they dare to remain where they were, for they would be discovered at any moment. Lord George ordered a retreat.

It is best not to think of that march back to Culloden House. It is sufficient to say that many a weary soldier never arrived at all, and that those who did arrive dropped without a sound to the wet earth and slept like dead men.

Only three hours were they permitted to sleep. Then the gentlemen went around among them, shaking shoulders, hoarsely calling commands, while the pipers put what wind they had left into their bags and summoned the clans to battle again. For the giant was in sight on Drummosie Moor.

CHAPTER TWELVE

Black Culloden Day

THE Duke's men came on, colors flapping, bayonets gleaming, drums athunder, white gaiters swinging regularly, regularly, as the men marched over the moor, a grand mass of steel and scarlet that moved with the precision of a machine.

The Highlanders, standing in mud that was over their brogues, howled defiance. But it must have been a pitiful sound, for they had hardly strength to stand. They blinked, in the half-hearted sunlight, swaying in their places, aching, aching for some whiskey and some food. It was seven o'clock: they had been permitted to sleep about three hours. For days their food had consisted of crumbly little chunks of what passed for bread: it was made from the sweepings of a mill, and in it were dust and grit and even splinters.

Black clouds hurried in from the sea, as though to shield this business from the sight of God. The sun was obliterated. It became very dark, and the English bayonets no longer glittered. Harshly the wind stiffened: it was wet and sharp, and very cold.

Charles had about 5,000 men. The right was in charge of Lord George Murray, the left of the Duke of Perth. From the right there were the Athole Brigade, Lord George's own men; then the Camerons, the Stewarts, those Frasers who weren't back in the hills looking for food, the MacIntoshes, the Farquaharsons, a few Macleans and Macleods and Maclachlans, new recruits, the Chisholms, and the various Macdonald septs. A pathetic little clump of cavalry hung on each wing tip. The second line consisted of some 800 men under Glenbucket and Lord Lewis Gordon. There were two little groups of flank guards, and two little groups of reserves, men with muskets but no sidearms.

The Duke's army numbered more than 9,000. Previous to this conflict, and subsequently, Cumberland proved himself a poor general. But on Black Culloden Day he appears to have done a good job of it. To be sure, the stupidest general in the world could not have lost that battle for King George. The English army was well equipped, well fed, well drilled, properly supported by cavalry and artillery—a navy had been moving north with it, along the coast—and it was on higher ground, with the wind at its back blowing straight down into the faces of the wild Scots. Nevertheless, Cumberland arranged his men well, taking no chances. The Earl of Aldemarle commanded the center, Major General Bland the right, Colonel Lord Ancram the left. Artillery was placed between the front line regiments (Charles had placed his few pieces on either flank), and the Duke's second line, under the veteran Major General Huske, was so arranged that each regiment was behind one of the spaces between the first line regiments. Beyond this second line were the reserves, under Brigadier General Mordaunt. The dragoons were on the flanks; and the Campbells, because in the fray their kilts might be confusing, had been given charge of the baggage.

It must have been a great hour when these two armies faced one another. The wind grew colder and colder, and a wet snow, half rain, had begun to fall diagonally, stinging the faces of the Highlanders. The hills of Ross looked bleakly down upon them; in the gray sea was an English supply ship; the Nairn, swollen with the waters of Spring, moved past with a roar.

It was to be the last battle of its sort, one of the most curious in history. Here was Chivalry, there Common Sense. Of course common sense would win. It is one of the terrible truisms that common sense always does win, in the long run. Meanwhile, however, there would be excitement.

The clansmen were impatient. In and out among them passed the gentlemen, haranguing them, reminding them of their tribal traditions, reminding them of how their forefathers had battled with the English and had conquered, or had lost and died with honor. "Scrug your bonnets, laddies! We're going to read the riot act to 'em this time!" The clansmen shivered. But if they were physically cold, they were emotionally at white heat. What was the trouble? When would the fighting start? The clansmen could not see any reason for this shifting back and forth, here and there, as each side made the customary passes toward outflanking the enemy. What was holding Charlie back? Who cared if the flanks weren't just right?

Now the Prince had no other thought than to order a charge. He could do nothing else. He was commander of a one-way army. The victors of Prestonpans and of Falkirk knew nothing about defense. Their idea of war was to rush down upon the enemy and kill everybody in sight—an old-fashioned and often effective method to which their ancestors had always been accustomed. The fact that the odds were all against them did not diminish their ardor. The ancient Highlanders, dressed only in kilts and often naked to the waist, had time and again charged the ranks of mail-clad men-at-arms.

First, though, the Prince wanted to make sure that everything was ready. He sat on a horse, on a slight rise of ground behind the center of the first line. Tall white feathers nodded on his bonnet; he wore the white plaid of the Royal Stuarts and on his breast gleamed the Star of St. Andrew. No wonder the men worshiped him! They knew nothing about the council squabbles, or the pettiness of the young general. Most of them, indeed, did not even know what the war was about and didn't care. But there was Charles: the chances were a thousand to one against him, yet he was as debonaire as though he were about to lead a lady through a minuet.

He must have been wondering whether he had done the right thing. Up until the last minute there had been an opportunity to retreat across the Nairn to the hills, where Cumberland would not be able to carry his artillery and where cavalry would be of no use at all; there the Highlanders would have been in their own country. But this would have meant giving

BATTLE OF CULLODEN

up Inverness and cutting all communication with France. Besides, the Prince had retreated too much already. He wanted no small, guerrilla warfare. He, too, was true to the ideals of his ancestors when he decided to fight it out on the open moor, man to man, and the Devil take the loser.

At last he nodded. The cannon exploded with a roar. They were badly handled and did little or no damage. The Duke's cannon, more numerous and much more effective, responded promptly. The air was filled with smoke, so that even the sky, which had been almost black, was hidden from sight.

The Duke of Cumberland stood on a high flat rock behind his lines. His plans were perfectly made, and he was delighted that these mad rebels had given him the opportunity to carry the plans through. "I own that I did not expect them to make a stand," he wrote later to the Duke of Newcastle.

The clansmen shivered, glancing impatiently back to where Prince Charles sat. What was the matter? Why didn't they charge? Must they stand there, in the snow and wind, and be cut to pieces by the Mother of Muskets without having struck a single blow?

This was true in the center and on the right. It was different on the left, where the Macdonalds were. In all previous battles since Bannockburn the Macdonalds had been given the right wing: it was their privilege, their post of honor. But on Drummosie Moor they were shoved over to the left. It seems (although it has never been established as a certainty) that Lord George Murray had insisted that his own Athole men, previously kept in the second line, be given the right wing for a change: Lord George had told the Prince that these fellows had been underrated and deserved a share of the glory. Whatever the reason, the Macdonalds were assigned to the left. That took the fighting spirit out of men who were ordinarily the most ferocious fighters of all; for these little matters were tremendously important to the old clansmen.

Now Cumberland's men had captured a wall which had protected the Prince's right flank, and they were tearing it down. Lord George was later blamed for not retaking it at any cost. He explained that he had tried to do so but his orders had miscarried. That excuse—in another battle weak enough—at Culloden was natural and understandable, for commands in the Prince's army that day were frequently miscarried or not carried at all. Anyway, the wall came down, and cavalry poured through the breach, taking the Athole Brigade from the side.

And at last Ker of Graden rode out with notice. that the command to charge was about to be given. He took this warning to the left wing first, since the left wing was further from the enemy.

The left didn't advance. The right did. The laddies on the right were moving before the formal command reached them. They were too impatient to wait any longer. The MacIntoshes, who had never before been under fire, started the rush. They fired a volley into the enemy, cast away their new-fangled muskets, and shrieking their war-cries and flourishing their broadswords, went sprinting toward the Saxon. The Camerons went with them, and the Macleans and all the others—all, that is, except the Athole men, who were attacked by flanking dragoons, and the Macdonalds.

Nobody has ever settled the question of why the Macdonalds didn't charge—a question which to this day offers an easy way to pick a fight in Scotland. Many writers say it was because they were sulky and peeved, not having been given the post of honor. Ewald calls them "passionless as cravens." It is said that the Duke of Perth, weeping, implored them to charge, promising them that he would thereafter call himself a Macdonald instead of a Gordon; but they did not budge. It is said that Keppoch also wept, crying, "Have the children of my tribe deserted me?"

If this be true, the descendants of Donald may well blush for shame. Lang says it probably is not true. He agrees with those who believe that the Macdonalds saw the right wing charge out of turn and shatter itself against the steel wall of bayonets, and that it was only too apparent, by that time, that a charge would be suicide and nothing more. Certainly something was wrong. The Macdonalds were not men to stand actionless, awaiting formal commands. When they saw fighting, they fought. It was not in the nature of them to watch a battle without lifting their own claymores in the thick of it. They had not waited for commands at Falkirk, where they had themselves charged out of turn, covering their clan with glory and their general with confusion. But at Culloden they stood still.

Not all of them. Scothouse and his kinsmen charged and were mowed down by bullets and cannonballs. Stout Keppoch, screaming "Claymores! Claymores!" bolted across the moor; and he, with the twenty-odd gentlemen who followed him, was slaughtered. But the rest did not move.

Meanwhile, the right and center men were making themselves immortal. Honor these heroes! They might have been mistaken, but certainly they were brave!

They crossed the moor, running uphill, their targets (when they had targets) held high over their heads, their bright swords flashing, their sporrans swinging. They shrieked wildly as they ran. The redcoats waited without a sound.

The clansmen hurled themselves upon the first line. They went down by the hundreds. Three deep, the soldiers of Common Sense met them anl slaughtered them; or rather, the attackers killed themselves against a wall of steel. The bayonets, thrust sideways, slipped past Highland targets and sank into Highland breasts.

Yet some, miraculously, broke through. These charged the second line with undiminished ardor. The pipes had been silenced, and there was no whiskey to warm their half-frozen limbs; but they charged magnificently. The army behind them was defeated. And in front of them the second line waited quietly, the men in front kneeling, the men behind them leaning over, and the men in back standing erect. A triple row of muskets. And when the clansmen were within a few yards of the bayonet tips, a volley was fired.

That ended the battle of Culloden. The Prince, who had been spattered with mud when a cannonball landed within a few feet of him, and whose horse had been killed underneath him, was obliged to quit the field. The baggage and artillery were deserted. Lochiel was wounded: a group of his kinsmen gathered around him in a circle, and carried him away, back over the Nairn, fighting like wildcats every step of the way. Great Macgillvaray took his stance in front of a well (men still point out the Well of Death) and swung his broadsword like a grand hero of the olden days, until he was beaten down by sheer weight of numbers and hacked to pieces. Lord George Murray, swept back from the fray, sword in hand, hatless, wigless, his coat cut to shreds, made one desperate attempt to bring up the second line; but it was too late; the men could only fire one volley and then retreat.

The Macdonalds, too, retreated. The Irish and French Scots retreated. Elsewhere, the retreat was a rout. Here and there a company was fairly orderly, marching away with some semblance of military rule, stopping occasionally to fire at their pursuers. Here and there a small group, chased too enthusiastically, turned like cornered animals and fought it out on the spot until all were killed. But most of the clansmen who were still on their feet, ran away. . . . Many of them (close to a thousand, according to one authority) never even woke up, but slept right through the battle, so utterly exhausted had they been.

On both flanks cavalrymen rode, shouting triumphantly, flashing their sabers, rising and falling as their horses heaved. It was a great day for the dragoons!

CHAPTER THIRTEEN

A Heroine Enters

THE Highland wounded were permitted to lie on the field, in a pouring rain, all that night, all the next day, and part of the next night. Then Cumberland remembered them and sent out little groups of soldiers to kill them. Most of the poor fellows had already perished of wounds, starvation, or exposure; but those who were left were dispatched by a bayonet thrust through the heart. Some thirty or forty had crawled into a ramshackle sheep hut near the battlefield and were lying there, unable to move: these were finished off all at once by the simple process of setting the place afire. Nineteen officers, who had concealed themselves in a wood, were taken to the park around Culloden House: they were given no chance to say anything, but lined up against a wall—those who could stand up—and pumped full of lead at a distance of only a few yards. Even then not all were dead, so the soldiers bashed in every skull to make sure of the job.

"A little blood-letting," Cumberland called it in his official report.

And so it was, comparatively. The clansmen who were slain during the battle, and the ones who were slain in cold blood after the battle, were the fortunate ones. Those of the wounded who had been able to drag themselves to nearby huts were hunted down the day after the bayonet work in the rain, and were dragged outside and shot. Still others—and there were many of these—had trusted to the woods and the hills, and had staggered or crawled away, to die alone. For weeks afterwards, at distances of ten, fifteen and even twenty miles from the battlefield, peasants were stumbling upon the decomposing corpses of men who had known that they could expect no mercy from the English.

The redcoats swarmed over the countryside. Prisoners were a nuisance and it was better not to have them. The attitude of the British government from the beginning had been that this was no war but merely an uprising, and that the men who fought under Bonnie Prince Charlie were not legitimate soldiers but beasts, vermin, who were to be stamped out entirely lest a few survivors breed again. Get rid of them! Cumberland knew his job. Strike while the public was still indignant and would applaud behavior which under ordinary circumstances would have horrified savages! For England and the people of the Scottish Lowlands had been frightened, thoroughly frightened, more frightened than anybody realized until now. Fear, indeed, seems to have rendered the English, at least, temporarily insane. There was no reason why the soldiers should stop at anything. The mountaineers were born rebels, traitorous scoundrels. Moreover, they could not strike back. Obliterate them!

"The only way to end this rebellion," Cumberland had written to Newcastle, before the battle, "is by the sword, and to punish the rebels so that they will not rise again."

The orders given to the soldiers applied not only to the clansmen who had been out under the Stuart banner: they applied to every member of every clan, man, woman or child. The soldiers stole and raped and burned in a frenzy of delight. They went into the homes of the men who had chased them at Falkirk and Clifton, and who were dead now; and they killed the cattle and the sheep, insulted the women, stole whatever was of any value, and burned the hut itself, afterwards departing with a laugh to do the same thing in the next glen. They made the Highlands one vast abattoir.

Associate director of the slaughter was General Hawley, the *real* soldier, whose methods had long been Cumberland's delight and example, and who probably owed to the Duke's friendship his escape from court-martial after Falkirk. Lieutenant-Colonel Howard, Captain Caroline Scott, and Major Lockhart, were also assistant butchers.

But the genius of it all was the Duke of Cumberland. It was no fever of fright that inspired him; for this much may be said for the young man: he was not a coward. No, it was deliberate, cold-blooded. He even had prepared an excuse before the commencement of the slaughter. He told London that he had found upon a Highlander an order from Lord George Murray, signed before the battle, in which the clansmen were instructed to give no quarter to the English troops. This letter was a forgery, and not even a clever one. But it served Cumberland's purpose well.

Chambers writes of Cumberland: "He had that persevering and insatiable appetite for prey, that, not contented with sucking the blood and devouring the flesh of his victims, he could enjoy himself in mumbling the bones; and even when these were exhausted of sap and taste, he would gnash on for the sport, and was only to be finally withdrawn from the horrid feast when putridity had rendered it disgusting to his senses."

There are hundreds of anecdotes told about the killings after Culloden, but I have been able to find only two which show any Englishman in a good light. One concerns that gentleman-soldier, Wolfe, later a general and the hero of Quebec, but at this time a colonel under Cumberland. They say that he was riding by the side of the Duke, just after the battle, when a wounded Highlander, his spirit still strong, lifted himself on one elbow and frowned defiance upon the victor. Cumberland pointed to him. "Kill that man for me." But Wolfe replied, "Sir, my commission is at your feet, but I cannot stoop to become an executioner." Presumably some less scrupulous person did the job. And presumably, too, Wolfe was too well connected and too well thought of to be cashiered for his refusal—although he was never afterward in Cumberland's good graces.

The other story concerns a group of prisoners, common clansmen, who were to be killed. The captors were amusing themselves by insulting their victims and the nation they represented. The English soldiers could not believe that these raw-boned, ragged, barefooted savages had terrified disciplined soldiers, veterans of the wars in Flanders. Colonel Campbell of the Argyle Militia (the Campbells, who fought for the government) happened along. This officer could not bear to hear his own countrymen treated with such derision, and he offered to wager the officer in charge of the English soldiers that any one of these Highlanders would defeat any of the Englishmen in a hand-to-hand combat with swords and no targets. The Highlander, if he were victorious, was to be given his freedom. The English officer accepted, and the best swordsman of the company put himself on guard. A Highlander was given a weapon and told what the wager was. The Highlander struck once and the Englishman was dead. The victor was given his promised freedom.

But the rest is a story of unbridled brutality and thievery on the part of the common soldiers, and deliberate insults on the part of their officers. For example, as a travesty of military glory the fourteen stand of colors captured from the Prince's army were carried by chimney sweeps from the Castle down to the old cross behind St. Giles', and there burned by the public hangman!

The measures of the government itself were less spectacular but much more effective. A general order went forth, threatening with punishment any and all who harbored escaped rebels. Preachers over all Scotland were commanded to submit to the government lists of the known rebels in their congregations or elsewhere. Rewards were offered for the capture of escaped fugitives in Ireland and the Isle of Man. Ministers in foreign courts where England had influence were instructed to demand the arrest of any rebels who made their way to those nations. Parliament passed a law forbidding the carrying of any sort of arms in Scotland, even though some of the poorer Highlanders in the extreme north, who had only heard of the uprising in a vague way, were accustomed to shoot game for their dinners, and indeed for almost all their meals. Bagpipes were forbidden: they might stir the ancient spirit again. Even the use of any sort of tartan anywhere, was prohibited. A whole people, always poor and now made literally penniless by the looting of the redcoats, was obliged to change its clothes; and muscular Scottish legs which had always been free to the air, now were forced by legislation to encase themselves in the abhorred and altogether inconvenient breeches of the Southron. The Highland dress, at all times one of the most distinctive and most picturesque in the world, was absolutely barred. The official penalty was a fine (as though these starving peasants could pay a fine!) but the actual penalty was often a bullet through the brain.

But the refugee the English went after with the greatest zest, the one, in fact, that the whole army and the whole navy concentrated upon, was our hero, Charles Edward Stuart.

Better for him had he fallen at Culloden! It would have left him an orthodox hero, and saved all those unpleasant things I shall have to tell you about him before this book is finished. And had he been able to see what was ahead of him, to understand that Culloden was the end of all his hopes, he would have dashed into death: there can be little doubt of that.

But always he had hope. Even when the battle went against him, and the clans were broken, he was throwing all his spirit into plans for a second expedition. It was clear to him at last that he could not succeed without substantial help from France. And already he was planning to go to France, to get an army on the strength of his solo achievements, and return to conquer. So when defeat was certain at Culloden, he rode away, attended only by Lord Elcho, Sheridan, O'Sullivan, Edward Burke, a guide, and a few others. His cavalry escort he dismissed after fording the Nairn at Falie. Thence he rode by Tordarroch, Aberarder and Faroline, to Gortleg, the seat of Simon, Lord Lovat.

That old scoundrel was anything but pleased to see him. Everything was lost now, and Lovat could only think of his life and his estates. He begged the Prince to depart immediately. Poor Charles! He accepted one tall beaker of wine, and then rode on past Fort Augustus to Invergarry Castle, the seat of

Macdonald of Clanranald, which at the time was deserted.* It was night, or early morning, when he arrived there, and he remained most of the next day. Edward Burke caught a salmon, and the whole party ate. When they left Invergarry it was for the estate of Young Lochiel, on Lake Arkaig. They were going west, toward that wild Lochaber country where the whole uprising had started.

The next afternoon, April 18, they quit their horses and went on foot over the hills for the Braes of Morar. It was an all-night tramp over rugged, desolate countryside. They were put up in a tiny hut the next day and, the following night, they walked to Borrodale, the farmhouse where Charles had stopped after his landing and before the raising of the standard at Glenfinnan. They did not dare to travel in the daytime. The Prince wrote a letter from Borrodale to the clan chiefs, who had gathered the remains of his army at Ruthven. He thanked them for their services and suggested that each chief defend himself as best he could: he told them that he was returning to France, and promised to come back soon with a French army.

The Prince has been much criticized for thus slipping out of the country, or trying to, while the faithful Lord George Murray was checking up the missing at Ruthven and still prepared to fight it out to the end. But Charles, in spite of his romanticism, knew now that without the assistance of some foreign force his cause was hopeless. He might have done the heroic thing and remained to die with the last of his faithful followers. But he really believed—there can be no doubt of it—that he could get a French army and return to save the clansmen from absolute destruction. And so believing, it was obviously his duty to make the attempt, rather than to make a last stand which would have been in effect to commit suicide.

His temper was not improved by a message Lord George sent him from Ruthven. His Lordship tactlessly cavilled about this and that and repeated, in effect, many "I told you so's" for the edification of his Prince. Murray was brave, and admirable

* The castle was destroyed, a few days later, by Cumberland's soldiers when they learned that Charles had stopped there.

in many ways; but he was no diplomat. To slap Charles in the face with a review of past errors, at this stage, was in the worst possible taste; and Charles never forgave Lord George for it.

Charles believed he would be safer, and would have a better chance of being picked up by a French ship, on one of the numerous islands that cluster around the west coast of Scotland. So he sailed by night out of Lochnanaugh, where a year earlier the *Doutelle* had anchored. With him were O'Sullivan, O'Neil, Allan Macdonald, a priest, and Donald Macleod and Edward Burke, guides, besides seven boatmen. Promptly a storm arose—and such a storm! Macleod, who was sixty-eight years old and had fished and piloted among the Hebrides all his life, averred he had never seen a worse one. The boat filled as fast as they could bail it out. Charles suggested that they land as soon as possible; but Macleod said it would be better to stay out in the open sea and drown than to be dashed to pieces against the rocks. The Prince, when it was not his turn to bail, sang the others a little Highland song, in Gaelic, to encourage them at their labors.

Morning came, and they were still afloat. Finally they put in at Rossinish, on the Island of Benbecula, where they remained for two days. Clanranald, himself a fugitive from justice but well taken care of by his many relatives in these parts, visited Charles at Rossinish. He found Scotland's Heir in dirty clothes, reclining in a hut with a doorway so low that the visitor was obliged to crawl through it on his hands and knees: the hut was "little larger than an English hog-style, and perhaps more filthy." Clanranald brought a couple of bottles of Spanish wine, half a dozen shirts, and some shoes and stockings, for the Prince. He suggested Coradale, at the south end of the Long Island, as a hiding place. But the others advised trying Stornoway, a wretched little port; so the next night they set sail for the north. They landed in the morning at Scalpa, another dreary little place, where Donald Campbell opened his house to them. Campbell himself was loyal to the reigning family, but he would not break the ancient law of hospitality for any government on earth. When a party of armed men (incited by Aulay Macauley of Harris, great-grandfather of Lord Macaulay the author and historian) arrived at the house with a design to seize the Prince and win the £30,000 reward, Campbell not only refused to deliver up his guest but warned the visitors that Charles was accompanied by a large number of desperate men who were armed to the teeth and would stop at nothing. The invaders departed.

Charles lingered at Scalpa for several days. While he was there, two French ships dodged three English men-o'-war and landed 40,000 louis d'or at Borrodale for him. This treasure was carried to Loch Arkaig, in Lochiel's country, where it was buried. You will hear more about it later.

Donald Macleod had been sent to Stornoway to hire a larger vessel. He got one: but after Charles and his gentlemen had walked across a wet moor in a pouring rain all night, they found the inhabitants of Stornoway up in arms against them. Either Macleod or one of the boatmen he had let in on the secret, had got drunk the previous night and had revealed the identity of the person for whom this vessel was intended. Whereupon the inhabitants, fearing that their village would be burned to the last stick if they permitted the Young Pretender to enter it, chased him away. Charles was furious, but there was no remedy. They started back for Scalpa in a small boat.

By this time, a good portion of the British navy was cruising around these islands and in and out between them. Cumberland had suggested this, in order to keep the Pretender within searching distance. Two ships of war got between their boat and Scalpa, and they were obliged to put in at the uninhabited island of Euirn, where they lived four days and four nights in a low hut with no roof. Of course it rained most of the time: it always rains in the north and west of Scotland, where the climate has a ferocity which blends well with the bleak grandeur of the hills. England is California compared with it! You would suppose that all the gods but one had combined to make this country attractive; but that Jupiter Pluvius played his worst tricks on Scotland in an effort to undo the good works of all the rest.

In the Highlands and in the Hebrides there are not only snow and rain and hail and sleet and fog: there are at times, literally, all these things together. This minute the sun is shining, the sky clear, the air, although biting cold, fresh and stimulating. You raise your head—and at the horizon you observe one small dark cloud. The cloud slips a little way up into the sky, catches sight of the sun, turns and summons from behind the horizon a flock of its fellows, and then leads the rush across the heavens. Before you have an opportunity to turn up your coat collar, black clouds have swarmed around the sun, blotting it from sight. The hills disappear in a rush of fog. It rains. It snows. It hails. The winds howl mournfully. Nothing whatever is visible; and walking against the wind, you are afraid your nose will collide with a rock or a tree.

Ten minutes later, perhaps, the storm clouds, as though they had expended themselves, dissolve like steam; the fog goes curling off around the hills; the wind ceases; the sun shakes itself, smiles to recover sight of fair Scotland again, and begins once more to shine with a generosity truly regal.

It is never very warm in the Highlands, and it is usually very cold. At night it is always cold. Moreover, the air is wet; and this makes a considerable difference. Inhabitants of dry northern sections talk with great unconcern about zero temperatures. But in such sections one does not notice the cold. But the wet cold of Scotland pounces upon you with the fury of a malevolent dragon; it gets down between your neck and your collar; it twists its way up underneath your overcoat; it unbuttons your gloves and encases your hands instead in firm chunks of ice. There is no escaping it. Sit by a fire and the cold will stand behind you, rubbing your back with icicles. Walk fast, or run, and the cold will walk or run with you, finding another crevice in your sartorial armor at every stride you take.

This was the land that now harbored the high-born young man from Italy. Yet Charles was thriving on it. He had never been so happy before; he was never so happy again. With his back against a wall, he was at his best. Tramping all night over countryside now rocky, now boggy; tramping through the cold rain and the fog; hiding by day in ramshackle huts that smelt of fish and had leaky roofs, if they had any roofs at all; afraid to light a fire sometimes, always afraid to venture out into any open place in daylight, always with pistols cocked;—he loved it! He insisted upon sharing every hardship. The men who accompanied him, a group constantly changing, were as uncomfortable as he, but never more so. They were all penniless outcasts, with no hope of regaining their places in the world; and any one of them could, by betraying Charles' whereabouts, make peace with the government, and render himself independently rich for life. But they loved him, they worshiped him.

When the party did get to Scalpa again, it was to learn that Donald Campbell had been forced to retire into hiding because the government threatened to arrest him for having given the Pretender hospitality. After that, they took Clanranald's advice at last, and sailed for Coradale.

Another man-o'-war intercepted them, and this time they were seen. They rowed ashore, and Charles with a few others took to the woods while the boatmen concealed the boat. Later they ventured out again, dodged still another ship, and spent the night at sea. The following night they spent in a tiny hut on an island in Lochwiskaway. From there they walked across South Ulst, the lower part of the Long Island, to Coradale, where they found an unoccupied forester's cottage.

Here Charles had breathing space and comparative comfort. Here, too, he heard about the Loch Arkaig treasure, and sent the sturdy Macleod to get some of it, for he badly needed money.

He was twenty-one days in this cottage. He slept on a bed which consisted of cows' hides stretched between two pairs of stakes driven into the ground that was the floor. Yet he was comfortable, and happy. There were scouts posted here and there to warn of the coming of the redcoats or the militia; and there were guides prepared to lead him back into the most inaccessible recesses of the interior of the island. A boat, too, was kept in readiness at all times. The Prince often went gunning, amazing the Scots with his ability to shoot birds on the wing: he had always been a crack marksman, even as a boy.

He had visitors at Coradale, too. Alexander Macdonald of Boisdale, that stern old fellow who had first waited upon Charles in Scotland, and who had then refused to help him, now called on him in his difficulty. Boisdale had not approved the expedition, but assisting a braw laddie in distress was something different, and the Macdanold did everything within his power to make Charles comfortable and as safe as possible. His nephew, Young Clanranald, was another visitor.

But perhaps the greatest assistance was given by Lady Margaret, wife of Sir Alexander of Sleat—the Macdonald of the Isles and of Sleat, who had refused to join the young Pretender. Sir Alexander, at this very time, was seeking the Prince in the neighborhood of Fort Augustus, at the head of his militia of clansmen; but his wife, a Jacobite through and through, was sending the royal fugitive newspapers and brandy and other acceptable things.

Macleod returned with bad tidings. He had not been able to get his hands on any of the money (why, is not clear). All he brought back was a letter from Donald of Lochiel, another from Murray of Broughton, and four bottles of brandy.

By this time the government had learned that the Young Pretender was somewhere in the Western Isles. Up and down the coast went men-o'-war and frigates. Every fisherman's craft was examined; and small boats filled with armed men went ashore every time an officer's suspicions were aroused. For six weeks now the Young Pretender had eluded the army, the navy and the militia. But he could not dodge them forever. And how could a French ship get to him? The poverty-stricken peasants were seldom able to assist him. He could not keep sailing from island to island without being captured. Yet if he managed to escape to the mainland again, he would find still more redcoats and militiamen, and every bayonet sharpened for him. To capture the Pretender was the one ambition of every army and navy officer, for each knew that promotion, the adulation of the populace, and a sinecure for life, besides the reward in money, were waiting for the man who marched in with the Prince as prisoner.

The government was landing soldiers on the Long Island now—seemingly it had caught the scent—and the place was not so big that Charles could long escape them. Lady Margaret Macdonald, always watching for danger, heard of the landing of these troops, and hastily dispatched Hugh Macdonald of Balshair to Coradale to warn the Prince.

Balshair found him still cheerful in the forester's cottage. Charles immediately called for a dram (this is an old Caledonian custom, and even now the guest may feel insulted who is not offered whiskey soon after he enters a Scottish home). They drank. Then Boisdale appeared. Charles greeted the old fellow with enthusiasm, ordering Edward Burke to make up a bowl of toddy. "Then we began with our bowl, frank and free," Balshair later told Bishop Forbes.

Now there are no better drinkers in the world than the Highland Scots. But they found this cheerful young Prince, presumably accustomed only to the fancy wines of the Continent, actually their master at this gentle sport, as he was at least their equal in sharpshooting and long distance tramping. He was adopting Highland customs with a vengeance, not simply learning Gaelic and wearing the kilties. "He took care to warm his stomach every morning with a hearty bumper of brandy, of which he always drank a great deal," writes Neal MacEachain, who joined the party about this time and came to know the Prince very intimately.

So this group in the forester's cottage started to drink from the punch bowl. Several other visitors, all gentlemen, dropped in, and they did not, of course, refuse the prompt invitation to participate in the sport. Again and again Ned Burke was called upon to refill the bowl.

Balshair, emboldened no doubt by the liquid, asked the Prince if he would take it amiss if he told him what were the two chief objections to the Stuarts. The Prince said not at all. Balshair named popery and arbitrary government. As to the latter charge, Charles said, it was chiefly a case of bad constructions his enemies put on ancient happenings. As to popery:

"Do you know, Mr. Macdonald, what religions all the princes of Europe are of?"

"I suppose the religions of whatever countries they govern."

Charles shook his head. "They have little religion or none at all," he replied.

This applied to Charles himself. Technically he was a Roman Catholic. Actually he was like most of us today—nothing in particular, with a certain belief in God, but not inclined to give much thought to the formal differences between sects and, in fact, but little interested.

"If you got to be king," one of the gentlemen said, "you'd forget all about us anyway."

Charles assured them that if he ever came to his own at St. James' palace, he would set aside a night for the entertainment of his faithful Highland friends, and that the bowl would never be empty for them.

"One of my ancestors," said another Highlander, "fought seven set battles for one of your ancestors, but when he went down to court he wasn't even received."

Charles laughed, shaking his head. "Don't be rubbing old sores. . . . I wasn't there then, was I?"

So it went. They talked over the campaign, crops, politics, religion, anything or everything. The conversation was amazingly frank, but the Prince never took offence. Often they sang the old songs over again, lifting their voices as they lifted their glasses, like sturdy gentlemen.

"We continued this drinking for three days and three nights," Balshair relates. "He (the Prince) had still the better of us, and even of Boisdale himself, notwithstanding his being as able a bowls-man, I dare say, as any in Scotland."

Nor do we have to depend wholly upon Balshair's word. After the three days and three nights, Neal MacEachain tells us, a Highlander came visiting and found "all these lying in their bed, very much disordered by the foregoing night's carouse, while his royal highness was the only one who was able to take care of the rest, in heaping them with plaids, and at the same time merrily sung the *De Profundis* for the rest of their souls."

But this could not be kept up. Balshair's warning had gone unheeded long enough, almost too long. Charles, the following night, sailed with O'Neill, Donald Macleod and Neal MacEachain to another tiny island, a deserted place, where they lived a few days on nothing in particular. Still the soldiers were near. So they went back to the Long Island, for three more days of hiding. Then they tried to make for comfortable Coradale again, but a storm forced them ashore in a deserted spot, where they spent a whole night crouching in the cleft of a rock to keep as much as possible out of the rain. The enemy was but two miles away.

They went on, later, to a place near Coradale, hoping to get some further assistance from Boisdale. But he had been taken prisoner by the British when they learned he had helped the Prince. It was often so. The Prince would seek out a man he knew to be faithful and hospitable, only to learn that his friend was in the hands of the enemy, and that his house, often enough, had been burned to the ground, and his cattle and sheep slaughtered. Boisdale's wife, however, gave them four bottles of brandy; and they skulked in this neighborhood for five or six days, unable to move because of the soldiers who were everywhere about them. They hid in wooded ravines by day, not daring to fall asleep; and at night they slept in open fields, with their boat sail rigged up over them to protect them from the rain.

They ate oatmeal and brandy. That was their principal article of diet throughout these wanderings. Sometimes they had whiskey instead of brandy, or usquabaugh; sometimes they had sugar, or even butter. When they went out in the boat they usually carried dried fish with them. Occasionally they caught crabs and ate those raw when they didn't dare to light a fire; and one happy day they came upon a cow all alone, and then they feasted. But mostly they lived upon brandy and oatmeal, or just brandy.

On June 21, when the notorious Captain Caroline Scott

landed within a mile of them, they decided to attempt to get to the Island of Skye, where they thought they would be safer. Now they no longer had a boat, and their situation had never been so serious. Apparently every avenue of escape was cut off.

Neal MacEachain, a quiet, bashful young man, who knew Latin, Greek, French, English and Gaelic, and who had once studied for holy orders, guided Charles and O'Neill across the mountains to a hut near the ruins of Ormaclett. Before they went, they said farewell to old Donald Macleod, who wept like a woman at parting from his Prince.*

Somebody had suggested that they appeal to Flora Macdonald for assistance. This young woman—she was hardly more than a girl—was, by every report we have, the very soul of sweetness and beauty. She was a cousin of Lady Margaret Macdonald and a step-daughter of Hugh Macdonald of Armadale, who was in command of a company of militia at that very hour seeking Charles not many miles away. Flora lived on the Isle of Skye, and was visiting near Armaclett. O'Neil approached her cautiously, at night, when no other person was near, and asked whether the independent companies were to pass that way the next day. Miss Macdonald said no, that they were to pass on the second day. O'Neil said, "I have a friend to see you." The girl must have known from his face and manner, who the friend was.

"Is—is it the Prince?"

Charles had been hiding nearby, with MacEachain. They brought him in, and he met Flora Macdonald. He smiled, holding out his hand. That clinched her decision; for no woman had

* He was arrested soon afterwards and sent to jail in London. I have not been able to learn whether he was ever released. O'Sullivan and Ned Burke, who had been sent away by the Prince when he quit Coradale, were more successful in avoiding the soldiery. O'Sullivan, after skulking in the neighborhood for some time, finally caught a French ship and got safely back to the Continent; he plays no important part in Charles' life after this. Edward Burke wandered alone, living for some weeks on shellfish. Then he hid in a cave for a considerable time, and a cobbler's wife, a Jacobite, brought him food every night. In time there came a general act of grace from which Burke was not excluded, so he returned to Edinburgh where he was made much of by the surviving Jacobites. He had previously been a chairman by trade; and now his friends put him up in business again by raising a fund and buying him one of the best sedan chairs in the city. For the rest of his life he was one of Edinburgh's most pointed-out citizens.

yet been able to resist that smile. Flora was frightened. But she agreed to do everything within her power to get Charles to Skye, where there were no government troops and very few militia, and where he would be nearer to the mainland.

This was at midnight. The three fugitives bowed, and slipped out of the candlelight and back into the satisfying darkness of the forest, while Flora quit the house for Benbecula to make arrangements.

There was need for hurry. Charles and his two companions slept in the forest atop a hill that night, and remained there most of the next day. The next night it rained and Charles took refuge under a rock while Neal MacEachain went down to learn whether Flora had succeeded.

But the militia came sooner than they had been expected. The gentle MacEachain fell into their hands and was taken to the barracks, a prisoner. And there he met another prisoner—Flora Macdonald! She had not been properly equipped with a passport and had been arrested on suspicion.

It was a piece of luck, however, that the captain of this company was no other than Flora's stepfather, who, when he discovered the prisoners, ordered them both released and provided Flora with a passport for her mother's home in Skye. Whether or not Captain Macdonald was, as some say, actually a Jacobite and in on the secret, we do not know. But the passport was made out to Flora Macdonald, Neal MacEachain, and Betty Burke, an Irish maid who was to attend Miss Macdonald. Of course, there was no such person as Betty Burke: it was for Charles to impersonate that female as best he could.

The agreement was that Flora should meet Charles at Rossinish. MacEachain, who knew every foot of this country, returned to the Prince, who was hiding back in the woods, and guided him to the rendezvous. It was a terrible trip. The fords of the loch were all guarded; and only after much tramping in a heavy rain did the three men find a wherry whose crew they prevailed upon to carry them across a wide part of the loch. After that they had a long hike over the soggy moor. Charles was almost exhausted. Once he fell to the ground, unable to move. The others carried him to the only shelter in sight, a shepherd's hut, where, posing as officers making their escape from Culloden, they were filled with black bread and dried fish, the first food they had tasted for many hours. They rested a short while before pushing on; but by five o'clock in the morning they were within sight of Rossinish.

Yet it hardly seemed safe to venture there in daylight, so they sank to the heather and, in spite of the cold and the wet, slept half that day. When darkness came they went down to the house of Clanranald's boo'man. The next morning O'Neil was sent to fetch Flora Macdonald. Soon afterwards the militiamen approached, and Charles was obliged to go outside again. MacEachain, as a tutor in the Clanranald family, was sufficiently well known to be safe in the house. But the Prince spent all that day crouching beneath a rock which did not protect him from the pouring rain, while a swarm of gnats pressed a constant and painful attack upon his face, neck and hands. He had originally taken refuge in the hut occupied by a dairymaid, but the soldiers came there for milk from time to time during the day, and it was not considered safe; so his young and homely hostess led him to the hiding place nearby and, whenever she found an opportunity, slipped away from her tasks to bring him hot milk and encouragement. At night, when the soldiers had gone, she went to tell him that he was safe again for the hour.

This girl might, with a few words, have won £30,000. That sum would be a fortune today: it was triply so in those days. With it she might have lived like a duchess for the rest of her life. But she would not betray her Prince, who had entrusted himself to her hospitality. Had it been discovered that she was concealing him—had one of the soldiers happened to wander a short distance from the hut and find His Royal Highness under that rock—the girl would have been thrown into prison, stripped of everything she owned. But she kept the faith. And we do not even know her name!

Two days afterwards, back in the boo'man's house, they were joined by Flora Macdonald, O'Neil, and Lady Clanranald with her two children, Peggy and Milton. The women wept when they saw the Prince's pitiful condition; but he tossed it off with a laugh. "It might be well for all kings if they had to go through such an ordeal," he remarked.

They sat down to dinner, Charles placing Flora on his right and Lady Clanranald on his left. He was always a Prince, even in a hovel.

The meal was interrupted by a messenger who informed Charles that General Campbell, Captain Scott and Captain Ferguson were closing in upon them with a large force. They quit the house hurriedly, crossed Loch Uskevagh in a shallop prepared for the escape, and finished the meal at five o'clock the next morning.

At eight o'clock Lady Clanranald learned that General Campbell was at her house and demanding to know what had happened to her. It would be best to amuse him, she said, and hurried away: she passed through the lines by explaining that she had been visiting a sick child in her capacity as lady of these lands.*

That night everything was in readiness—the boat, the four boatmen, and the passport. Prince Charles, he whose baby diapers had been blessed by a Pope, retired behind some bushes and changed his ragged, dirty clothes for a linen gown with a pattern of purple flowers on white, a light-colored, quilted petticoat, a white apron, and a mantle of dun camlet, made after the Irish fashion, with a hood. The getting-together of this outfit had been the cause of Flora Macdonald's delay in arriving at the rendezvous. Charles must have presented an odd figure with his broad shoulders, his long legs, and his long muscular arms!

As they were about to depart, four wherries filled with soldiers came along the shore. The plotters quickly stamped out their fire and retired to Charles' rustic dressing-room, holding their breath while the wherries moved slowly past. But all was well. They had not been seen.

There was no passport for O'Neil, and they said farewell to

* Clanranald and Lady Clanranald were arrested a few days later, and sent to London, where they were kept in prison for about a year, being released in June of 1747.

him on the shore. There were tears in his eyes, as there had been tears in the eyes of Macleod.

The night was very dark—no moon, no stars—when they pushed out into the open sea; and a storm was coming up.

CHAPTER FOURTEEN

More Oatmeal and Brandy

THIS being one of the great scenes in our story, it is a pity we cannot forget what a preposterous costume Charles was wearing. The crossing to Skye has been sung by many poets, painters have loved it; and not so many years ago novelists were wont to drag it into their stories at all costs. But for me, at least, it is made grotesque by the remembrance of that dress with the purple flowers. It is as though one tried to picture Washington crossing the Delaware in bell-bottomed trousers, or Sheridan dashing up the Shenandoah Valley astride a jackass.

However, the passage was tragic enough to the seven persons in the boat. They could not see anything at all: they might as well have been floating at the bottom of Abbadon's pit, so utter was the pitch of the night: they were alone in an immensity of blackness. The wind rose and the waves with it. The frail craft was battered mercilessly, until even the oarsmen glanced nervously at one another. Neal MacEachain, that gentle young man, sat in the bow and said never a word. Naturally Flora Macdonald was frightened. Prince Charles felt for her in the stern, and sat beside her. To quiet her fears he sang ballads and, in a low voice, told her stories of the European courts he had visited, while the wind shrieked and the waves crashed against the boat with a terrible persistency, to back away hissing like vipers.

When the dawn came there was no shore in sight. But soon they saw the dark hills of Skye, most celebrated of all the Hebrides. It was the northwestern tip of the island, a place called Waternish. Apparently it was deserted. The storm had subsided, and they sailed confidently for this piece of land.

But just as the boat was about to ground, one of the boatmen saw scarlet specks moving in the underbrush, and shouted a warning. They turned hastily.

And now the soldiers came out of hiding and called for them to stop or be shot. "Don't mind the villains," cried Charles to the boatmen, who replied that they feared only for him, not for themselves. "Oh, as for me, don't mind me," said Charles. But he begged Flora to lie flat on the bottom of the boat. This she refused to do, saying that it would ill behoove a Macdonald to hide from danger to which her Prince was exposed.

"Please. . . ."

A bullet, then two or three more, lifted tiny silver spearheads out of the water near the boat. The oarsmen strained every tired muscle. Still Miss Macdonald refused to shelter herself, until the Prince should do so. The shots from the shore multiplied. The water about the boat was chopped with angry little splashes.

At last they compromised. Prince Charles agreed to lie down in the bottom of the boat provided Flora Macdonald lay next to him. It was hardly conventional, but it was much safer than sitting in the stern. Fortunately for the voyagers the soldiers were not good shots. Passengers and crew came out of the danger zone untouched.

They rowed on for three hours, and then beached near Monkstat House, the seat of Sir Alexander Macdonald who, at the time, was in attendance on Cumberland near Fort Augustus. The boatmen were thanked and sent away, and Flora and Neal MacEachain walked to the house, while Charles remained hidden among some rocks near the shore.

Lady Margaret Macdonald, that good friend of Charles, was entertaining, and some of the guests were militia officers. But Neal MacEachain, as a tutor, was accepted without suspicion, and so also, of course, was Miss Macdonald. That young woman, with rare courage and presence of mind, chattered with the vistors, as if wholly unconcerned. Finding it impossible to get Lady Macdonald aside, she confided in Macdonald of Kingsburgh, Sir Alexander's factor, and he put the matter up to Lady Margaret herself. That worthy lady was frightened when she learned that the royal fugitive was lurking on her husband's property and so near to his house. She knew what it would mean if the government discovered this; for the authorities were in no mood to accept excuses. She insisted that the Prince go elsewhere. She was willing to help him all she could—at a distance.

Macdonald of Kingsburgh was an old man. He did not greatly care whether he died in bed or dangling from a gallows tree. He offered to harbor the Prince himself. Neal MacEachain hurried down to the hiding place to inform Charles to expect the coming of Kingsburgh, whom he had never seen; and then returned to the house. Presently Kingsburgh slipped away and walked to the shore. The hiding place had been described to him, but he had some difficulty in finding it. He was searching among the rocks when he was suddenly confronted by a tall, ferocious-looking female, who brandished a thick black club and cried in a masculine voice, "Are you the Macdonald of Kingsburgh?"

"Your Royal Highness," said the factor, "I am."

Charles apologized. He had been getting a bit panicky, alone in that desolate place after so many nerve-racking adventures. Kingsburgh had brought with him some meat and bread and a bottle of Burgundy; so they sat by the shore and had a little feast by themselves. They then encircled the house and started off on the road to Portee, by way of Kingsburgh, where they were to spend the night. Donald Roy, a young man who had been wounded at Culloden, had been sent ahead by Lady Margaret to inform the Macleod of Raasey that this party was coming, and to engage a boat at Portee.

A few hours later, Flora Macdonald excused herself, explaining that she was eager to see her mother again. "Mother isn't well, you know." "Oh, but you must stay a little longer!" "No, really I can't." And much more of this, all well done for the benefit of the officers and guests. Then the horses were brought around, and Flora and MacEachain, together with the Macdonald of Kirkibost, who happened to be going that way, and a few servants, set out on the road to Kingsburgh.

Charles made but a poor woman. It was Sunday, too, and

FLORA MACDONALD

rom time to time they would pass little groups of Presbyteri-
ns coming home from church. These good people were scanda-
ized to see Sir Alexander's own factor walking side by side with
common serving girl—or rather, an *uncommon* serving girl,
or she strode along next to Kingsburgh with all the assurance
f a lady, and he did not seem to object at all. The good people
vere even more scandalized when, this pair coming to a brook,
he woman, brazen hussy! lifted her skirts almost to her knees
o wade across.

Kingsburgh spoke to Charles about that. "It will not happen
gain," Charles promised; and at the next brook the Prince did
ıot lift his dresses at all, so that the bottoms of the skirt and
etticoat were soaked, which made walking in them a task
ven more difficult than before.

Kingsburgh also censured Charles for replying to the salu-
ations of the church folk with bows, instead of with curtseys.
They call you Pretender," said Kingsburgh, "but all I can say
that you are the worst at your trade I ever saw."

Charles laughed. "I expect to manage three kingdoms, and
et I can't even manage these skirts," he admitted.

After the second brook, they turned off the highway and
nade their way through the woods to avoid raising any further
uspicions. They came to Kingsburgh's home at about 11 o'clock
t night. Lady Kingsburgh and all the servants were in bed.
lora Macdonald, however, was waiting for the party.

Kingsburgh lighted candles. His wife, hearing him come in,
nd hearing too that he had guests, sent their seven-year-old
aughter down with her apologies for not rising and her sugges-
ion that they take whatever food they could find. The child
elivered the message, but ran back to its mother crying with
right at the horrible looking wench who was pacing up and
own the hallway with the strides of a giant. Soon afterwards,
Kingsburgh himself entered the bedroom and insisted that his
vife rise immediately, get dressed, and descend. This was in the
Eighteenth Century. She obeyed without question.

Charles rose to greet her, and after the French fashion,
ussed her on both cheeks. She felt the unshaven chin, and went

white in the candlelight. She said not a word, but drew he
husband aside into the hallway and asked, "Is he one of th
gentlemen who fought at Culloden?"

Kingsburgh said, "He is."

"I knew he was a man. Does he bring any news of the poo
Prince?"

Kingsburgh took his wife's hand and said very quietly, "M
dear, he *is* the Prince."

If she had been frightened before, she was doubly so now
They would all be hanged, she whispered. But her husban
shrugged, saying something about a good cause anyway.

Then the hostess came to the top. Lady Kingsburgh, wit
tears in her eyes, informed her lord that there was nothing i
the house to eat except some eggs and butter and cheese. Sh
couldn't think of placing that before Royalty! Kingsburgh
who had been talking with the Prince all afternoon, laughe
and assured her that Charles would be delighted.

"Get the meal ready, and then come and sit with us," he saic

"*I* sit with you! How should *I* ken how to act before
Prince?"

"Come. The Prince will refuse to eat a bite without you
Don't worry about behaving before him. Be natural—he is.

So the meal was spread, such as it was, and they all fell to
Charles was gay. With Flora Macdonald on his right side, an
Lady Kingsburgh on his left, he ate four eggs and a lot o
bread and butter, and drank two bottles of beer. Then he calle
for a dram of brandy and toasted "the health and prosperity o
our landlord and landlady."

Later, when the ladies had retired, he brought out his pipe
lighted it, and sat down before the fire while his host mixe
usquebaugh, hot water and sugar into a Highland toddy. Ther
the two men sat talking about this and that and the othe
thing. Charles was very happy. If I linger on these homely par
ties, it is because we do not again find Charles as comfortabl
as this; and there is so much of misery and bitterness ahead tha
I am reluctant to move on from this part of the story.

Before they realized it, then, it was three o'clock in th

morning. The host suggested bed: there was a toilsome day ahead of them. "We must empty another bowl first," said Charles. No, said Kingsburgh, bed. No, said Charles, another bowl of that delicious toddy. Kingsburgh rose and started to put the bowl away. Charles rose and tried to take it out of his hands. There was a friendly struggle and the bowl broke in half, ach man holding a piece. Then they were obliged to retire.

Charles said, "Sheets. . . . I had almost forgotten what a bed was like."

It was his habit to sleep only about four hours, but what with the exhaustion of the trip, the nervous strain of so many perils, and the notoriously soporific effect of usequebaugh, coupled with the fact that he was sleeping in a real bed again, he did not rise on this occasion until one o'clock the next afternoon, a full ten hours after his retirement. "The best sleep I've ver had," he assured Lady Kingsburgh.

Charles donned his feminine dress once more, and called for he ladies to help him with the finishing touches. They fussed around him, giggling at his awkwardness, and whispering beween themselves. Lady Kingsburgh was urging Flora to ask the Prince for a lock of his hair, and Flora was urging Lady Kingsburgh to make the request herself. At last Charles inquired; and, blushing, they told him. He promptly placed his head in Flora's ap and told her to cut off as much as she wanted. She clipped one lock, and gave half of this to the hostess.

It was agreed that Charles should get into man's apparel as soon as he was out of sight of the house and its servants, since he story of the extraordinary Irish female who lifted her dresses to her knees when she waded through brooks, was well distributed over the countryside and might fetch snooping soldiers. Meanwhile, he certainly needed another pair of shoes, for he ones he wore were barely holding together and his toes were ticking out at the ends. Kingsburgh supplied him with a fresh pair, and hung the old ones in a corner, remarking as he did so hat these would come in handy some day.

His Royal Highness asked, "What do you mean?"

"Why," said Kingsburgh, "when you're in St. James', and I

come to call, I'll wave these shoes at you and you'll remember who I am."

"I certainly will," Charles promised.

Half a mile or so up the road, the party stopped, and Charles dodged into the bushes, to emerge a few minutes later, a man again. He handed the woman's clothes to Kingsburgh, who took them back to his home and burned them—all except the dress, which his wife insisted upon keeping as a memento.* Soon afterwards Charles said goodbye to Kingsburgh. So overcome with emotion was the Prince that his nose began to bleed profusely. Kingsburgh expressed concern. "This often happens when I saw farewell to anybody I like very much," Charles assured him.†

At Portee, Donald Roy had a boat ready. He had obtained it in Raasey only with the greatest difficulty, for the laird there was himself an outcast, proscribed and hunted, as were most of his gentlemen, and the island itself had been burned over. Donald Roy brought the two parties together, and they retired to the one inn at Portee—which village, incidentally, got its name from the fact that Charles' great-great-great-great-grandfather, James the Fifth, had touched there on his cruise of the Hebrides.

They were soaked to the skin. Charles had a drink and changed his shirt. He bought some tobacco, and did not want to take the change of three halfpennies; but Donald Roy made him take it, explaining afterwards that a person in Scotland who refused to accept change was sure to attract attention. To make matters worse Charles wanted to have a guinea changed

* Some years later, a merchant of Leith, one Carmichael, got a copy of the pattern of this dress and reproduced it. He became rich on the sale; for every Jacobite lady wanted to have one, and purple flowers on white were all the rage. The shoes Charles had worn through were cut into strips, after the death of Kingsburgh, and were given to various women, friends of the family, who carried them away next to their hearts. The sheets between which the Prince slept were not washed but were saved as they were, the one to serve as a winding sheet for Lady Kingsburgh, the other to serve in a like capacity for the beautiful Flora Macdonald.

† Kingsburgh was arrested a few days later. The government was always a few days behind Charles. They imprisoned Kingsburgh in Fort Augustus, and later in Edinburgh Castle, for about a year. The factor was afterwards pardoned and died at his home in 1772.

into silver. In all Portee there were only thirteen shillings. Charles would have accepted these for the guinea, since what he wanted was the silver, but his horrified companions prevailed upon him to give up this idea, since the possession of a guinea would instantly mark him as a person of great consequence—comparatively a millionaire—and would no doubt arouse the suspicions of everybody in the village.

Later, when Donald Roy returned to the inn, the proprietor wanted to know who that tall young man was. Donald said he was an Irish gentleman who had escaped from Culloden. The proprietor remarked, "You know, I thought that it might have been Prince Charles himself."

The Prince asked Donald Roy to accompany him. "When I have a Macdonald with me I always feel safe," he declared. But Donald explained that with his injured right foot—which had been struck by a ball at Culloden—he could not walk far and would be a hindrance rather than a help.

In the party now were Charles; the Macleod of Raasey, and his son, Raasey the Younger; two kinsmen, Murdoch Macleod, a brother of the chief, and Malcolm Macleod, a cousin; and two boatmen, John Mackenzie and Donald Macfriar. They were all veterans of the campaign and all hunted men, excepting Young Raasey, who had remained at home to safeguard the family's title to its estate, and who took a desperate chance when he accompanied this party. Neal MacEachain was left behind, Charles bidding him a fond farewell.

There was another farewell to be said, a more painful one. Charles took both of Flora Macdonald's hands in his. . . . He could say nothing to the beautiful girl, and she could not speak while she looked up at him. Tears rolled down both faces: the men who waited in the boat looked the other way. Charles took off his bonnet, and leaning down to the little face, kissed it twice. Still without a word, he jumped into the boat, nodded to the oarsmen, and sped away over the choppy waters toward Raasey. And Flora Macdonald sat on a rock and watched the boat until it was out of sight, and stared at the horizon for a long while afterwards.

It was not a long trip. Three hours later they were stepping ashore at Glam, where they took refuge in a shepherd's hut. Some oat cakes, a few drinks, and a pipe again, and they were comfortably settled. The boatmen were posted outside as guards. Inside, the gentlemen discussed all manner of things, but particularly a suspicious stranger on the island: this fellow had come to sell a roll of tobacco, had sold it, but had lingered for no apparent reason. He might be a government spy.

The Macleods told also about the destruction Cumberland's men had wrought upon almost everything in the island—burning huts, killing cattle, driving the peasants to the woods. This very hut they were in had been built only a short time previous and after the redcoats had departed; it was one of the few on the island. The chieftain, old Raasey, did not dare to occupy his ancestral home, where his son was now an unwilling master; the father skulked in the forests, supported by the son, who smuggled food and whiskey to him as often as he could.

It was a sad tale, and all too familiar in those parts. Charles' spirits were not high when it was finished. He matched it, however, with the story of his own wanderings. "Why, since the battle I've endured enough to kill a hundred men. Sure, Providence didn't design all this for nothing. I'm certainly being reserved for some good yet!"

He remained in this hut for several days. He was now getting news with some regularity from other parts of the two kingdoms. Young Lochiel was still alive, nursing a wound in a little hut on Ben Alder. Cluny Macpherson and Young Macpherson were with him. The Duke of Perth had managed to get a ship for France, but worn out by the privations he had endured, had died before anchor was cast. Lord George Murray was somewhere in hiding. Lord Elcho and Lord Ogilvy had managed to escape to France. But Kilmarnock, at Culloden, blinded by cannon smoke, had stumbled into a regiment of dragoons, thinking they were his own men: he had been taken prisoner to London. Stout Balmerino, too, had fallen into the hands of the British—or rather, had surrendered himself to them after a few weeks of terrible hardships and near-starvation. John Murray of

Broughton had ventured into the Lowlands and had been captured. The old Marquis of Tullibardine had been found in a cave and now was pining his life away in the Tower of London. In the same prison were Lord Cromarty, Lord Lovat, the Earl of Derwentwater, and many other gentlemen.

Then the men of the Carlyle garrison, poor devils! What mercy could they, or anyone else, expect from such a government? The formal executions began with these men. Eighteen of the gentlemen were put on trial in Southwark on July 15, and all but one were condemned to death. On July 30, nine were executed. They were perfectly calm: only one displayed nervousness for a moment, which he quickly covered by taking a pinch of snuff. In the presence of a huge crowd, they were hanged. That was not enough. Before they were dead, they were cut down, and one by one disembowelled. The executioner ripped open their bodies and pulled out the hearts and these, with the testicles, he threw into a fire, crying, as he did so, "God save the King!"—a cry the populace piously amened. The heads were then cut off and used for purposes of public ornament: some were posted on the Temple Bar; others were preserved in spirits and sent for similar display to Manchester and Carlisle.

But this was only the beginning. Not since the time of Jeffries had the Assizes been so busy or so bloody. The justices all over England—for the men were tried in England where convictions were certain, instead of Scotland where the crimes were committed and the arrests made—were hoarse with the recitation:

". . . you must be hanged by the neck; but not till you are dead; for you must be cut down alive; and your bowels must be taken out and burnt before your faces; then your heads must be severed from your bodies; and your bodies must be divided each into four quarters; and these must be at the King's disposal, and God Almighty be merciful to your souls!"

This was what was called "hanging and quartering," and was England's favorite method of warning these Highland savages against ever again venturing to attack a civilized nation.

Some of the prisoners were treated with what was technically known as clemency. That is, they were permitted to sweat the rest of their lives out below decks in the navy, or on the plantations of America or the West Indies.

All this the Prince heard about, from time to time, in his wanderings. What must have troubled him still more, though, was the treason of some of his followers. The great majority were faithful to the bitter end. But Macdonald of Barrisdale offered to assist Cumberland to find Charles, if guaranteed his own life; Aeneas Macdonald, the nervous little banker from Edinburgh, told at least some of the things he knew; and John Murray of Broughton told everything.

Murray of Broughton must be ranked below Barrisdale and the banker, even below Hawley and Caroline Scott and Cumberland—below them all. Your good Scotsman would prefer the company of Satan himself. For this miserable maker of plots, a man with a keen brain and no backbone at all, had been James' and Charles' Secretary of Scottish Affairs and he now revealed to the government every scrap of correspondence in his possession. It was damning evidence. There could be no appeal from it. Murray of Broughton not only told his entire story, implicating everybody he could implicate, but he also confirmed all this in black and white. Many a brave man went to death because of this despicable treachery.

Derwentwater, whom James in Rome loved better than any other Jacobite, lost his head literally but not figuratively: he was cool to the end, a perfect gentleman. Cromarty, Kilmarnock and Balmerino, tried at one sitting, were condemned together. Cromarty, whose wife was with child, was pardoned at the last minute. The countess who had entertained Hawley pleaded on her knees for the life of her husband, but she pleaded in vain. Nobody said anything about stout Balmerino. King George, besieged on all sides by petitions for mercy in the cases of Cromarty and Kilmarnock, once demanded, "Does no one speak for Balmerino? He's a rebel, but at least he's an honest one."

The two noblemen went to the block at Tower Hill on August 18, 1746. Kilmarnock, resigned, pious, drew many a tear as he walked across the square toward the platform. The executioner found himself obliged to down three stiff drinks before he could behead this charming man. Kilmarnock took off his coat and vest and carefully arranged his hair so that it would not interfere with the blow. He informed the executioner that he would give a signal by dropping his handkerchief. Then he knelt gracefully, placed his neck on the block, and prayed for two minutes, at the end of which time the bit of lawn was dropped and so was the axe. The executioner, for all his earlier qualms, did a neat job: only a tiny bit of flesh remained to be cut after the blow.

Then the platform was strewn with sawdust, the people shouted "God save our gracious King!" and out came Balmerino. It is impossible not to admire this bluff old fellow. He had dressed for the occasion in his most brilliant uniform, blue turned up with scarlet: he called this his "damnation regimentals." When the death carts were quitting the Tower, it was discovered that the executioner had left his axe behind, and there was some embarrassment as to which of the carriages should carry it. Balmerino cried, "Here, I'll hold it"—and he did.

"I won't detain you long," he promised, as he ran up the steps of the platform. Like a popular boxer before a bout, he walked around the railing, bowing to friends, calling farewells. Then he glanced at the block. "Is that my pillow of rest?" He read the inscription on his coffin, and pronounced it correct Latin. He chatted with the executioner, tipped him three guineas, regretted that he could not give more but told the fellow he would throw in his coat and vest—"I won't need them any longer." He felt the edge of the axe. He promised to drop his arms in signal for the blow. And then, still swearing that he loved the Stuarts and only regretted that he had ever served in the army of George the First, he laid his thick Scotch neck across the block and accepted death.

One more execution and I will proceed with our story. You must know what happened to Simon, Lord Lovat.

This old rascal was over-optimistic when he supposed that

the government would believe him any longer. The fact that clansmen had taken the field was enough for Cumberland. Simon might write all the letters he pleased to Duncan Forbes, but Simon's men had worn the white cockade.

Cumberland, soon after Culloden, ordered the destruction of Beaufort; and from the top of a nearby mountain old Simon had watched the hereditary seat of the Fraser chiefs go up in flames. His end, he must have known, was near at hand. He had played crooked once too often.

With sixty retainers, he tried to get down to the sea, hoping to find a French vessel. But a troop of cavalry routed the retainers in a wild and desolate glen in one of the remotest corners of Invernesshire. Where was Simon? They searched well for him; and finally they found him wedged into the hollow of a dead tree. It took four men to get him out, he was so fat and heavy that he stuck there. Too weak to walk, or even to ride, he was carried back to town in a sort of cage-litter; and from thence to London by boat. On August 15, 1746, he rode up to the Tower in an open landau drawn by six horses. "Were I not so old and infirm," he boasted, "you wouldn't keep me here long!"

The House of Commons impeached him December 11, 1746, and his trial by his peers started March 8, 1747. It lasted seven days. Simon laughed and joked, the jokes being mostly obscene. His raucous voice disturbed the placidity and stern formality of Westminster Hall. The peers did not think it was proper for a man to laugh on such an occasion; and only ladies who didn't care much for their reputations dared to attend the trial. The galleries were packed with ladies every day.

Yet Simon played every trick he knew. He was eloquent on occasion. He was watchful, for all his levity. He tried to wriggle out from under with technical objections and too-familiar lies —told, however, with an adroitness which was not familiar in those days of promiscuous perjury. When asked whether he wanted to cross-examine Sir Everard Falkener (for Simon was his own lawyer), the defendant said, "No—only tell him I am his humble servant and wish him joy of his young wife." But when the time came for summation, he was masterful. But there were the letters Murray of Broughton had sold to the government. Their eloquence was greater than Simon's, and Simon was sentenced to die.

The night before the execution he ate a hearty meal. His flow of lascivious stories never stopped. He dressed carefully the next morning, and went to the block in state. On the way, a hag thrust her head into the carriage window, shrieking, "You damned old rascal, I begin to think you'll be hanged at last!" Simon smiled. "You damned old bitch," he replied, "I begin to think I will too."

At the very end he showed some dignity. Two men had to help him up the three steps to the platform. A great crowd had gathered. Simon nodded and smiled. He shook hands with the executioner, and tipped that fellow ten guineas, admonishing him to be sure to do the job with one stroke. When there were big crowds, and persons of high rank were being executed, the headsmen sometimes lost their nerve at the last moment and missed the neck; this made for a nasty hacking, during which the shoulders were sometimes mutilated and the victim suffered not a little. Simon didn't want that. He felt the edge of the axe to make certain it was sharp. "Look out for my shoulders," he said to the executioner. "I'm so fat there isn't much room for you. Do be careful." He knelt in prayer for a reasonable time, and then placed his head across the block. He repeated, over and over again, his favorite line from Horace: "Dulce et decorum est pro patria mori." The executioner did the job with one clean stroke.

Horace Walpole wrote: "He died extremely well, without passion, affectation, buffoonery or timidity."

CHAPTER FIFTEEN

Robbers in a Cave

MEANWHILE, Charles Edward Stuart was at Raasey, a fact of which less than a dozen persons were aware; all the rest of the world, for almost three months now, had been breathlessly inquiring about this extraordinary young man. It was established that Charles, or his corpse, was somewhere in Western Scotland, that was all. As well say somewhere in central Mongolia! His father, his brother, the hundreds of Jacobites on the Continent and the thousands in Britain, were without any reliable news about him. Now he was reported dead; again he was reported rescued. But nobody knew where he was, and nobody except the Prince himself, knew accurately where he had been all this time. The government was quite understandably eager to lay hands on him; for once he got to France he would be lost to England and still dangerous, and as long as he was in the Highlands he was a potential source of trouble. The government could not understand why somebody had not betrayed him. Gentlemen might prove faithful, but that much was hardly to be expected from penniless and illiterate mountaineers. The loyalty of the Highlanders was very annoying.

France continued to send out vessels to search for him. Some of these were official, most were private enterprises. None of them had much chance of finding him as long as the English men-o'-war were patrolling the Hebrides so diligently. They did manage to pick up other outcasts from time to time, but the Prince himself remained among those missing.

Today, thanks chiefly to Bishop Forbes and Professor Blaikie, we know where Charles was almost every minute of this period. But at the time, nobody but Charles knew this—not even the persons he took into his confidence, for he was constantly changing companions and he never announced his next move until circumstances made it imperative or until his mind was fully made up on it. He was developing that ability—the most conspicuous he had, perhaps—of keeping other people guessing about his whereabouts and his plans.

We left him in Raasey, sitting in a hut talking with a little group of Highlanders.

They were still talking about that mysterious stranger who had been prowling in a suspicious manner about the island. The Highlanders were convinced that he was a spy. And when John Mackenzie, one of the boatmen, who was acting as a lookout, stuck his head inside the hut to announce that this fellow was approaching, they were doubly certain.

"Kill him," was the verdict. Charles objected vehemently. How could they kill a man in cold blood when he might be perfectly innocent? The Highlanders conceded that he *might* be innocent but, on the other hand, he might be a spy. It was best to shoot first and ask questions afterwards. Charles protested. They informed him that although he was the King, they were the Parliament, and the man must die. Charles said he wouldn't tolerate it. The Highlanders, at the doorway, cocked their pistols and waited for the intruder to get a wee bit closer. Fortunately for him (he later turned out to be a wearer of the white cockade who had fled after Culloden and was seeking nothing more than a safe place to hide) he turned away just before he reached the hut, and was seen no more that day.

Still, it seemed that the place was not altogether safe. Skye, Charles thought, would be safer. He had been at Raasey two days when he pushed off for a return to that big island. With him were John Macleod, Murdock Macleod, Malcolm Macleod, and two boatmen. They landed at Nicholson's Rock, near Scorobreck, where they spent the night in a cow-byre (or according to some authorities, a cave). The next evening he sent the boatmen away; the old laird returned with them; Murdock Macleod was dispatched on some trifling errand; and with Malcolm Macleod, Charles made his way across country, on foot, for the Mackinnon's territory. His alias was Lewis Caw, and he was to pass as Macleod's body servant. In order to look the part, he changed coats with his companion, unbonneted and wrapped a dirty white handkerchief around his head, tore the ruffles from his shirt, and ripped the buckles off his shoes. He was proud of his disguise. But Macleod insisted that Charles, whatever his clothes, had the manner natural to such a high-born prince, and would be recognized anywhere. In fact, Charles later was able to pass through many places in disguise, without being recognized; but on this occasion, it may be, he had not yet learned the knack of pretending to be somebody he wasn't, for when they came upon two Highlanders, veterans of the campaign, these fellows, after a preliminary stare of amazement, dropped on their knees before him and offered their services. Macleod informed them that they were not needed, and made them swear on their naked dirks that they would not tell anybody they had seen Prince Charlie.

Then he and Charles walked on. Macleod, himself no mean hiker, was obliged to strain himself to keep up with Charles and commented upon the fact. The Prince said he never feared pursuit by English soldiers, provided he was out of musket shot, but Highlanders, he admitted, were the best walkers he had ever known.

Charles asked Macleod what he would do if they were to come upon their enemies.

"That depends upon how many there are," said Macleod. "If there are only four, I'll answer for two of them."

"And I'll answer for the other two," the Prince said.

But there were no enemies. The two men helped themselves to the contents of the one brandy bottle from time to time, and once they stopped for a short rest. Charles told Macleod some of his adventures and waxed indignant over the behavior of Lord George Murray, particularly towards the end of the campaign, when, he said, Lord George either ignored or deliberately disobeyed all his commands. Macleod told something about the condition of the Highlands after Cumberland's soldiers had passed. "I can't understand it," the Prince exclaimed. "Surely a man who calls himself duke and pretends to be so great a general, cannot be guilty of such atrocities." And he really seemed puzzled. For Charles found it difficult to believe that any royal person, even an enemy, could act in an unroyal manner.

When they rose to renew the walk, they discovered that the brandy bottle contained only one more drink. "You take it," said Charles. "No, you take it," cried Macleod. "But you are more tired than I." "But *you* are the son of my king!" At last they settled the matter by throwing away the bottle with the drink in it. Three years later Macleod returned to the spot and found the bottle, and the drink.

Early on the morning of July 4 they arrived at the home of John Mackinnon, in Elgol. This gentleman was married to a sister of Macleod. She was at home, but Mackinnon wasn't. The servants must be kept in ignorance of Charles' identity. He and Macleod had been obliged to wade through a bog part of the way, and their brogues being well worn, their feet were very muddy. A serving woman with water in a basin washed Macleod's feet; but when they asked her to do the same for Charles, she was indignant. She would serve gentlemen and ladies, but not common servants. Evidently the long tramp had worn away that majestic mein which was supposed to show through any clothes however ragged.

Mackinnon himself soon returned, and his brother-in-law went out of the house to meet him. Macleod pointed to some English ships cruising slowly nearby, and observed that Prince Charles might be a prisoner on one of those. The ships wouldn't be there if he were, Mackinnon replied, they would be hastening back to London.

"What would you do if the Prince were here?" Macleod asked.

"I wish he were," said Mackinnon. "He would be safe here."

"Well, he is here. He's inside your house this minute."

The delighted Mackinnon had great difficulty restraining himself when he came into the Prince's presence. What a terrible thing to have a Stuart in your home and yet be obliged to treat him like a commoner because of the servants!

Charles lived up to his rôle, keeping himself unbonneted, and sitting humbly in a corner. He refused to sit at table with the others, informing them obsequiously that he knew his place with gentlefolk. He seemed to enjoy the mummery.

The travelers were tired. But Charles slept only two hours. When Macleod awoke he found the Prince gaily dandling little Neil Mackinnon. "I hope you'll be a captain in my army some day," he was telling the child. Presumably there were no servants present.

They had agreed not to inform the old chief about the presence of Charles, for although he was a man of the greatest integrity and devoted to the Stuart cause, he was considered too old to be of any help at this time. But The Mackinnon learned, and insisted upon taking over the arrangements himself. Aged as he was, he knew his duty. He got a boat and four boatmen, and went with John Mackinnon and Charles when they crossed to the mainland that night. Macleod, who was left behind, was captured a few days later and kept a prisoner in London for about a year.

Charles still wanted to get back to France and persuade Louis to grant him an army. His chances of getting a ship, he estimated, were better now on the mainland.

The boat trip, about thirty miles, was a rough one. Once they came upon a wherry filled with militiamen, who, however, were prevented by the storm from examining closely the occupants of the smaller craft.

They landed at Little Mallaig, near the mouth of Loch Nevis, only to find the countryside overrun with militiamen. For three nights they slept in the open fields. Then the chief and one boatman went off to look for a cave or some other shelter, while John Mackinnon, the Prince, and the other three boatmen took to the water again for the same purpose. Rounding a sharp point, this party came upon a group of soldiers with a beached boat.

"Where do you come from?"

"From Sleat," John Mackinnon called back.

"Row ashore while we question you."

That would never do. Mackinnon snapped, "Row for your lives," and the three boatmen bent their backs manfully. The soldiers jumped into their craft and pushed off after them. For a quarter of an hour it was a dead heat. Mackinnon shouted encouragement to the straining oarsmen, and prepared the muskets and pistols. If the soldiers won the race they could count on a warm reception. Charles begged Mackinnon not to shoot unless it was absolutely necessary.

The pursuers did not have desperation to lend them strength. Soon they fell behind. John Mackinnon kept close to the shore, and when the militiamen had fallen back a short distance, he steered sharply into a little cove, cutting them from sight. Then he beached the boat, and afterwards cocked triggers and waited with two of the boatmen, while Charles and the other boatman scrambled up through the woods to the top of a hill, from where they soon had the satisfaction of seeing the soldiers return disappointed. No shots had been fired. But an alarm would be given, and Charles might expect extra-special diligence on the part of the military in this vicinity.

It happened that old Clanranald, the father of Young Clanranald, was in the neighborhood. Charles sent Charles Mackinnon to him, but the old chief refused to assist the Prince in any way. He had suffered enough already, he said. Mackinnon was furious. But Charles shrugged. "There's no help for it. We'll have to do the best we can for ourselves."

They rejoined the old chief of the Mackinnons and made their way to the home of the Macdonald of Morar, whose wife was a sister of Young Lochiel. He received them cordially enough at first, feeding them and conducting the Prince to a small cave about a mile from the house, where Charles would be safer. Morar then went in search of Young Clanranald, whom he could not find. When he came back his manner was suddenly cool; he refused to be of any further service to poor Charles, whose situation now was as bad as it had ever been. "Almighty God," he prayed, "look down upon my circumstances and pity me." He remarked that he hoped the Mackinnons, at least, would not "leave me in the lurch."

"I'll never leave your Royal Highness in danger," exclaimed the old chief, tears in his eyes.

"With the help of God, I'll go through the whole wide world with you," said John Mackinnon.

Morar did lend the services of a son as a guide, and the party walked to the home of the Macdonald of Borrodale. That home, however, had been burned to the ground by the redcoats. Borrodale himself they found lurking in a bothy. Charles said goodbye here to the Mackinnons, who, like the others who had befriended him, were soon afterwards captured and imprisoned in London,* and he remained with Borrodale for three days. Where to go next was a question. For the hour, he seemed to be safe; and the poor lad wanted to catch his breath. But the rest was not long. Word came to him of the capture of the Mackinnons, and he removed to Macleod's Cove, on a hill, where he remained for another three days, in the open. Here he was joined by the Macdonald of Glenaladale, for whom Borrodale had sent: this Glenaladale had been one of the first to pledge allegiance to Charles that momentous afternoon on the deck of the *Doutelle,* and he was a veteran of every battle of the uprising.

The capture of the Mackinnons and the chasing of the boat which had disappeared, had by now warned the military that the Young Pretender was somewhere on the mainland. Charles now did some of his most brilliant dodging in this grim game of hare-and-hounds, with the advantage of being in some of the wildest country he had yet visited. It is important that you understand the nature of this country. There are five promon-

* Two of the boatmen were also captured, and according to Chambers, one of them, when he refused to divulge the secret of the Prince's whereabouts, was stripped to the waist, tied against a tree, and scourged with a cat-o'-nine-tails until his back was a mass of blood and chopped flesh. Still he shook his head. The soldiers threatened to do the same thing to John Mackinnon, but he laughed at them.

It is worth noting that none of these persons who were arrested for assisting Charles to escape—Clanranald, Flora Macdonald, Malcolm Macleod, Donald Macleod, the Mackinnons, and the others—was accorded a trial. Excepting Kingsburgh, who was none too well treated, they were all taken to London and kept in confinement until the passage of the Act of Grace in July, 1747. No charges were brought against them, and most of them were not even questioned, except at the preliminary examination when the arresting officers were keen to learn the whereabouts of Charles. The Habeas Corpus Act had been suspended, of course.

tories projecting into the sea at this point on the west coast of Scotland, which, on the map, resemble the fingers and thumb of a great hand. Each was wild, wooded, and desolate. Charles was on the ring finger, without a boat. The sea was alive with gunboats: escape in that direction was impossible. Escape on the land side also seemed impossible. The government, elated to have bottled up the Young Pretender at last, had established a cordon of guards across the entire space where the fingers, or promontories, joined the rest of the countryside; these sentries, posted only a short distance apart, would allow no one to pass without rigid examination. Groups of inspection officers passed up and down the lines constantly to make certain that each man was keeping good watch. At night? But at night there were huge fires built along the line, short distances apart, and a soldier was stationed at each fire: each soldier marched from his fire half the distance to the next fire, where he came face to face with another sentry: both men saluted, turned, and marched back to their respective fires. A shot from any one of these sentries would bring a large party of soldiers, all eager to get the reward. The guard was well maintained, too, and each inch of ground along the twenty-mile front—the knuckles of this geographical hand—was covered by a soldier every five minutes. It would seem that no human being, no, not even a rat, could escape from this trap.

From the hilltop, Charles could see the fires every night.

Yet he could not remain where he was, for the reserve soldiers, although never breaking the line, spent their days carefully searching the countryside between the line and the sea. Sooner or later they must get him. He could not fly, and he could not evaporate and then solidify in another place. Angus MacEachain, Borrodale's son-in-law, offered a place of concealment he had prepared near Meoble, in the Braes of Morar; one of Borrodale's sons, Ronald, was sent to examine this place and report on it. Before Ronald could return, however, the military were seen coming up the side of the hill upon which Charles had taken refuge. So Charles, Borrodale, Glenaladale, and Borrodale's other son, John, not able to wait for Ronald's report, descended the hill on the other side and made for Meoble. There, for the first time, they realized how thorough had been the government's work in setting their trap.

There was one man who might be able to help them, and he was Donald Cameron of Glenpean, who knew every tree and every rock of this countryside for miles around. They sent for him, but could not wait for him. They had sent John Macdonald, Glenaladale's brother, to Glenfinnan for intelligence, but they could not wait for *his* return either. The soldiers were steadily closing in upon them, and besides, they had only a tiny bit of food. They stumbled on—anywhere to get away from the military, for a single shot would betray them now. By accident they fell in with John Macdonald, and he brought the discouraging news that a party of about 100 Campbells was approaching from the south to aid in the search!

In daylight they were motionless, not daring to light a fire, to look for food, or even to call to one another. At night they stumbled forward again, feeling their way between two hills. Then, in the moonlight, they saw a man coming down one of these hills. Anybody was an enemy. Charles and John Macdonald dropped quietly behind bushes, and Glenaladale, hand on pistol butt, approached the fellow deliberately.

Conceive their delight when the shadowy figure, coming nearer, proved to be Donald Cameron of Glenpean!

Cameron could see in the darkness, and knew forests like an Indian scout. It was about 11 o'clock when they met him, and they tramped with him all night to a place called Mamnynleallum, a deep spot on the side of a hill which had been searched the previous day and presumably would not be searched again. Thus, under Glenpean's guidance, they were following the military instead of permitting the military to follow them. But the line of sentries remained.

All that day, July 19, they did not move from their concealment. At nine o'clock that night they ventured forth again, following Glenpean. Once they were climbing a hill on one side while the soldiers were climbing it on the other side:

fortunately, one of the Glenaladales, sent ahead to reconnoiter, discovered this fact in time to warn them. They ascended another hill, and looked down to find the line of sentries almost at their feet, the yellow fires illuminating huge spots in the blackness of the night. They could hear the guardsmen calling the password to one another, and they could even see the sentries when they walked into the light of the fires and then walked away again.

And now some mathematically minded person in their midst, probably Glenpean, conceived a simple, if dangerous way to get through that line. Why had nobody thought of it before? The plan was this:

Select a place exactly half way between two of these big fires, a place where there was some sort of gully or stream. Wait until the two guards, one from a fire on each side, met at this spot, exchanged the password, and then strode back to their respective fires. Then slip through. For the space of perhaps two or even three minutes the backs of both men would be turned, and unless the inspection guard happened along at that time, or unless somebody's foot slipped, or a twig snapped, or a stone rolled over, or one of the guards chanced to glance over his shoulder—unless one of these things or some other accident happened—the party ought to be able to get outside the line.

They were sure to be captured, or starved to death, if they remained where they were. Within a few hours the dawn would be up, and another day would be too late. So they crept down the hillside and, on their hands and knees, approached as closely as they dared to the space between two fires. Fortunately there was a tiny brook here which had worn well down into the rock. The inspection party, which passed every fifteen minutes, had just departed.

Glenpean whispered that his nose was itchy, and averred that this was an infallible sign of great danger ahead. Like all Highlanders, he was highly superstitious. But he was also brave. Whispering in the darkness, he proposed to go through the line himself before the others tried it. If he returned, it was safe. If he didn't, it wasn't. He disappeared into the darkness without a sound just after the sentries had turned their backs to one another again. It seemed that he was gone for hours.

Then a wee hiss, a hunched shape straightening to a kneeling position, and their guide was back with them again. The sentries never knew: they walked patiently back and forth, back and forth.

And now the whole party—Charles, Glenaladale, Glenaladale's brother, Borrodale's son, and the Cameron of Glenpean—crept stealthily down the gully on their hands and knees. They kept close together. They were absolutely silent. For a long time they did not dare to straighten up, even when they were well beyond the line. Finally they rose to their feet, probably a bit pale in the darkness, probably a bit jumpy after their long strain, but sound and strong still. Charles broke the silence with a soft laugh. "Does your nose still itch, Donald?" he asked.

But this was only one of many adventures of the sort, some of them quite as exciting. That very morning, for instance, and still before dawn, the Prince came within half an inch of death when he slipped on a narrow path which wound along the edge of a precipice. I might write many more chapters of well-authenticated tales about the doings of Bonnie Prince Charlie as a fugitive in the Scottish Highlands. Let it suffice that the little party eventually got to Glenshiel, in Lord Seaforth's country, where they learned that the French ship which had been lingering at Poolewe had been obliged to put to sea again: Charles had hoped to get that ship. Donald Cameron was duly thanked and returned to his own country. He knew nothing of Seaforth's domains and could be of no assistance to the Prince, who was at all times anxious to keep his party as small as possible. With Donald Macdonald, a vassal of the Macdonald of Glengarry, as guide, the party started for Glenmoriston, which was further inland. The military, it was estimated, would not be so thick at Glenmoriston; and Charles hoped to meet with Young Lochiel and with Cluny Macpherson, who were in hiding somewhere near there.

Of course they started at night. They had not gone far

when Glenaladale discovered that he had lost his purse—or rather, the party's purse, which contained all the money they had among them. He insisted upon walking back over the same route to look for it, and Borrodale's son accompanied him. Charles, the guide, and John Macdonald of Glenaladale, sat down by the side of the path to await their return. A few minutes later a company of soldiers filed past, going in the direction of the two purse-seekers. Again Charles was saved by an apparent miracle. Had not the purse been lost, and had not Glenaladale discovered its loss at the moment he did, they would all have walked directly into the hands of these soldiers. It was not a matter of fighting, either, for a single shot would have brought additional soldiers on the run from all directions. Fortunately, Glenaladale and John Macdonald returned to the Prince by another route.

Another day of misery, and a night spent on the cold ground, with heather piled over him in order to keep out the midges; and then Charles was introduced to the famous Seven Men of Glenmoriston.

These men were robbers who lived in a cave. They were led by Patrick Grant, who was commonly called Black Peter of Caskie. They feared nothing; they were desperate men, outlaws, each with a price on his head, but each a crack shot. General Campbell would have given almost as much for them as he would have given for Charles himself. For these banditti, all men whose homes had been burned and who had been obliged to hide in the forest after Culloden, were taking their revenge upon the soldiers of the King. There are no more picturesque fellows in history. They stole only from their enemies, and to their friends they gave anything or everything they had. They were not robbers from inclination, but from hate. Familiar with every foot of land in Glenmoriston, they were able to post themselves at strategic points in the mountain passes, waiting for the soldiers who would be going out to beat some poor woman and drive away her cattle. When the soldiers came, when they reached a certain point in a narrow pass, the muskets of the Seven Men crashed in one explosion, like a shot from a cannon, and seven soldiers were stricken down. A moment of silence, while the smoke floated away, then another roar, and seven more soldiers fell. If the company was not too numerous the Seven Men would draw claymores and have at them on the spot. More often, however, they would continue a steady, terribly accurate fire from the darkness of the wooded hills, until the soldiers, completely demoralized, broke and ran. Sometimes the Seven Men would make a sally upon a military camp at night, appearing with the suddenness of fabulous demons, shrieking, shooting, swinging their swords. . . . Then silence again. And nobody could ever find the Seven Men. Search anywhere you wanted: they were not in that place, but many miles away. But there were evidences of their visits in every narrow glen and dale—rotting corpses, or dried heads stuck grotesquely atop tall pine trees. Do unto others as they did unto you, was the motto of the Seven Men of Glenmoriston.

To Charles they swore fidelity, swore it on their naked dirks. He was their guest, and no man ever met more faithful hosts. When he came to them he wore a ragged coat of coarse, dark cloth, a ragged waistcoat of Stirling tartan, brogues that were worn through in many places and held together only by thongs, a belted plaid, and around his neck a dirty clouted handkerchief. He wore a bonnet over his wretched yellow wig, and had but one shirt, and that saffron colored and very dirty. It is not unlikely that he was even lousy at this time.*

The Seven Men of Glenmoriston made him comfortable in a spacious cave, by the side of a sweet-singing subterranean brook. They fed him all he could eat, and they plied him with whiskey.

Whiskey? It was not good enough for their Prince! And the poor lad seemed to need a change of clothing. So the Seven Men excused themselves, took up their muskets, and went forth in search of something approximately worthy of such a brave

* At John Mackinnon's house in Skye, Malcolm Macleod observed Charles scratching himself. He took the Stuart scion to a quiet place outside the house, stripped his shirt from him, and picked more than one hundred lice from Charles' body. There were doubtless other occasions like this.

and high-born fellow. There was gunsmoke in a lonesome place that day, and General Campbell, when he received his next report, cursed the freebooters again. But Charles was well supplied. Now he had clean shirts, good shirts, which formerly had belonged to officers of King George. The wines those officers had intended to drink were Charles' also. Was there anything else he wanted? His hosts would get it for him.

For three weeks, they kept him in one place or another, guarding him with the jealousy of perfectly trained dogs. Nothing was too good for him. "He fascinated them," writes Ewald. "His coolness in moments of danger, his winning manners, his powers of enduring fatigue, his superiority in all manly exercises, won not only their devotion but their love." They were in tears, these fierce fellows, the terror of an army, when the time came for Charles to leave them. They begged him to remain. He would never be betrayed. He would have everything they could buy or steal for him—wines, laces, fancy clothes, anything. Why should he venture forth again into the dangers of the open heath and the guarded shore? They could equip him with claymore and target, with musket and pistols and the sharp *skene dhu,* and he could live with them and be their chief, forever adored, commanding them to do whatever he desired of them and certain of absolute obedience. This would be his kingdom, this cave, these glens and grim rocks, the heather strewn hills and the dark forests of pine. They would be his subjects: he had expected more, to be sure, but not in all the world would he find any others so faithful to him.

A tempting picture they drew for him! But there was one purpose in Charles' life. He must recover the three kingdoms for his family. He must get to France, persuade King Louis to put an army under his command, and return to call out again just such fearless fellows as the Seven Men of Glenmoriston. Then another dash for London—and this time he would win!

So he said farewell to them, and went off to try to find Donald of Lochiel and Cluny Macpherson.

Now a strange thing happened—the sort of thing you would never expect to find in a history, even a history like this. A peasant got drunk, or perhaps avaricious, and informed some soldiers that a tall young man with a handsome oval face and proud bearing, was hiding in the Braes of Glenmoriston. The soldiers sought him out, and beat him from cover. He tried in vain to escape; and when he found himself cornered he drew claymore and gave a good account of himself. But he was cut down by sheer force of numbers, and dying, he fixed his attackers with a haughty stare and exclaimed: "Villains! You have killed your Prince!"

The soldiers were filled with delight. Here, at last, was the Young Pretender, and to them would go the reward. Six feet tall, muscular yet slim, with hazel eyes, light brown hair that was blond at the tips. . . . They chopped off the head and sent it up to London for examination, afterwards getting drunk in anticipation of their shares of that £30,000.

The government sent for Prince Charles' *valet de chambre*, one Morrison, who was in Carlisle awaiting execution. They offered this fellow his life and freedom if he would tell them honestly whether or not the head was that of his recent master. But on the way to London, Morrison fell seriously ill, and for some weeks he was not able to try to identify the head. Meanwhile it had become badly decomposed; and when the valet was brought to face it he swooned without being able to utter a word. Later, however, he examined the head, and then he informed the government that it was not that of Charles Edward Stuart.

In fact, the head was that of one Roderick Mackenzie, son of an Edinburgh goldsmith. Young Mackenzie had served as an officer in Charles' own bodyguard; he was about the same age as the Prince, and his striking resemblance to that personage was often a subject of conversation among his friends. He was himself a fugitive after Culloden, when the soldiers cornered him. Presumably he realized that he was doomed when they caught him, and realized too that he could serve the white rose better by his death than he had been able to serve it in life. Presumably he shouted, "Villains! you have killed your Prince!" because he thought that this would assist Charles in escaping.

By the time the identity of the head was learned, the government, certain that it had nabbed its royal prisoner at last, had called in most of the military and naval forces stationed in the Highlands; only scattered bodies of militia remained to make mischief. So that Charles, when he quit the Seven Men of Glenmoriston, was as safe as he had been at any time since his landing in Scotland. He was not by any means out of the fire yet; but at least he no longer was obliged to go crawling on all fours between posted sentinels, or peek carefully around each rock before he ventured to walk there.

After sundry minor adventures, and several false alarms, he rejoined Donald Cameron of Lochiel, who had been been living in a comparatively comfortable hut on the side of Ben Alder, in company with Cluny Macpherson of Cluny, and his son, Macpherson the Younger of Breakachie, besides a few servants. From the door of the hut they could look out over a military encampment a few miles away. But they were not disturbed.

However, it was not considered safe enough for Prince Charles, who was removed to a much less comfortable abode, the "Black Hut," in another part of the mountain. Later he and Lochiel and the Macphersons and a few others moved to still another hiding place on this mountain, Macpherson's "Cage," which is still pointed out to tourists. The "Cage" was a sort of half-hut, half-cave, a two story affair, made chiefly of large slabs of rock and many tree branches. It accommodated six persons, four of them playing cards, one cooking, and the sixth keeping watch in the doorway. It was impossible to stand upright, but one was comfortable enough when seated. The "Cage" was an excellent hiding place. Nobody would think of looking for any person in that strange refuge, which, indeed, looked like nothing in particular from the outside, even when you were close to it. The upper story was a bedroom and dining-room; the lower story, a storeroom and kitchen. Young Macpherson rigged up an ingenious device for getting rid of the smoke: in the Black Hut the smoke had refused to go anywhere but into the eyes of the hut's occupants.

And there was Prince Charles in the "Cage" one afternoon, playing cards, humming a little tune, and perhaps dreaming about his eventual triumph, when they brought him the news that two French ships, privately chartered for the especial purpose of rescuing the Stuart, were at anchor in Lochnanaugh. This was on September 13, five long months after the conflict on Drummosie Moor.

It was almost a week's trip to Lochnanaugh. Other outlawed gentlemen joined them on the way, including John Roy Stewart and Young Clanranald. On September 19 they boarded one of the ships, along with various other gentlemen and 107 commoners. Cluny Macpherson of Cluny remained on shore: he would safeguard the interests of the Prince in the Highlands, take care of the buried treasure at Loch Arkaig, and keep in correspondence with Charles, until the coming of that glorious expedition which would restore James to his hereditary rights.

Shortly after midnight they weighed anchor and sailed out of this same hill-hedged harbor into which the *Doutelle* had carried an optimistic, battle-mad boy fourteen months previous. And the sailing wrote "Finis" to the history of Scotland, which has since consisted merely of footnotes to the history of England.

CHAPTER SIXTEEN

Gold Lace Again

"GO frowning forth, but come thou smiling home," his king told Theredamas.

The Persian didn't. Neither did Prince Charles Edward, who, instead, went smiling forth and came back frowning. But not for an instant did he permit the frown to show! not yet! His generalship on the field had ended with the dissolution of his army; but he calculated that his generalship at court and the council table was only beginning. How he hated France! That low, hypocritical nation! She had wanted a catspaw. She had wanted him to lose. He made a convenient club for her; but if, by any chance, he had actually attained that coveted seat in St. James', he might have waxed English and patriotic. And that was a chance Louis did not care to take.

You understand, these were Charles' feelings. What the exact truth was we do not know. Certainly France had promised something; certainly the promises had been well hedged with qualifications; but how much or how little they were exaggerated before they reached the ears of the Prince, and how much or how little he exaggerated them in his own sanguine imagination, the world probably never will learn. The point is, Charles believed himself to have been betrayed. He came back frowning.

He landed at Roscoff, on the Bretòn coast, and promptly moved a few miles to the village of Morlaix. Here he remained for two or three days to get his land legs. Meanwhile he wrote to his brother, Henry, Duke of York, stressing the importance of an early secret interview with His Most Christian Majesty Louis XV, King of France. Charles wanted to lose no time: a French expedition that month would without trouble fan up the not-yet-dead-ashes of Jacobitism, for the clansmen had nothing more to lose now and would willingly take another chance. But delay would be fatal.

On the way to Paris he was met by a group of French gentlemen headed by his brother. These two young men were entirely unlike one another. While Charles longed for the military life, the grand dash to glory, the flags, the drums, the roar of cannon and crackle of musketry, Henry was concerned only with prayer and study and quiet meditation. Henry went to mass and, if he also went to drill, it was only because royal princes were expected to do so; and as for Charles, he went to drill, but only because princes were expected to do so did he go to mass as well. Charles had no religion: except in its political aspects, that subject did not interest him at all. Henry, on the other hand, was deeply religious, as a boy, as a youth, as a man. Henry was quiet, patient, prematurely pompous. Charles was hot-headed, stubborn, easily annoyed and intolerant of delay.

Yet they were brothers, and it was their duty to love one another—publicly. When they met on the road to Paris, at first they hardly recognized one another. But they fell into embrace, as they were expected to do, and said the things they were expected to say. Henry remarked that Charles had unaccountably grown plump: his friends had supposed that the hardships through which he had passed would make him gaunt and haggard.

They went to Paris. Charles was afire with impatience to see the king. How he hated the French! But it was necessary to be suave, and play his part. He would be a public hero; and the acclamations might overcome Louis' timidity and the caution of his ministers and mistresses. The cheers of the street crowds might be sufficiently loud to serve as rallying cries for another army—a properly equipped, properly disciplined army.

His most Christian Majesty was presiding over an extraordinary council of state at Fontainebleau when they whispered to him that the Prince of Wales had returned: he quit the table and rushed out with open arms. There were fond embracings, and France's voice was heard to cry, "*Vous avez fait voir que toutes les grandes qualités des heros et des philosophes se trouvent reunies en vous; et j'espere qu'un de ces jours vous receviez la recompense d'un merite si extraordinaire!*"

A promising beginning. Charles immediately started to say something about the need for another invasion of Great Britain, but Louis gave him no opportunity, hurrying him, instead, to the Queen's apartments. The Queen was a kinswoman of Charles' mother. She showered the lad with compliments, tears and kisses. Every time Charles started to bring up the subject of another try at the throne, with French assistance, he was told again what a wonderful young man he was.

After the king and the queen came the whole court. It all would have been pleasant, had it been well placed. Charles, being human, liked to have people say flattering things about him; but just now he was impatient, for the time was short. There was black, black hatred in his heart, but he played his part well and his face smiled while his soul was cursing.

But he was in the very capital of Pomp and Circumstance. The Sun King's most distinguished guest and cousin must not think of talking business until he had been formally presented at court, and wined, and dined, and everything else. They would think of a lot of things to say to him yet. The Castle of St. Antoine was fitted out for him, and also a magnificent suite at the palace of Versailles. Did he want money? The King would settle a huge pension upon him. The King also fixed a day for his proper presentation.

Charles went through with it all. There was nothing else he could do. He dressed, for this occasion, in rose-colored velvet embroidered with silver lace; his waistcoat was of rich gold brocade with spangled fringe set on in scallops; diamonds glittered on his cockade and on his shoe buckles; his white wig was perfectly combed; and, his breast ablaze with the Star of St. Andrew, the Cross of St. George, the Garter, and a multitude of other decorations, he went to court.

In the first carriage were Lord Elcho, Lord Ogilvie, Gordon of Glenbucket, and Kelly. In the second carriage were the

Prince himself, Lord Lewis Gordon, and the Cameron of Lochiel, Donald's aged father. Two pages, resplendently attired, and ten footmen, dressed in the full glory of the royal English livery, walked on either side. In the third carriage were four chamberlains. Then came Young Lochiel and the other exiles, and the cream of the French aristocracy.

Paris went wild, shouting itself hoarse.

After the presentation ceremonies, there was a State banquet in honor of Charles.

Eventually he got the ear of the king. But Louis was evasive and non-committal on the subject nearest the Prince's heart. Lochiel, Lochgarry, Ogilvy, Maxwell of Kirkconnell and others, were granted commissions in the French army, and a fund was appropriated for the use of other exiles who had fought under the white banner. But 18,000 or 20,000 soldiers for an expedition: that was another matter. Louis the Grand presumably supposed that Charles would forget—that his ambition would slip away from him under the enervating influence of Parisian gaiety. Surely in this capital, if anywhere in the world, there would be sirens who could make him forget his ambitions and wines which could drown his bitternesses. Nothing was too good for this young man, who could have everything except what he wanted.

His ambition would die when he died himself, not sooner. Ladies with smooth shoulders, wine in golden goblets, and the adulation of the multitudes, were all acceptable, but Charles kept thinking of those 18,000 or 20,000 men. Starting at scratch, he had almost won a throne. And now that he understood matters so much better, now that he had behind him a stupendous prestige, he could, he was certain, unseat German George easily—if only France would help. He wrote to his father. "I never intend to give myself reste either in minde or body until I faile, or bring off our Business."

Louis made some uncertain gestures to keep the lad quiet—drilled a few regiments, ordered a few supplies shifted back and forth, caused some military stirrings in port towns. But Charles was not fooled. Charles, by this time, knew something about armies: he was not the boy who had been kept inactive for so many months in 1744 and 1745.

Charles talked expedition to the king largely through the mediumship of Cardinal Tencin, who, as already noted, was under obligations to the Stuarts. Once, Tencin hesitantly suggested that if Charles were willing to cede Ireland to France the thing might be arranged. Charles flew into a fit of anger. He was no damned political huckster! "Everything or nothing!" he screamed, again and again. Tencin, frightened, insisted that it was no more than a passing thought and did not in any way represent the king's attitude. But after that Charles hated the Cardinal for a sly, sneaking schemer.

France would do nothing for the present. Very well, and damn France! Charles was acting independently now; he paid little attention to his father's letters, and was no more than polite, if he was that much, when his brother fretted about all this drinking.

Spain might do the thing for him. Spain was a devout Catholic nation and had always professed the greatest sympathy for the Stuart family. Had the thing been put up to Spain instead of to France, in the first place, it was likely enough that Spanish ships would have come sailing in with the men Charles had needed. Charles went to Spain.

He went quietly, warning no one. But he found the nation decadent, rotten, filled with frightened whispers and half-promises. Spain was walking in a circle, on tip-toe, and always with her head turned and looking over a shoulder. Caravajal did not even want to take the Prince to the palace; and when he did do so, it was with elaborate secrecy, at midnight. Ferdinand Sixth and his queen were gracious, but they, too, were frightened. They begged the embarrassing guest to return immediately to France. They would do what they could, they said, pledging nothing definite. Charles flung himself away, disgusted, and wrote indignantly to his father.

Poor James! For three years he had not seen his beloved Carluccio. For six months of that time he did not even hear from him, did not know what to believe. False reports poured into the gloomy Roman palace. The news of Charles' safe arrival in France, at last, filled the father with delight; he caused medals to be struck in honor of the event, and for a time he was all smiles.

But Charles was acting strangely. James could not understand it. James was more than willing to let the boy have his regency: had Charles gained the throne, James almost certainly would have abdicated in his favor as soon as he could do so with safety. He who had so long worn an unreal crown was weary of being king.

But the boy needed some assistance, needed watching and good advice. He was reckless. He appeared almost to have gone mad with rage. Yet he would pay little attention to his father, but continued to stumble through the strange forests of Continental politics, aggressively confident that he knew what he was doing. James never had an opportunity to cease worrying.

The truth is that Charles was in the hands of advisers who were at enmity with James' court in Rome. The Jacobite party was split wide open. From the birth of this boy—indeed, from pre-natal days—there had been at least two Jacobite factions; they came to be known as the King's Party and the Prince's Party. The persons James recommended to his son, Charles slighted. The persons James warned him to beware of, Charles accepted as confidants. There was no personal feeling of enmity between the two: James was all fondness at all times, and Charles, although a bad son, often peevish, seems never really to have hated his father. But Charles had learned the extent of the anti-Catholic feeling in Great Britain, and he wanted to keep away from Rome as much as possible, to create the impression that he was not, at any time, a creature of the Pope.

For a while, after his return to Paris from Madrid, there was much talk of marriage. Hardly an unwedded female of exalted rank and the proper religious faith but was mentioned as a possible or even probable bride. Charles was not interested. Eighteen or twenty thousand soldiers were what he wanted, not a woman. He seemed to have some fondness for King Louis' second daughter—he had been known, in the Highlands, to toast her black eyes. But he was too proud to sue for her hand until he was a real, honest-to-goodness Prince of Wales in England. He wanted no pity. He wanted no wife either. All he wanted were those soldiers. He had promised the mountaineers that he would come back at the head of an army, and he was determined to make the promise good.

Yet while they were suggesting this princess and that grand duchess, with or without consulting Charles, the Prince himself was stricken with a matrimonial inspiration. Suppose, he thought, I offer my hand to the Czarina? If France and Spain won't help me, a Russian wife might!

This was about as silly an idea as he could possibly have conceived. His father practically told him so. Charles did not propose to Elizabeth; and it is as well that he didn't, for she would have refused and he would have been bitterly humiliated.

He was not interested in marriage as such. He had work to do before he could settle down with a wife and, unless he could get a royal princess or an actual sovereign, he wanted none at all. But it was important that the Stuart name be continued; and James, out of respect for his lost Clementina, had persistently refused to remarry. So Charles again and again urged his pious brother to take unto himself a spouse, pointing out to him that he could without embarrassment accept a duchess or minor princess—titles Charles felt would be impolitic for an older brother. Henry tried to avoid this embarrassing subject. He was not the marrying kind. Charles reminded him that princes of the blood royal were *obliged* to be of the marrying kind, whether they liked it or not, just as they were obliged to keep a straight face under musket fire and publicly pretend to believe liars. But Henry continued to dodge the issue. He had plans of his own. But he didn't tell Charles about them.

Charles was to learn those plans in due time; and he was never the same man afterwards.

Meanwhile, all sorts of plots were hatched around him, and the rumors about him were well-nigh innumerable. There was, for instance, the talk of Poland, a nation at that time governed by an "elective king." That throne was a favorite plaything of the monarchs and statesmen of Europe, and had served as excuse for many a war. The incumbent at this time was Augustus of Saxony, titled King Augustus III; and his family, and its backers, were eager to make the office hereditary. If they made a real step in this direction they would provide Louis with an excuse for stepping in. Louis had kept his hands off that Polish throne for some years now, and he was tempted to make another try at it.

All this gave the English statesmen something akin to insomnia. For one of the most probable candidates, according to rumor, was the Young Pretender, Charles Edward Stuart. Many years before, melancholy James had been asked to stand for election to the kingship of Poland, but had refused; half a loaf might be better than none at all, but James felt that it was his divine duty to be King of Great Britain and Ireland, and he would accept nothing less. But now here was Charles Edward, a young man of parts, with a brilliant background, an engaging personality, and a mother who had been a Sobieski. Tortuous feelers were put out; but it was learned, in time, that Frederick the Great and the King of Sweden, whose coöperation would be necessary, were lukewarm to the proposition, which was thereupon dropped.

Charles never expressed an opinion publicly on this matter. Certainly if the throne had been offered to him, James would have counseled refusal; for in Poland, Charles would be no more than a tool for Louis of France to use as he willed. Yet it may be that the Prince would have accepted, if for no other reason than that his father and his father's friends asked him to refuse. It may be that he would have convinced himself, or been convinced by his companions, that he could use Poland as a crowbar to pry open the door of Britain. But anyway, he wasn't offered *that* crown, and so English statesmen sighed with relief and turned to fresh worries in other parts.

Schemes like this—and there were many of them—never served to divert Charles from his single purpose. He continued to devote all his efforts to the one end. But the delays made him furious. Time was so valuable! Had he been able to strike promptly after his return to France, while the clansmen still were ready with their muskets and their grand fighting spirit, he would have been successful: of this he was certain. But every week now put him a step further away from that seat over the Stone of Scone. For the British government was relentless in its task of stamping out every last spark of rebellion and of sympathy for the Stuarts.

In the summer of 1747 the British Parliament passed the Act of Grace, pardoning generally those who had taken part in the uprising of 1745-46, with, however, a very long list of exceptions. But this meant little to Charles. The redcoats were still quartered in the Highlands, still intimidating the clans. The ancient spirit did not dare to show itself. Scotland was down, and England was kicking it—kicking hard, too. Hadn't England bought this nation outright, and wasn't England privileged to keep it in its place?

The executions, the burnings, the murders, the rapes, were only a part of the English program, and a comparatively unimportant part. By far the most effective measure was the law proscribing the Highland kilt—19 George II, Cap. 39, Sec. 17, 1746. That law was a deathblow to Scottish spirit. There was no way to evade it, no way to avoid its inevitable effect. To one who does not know Scotland as she was in the days before she began to say "yes" to England, the law seems harmless enough, even rather trivial:

". . . from and after the first day of August (this was old style) one thousand seven hundred and forty-seven, no man or boy within that part of Great Britain called Scotland, other than such as shall be employed as Officers and Soldiers in His Majesty's Forces, shall, on any pretext whatsoever, wear or put on the clothes commonly called Highland clothes, that is to say the Plaid, Philabeg, or little Kilt, Trowse, Shoulder-belts, or any part whatsoever of what peculiarly belongs to the Highland Garb; and that no tartan or party-coloured plaid or stuff shall be used for Great Coats or upper Coats . . . every such person so offending . . . shall suffer imprisonment without fail for six months and no longer, and being convicted of a second offense before the Court of Justiciary, or at the Circuits, shall be liable to be transported to any of His Majesty's plantations beyond the seas, there to remain for the space of seven years."

This was followed by a general order sent out to officers of the troops stationed in Scotland, directing them to report to London any magistrate who failed to convict on charges of violating this law. Persons who were even suspected of violating it in secret, were haled before a notary and made to swear this oath:

"I swear as I shall answer to God at the great day of judgement, I have not and shall not have in my possession any gun, sword, or arms whatsoever, and never use tartan, plaid, or any part of the Highland garb, and if I do so may I be accursed in my undertakings, family, and property, may I never see my wife, nor children, nor father, mother, or relations, may I be killed in battle as a fugitive coward, and lie without Christian burial in a foreign land, far from the graves of my forefathers and kindred; may all this come upon me if I break this oath."

And why all this trouble because the residents of a remote wilderness preferred skirts to trousers? Why did the government put more stress upon the abolition of the *breacan fiele* than upon the actual disarming of the Highlanders? They did not fight with their sporrans. Philabegs and trews, badges and eagle feathers and blue bonnets, never killed a soldier of the king. And who would be afraid of a bagpipe, which, under the new laws, was as much condemned as a musket or a broadsword?

Official London knew, and understood. Scotland in breeches! The thing was inconceivable. These long-legged, hard-muscled fellows who had caused so much trouble, and whose ancestors had caused so much trouble ever since anybody could remember—they would be harmless enough if they were stripped of the gear they loved and associated with battle. If no pipers blew up to stir them into action, they would be quiet, law-respecting persons. If the Lord of the Isles was not permitted to wear that exquisite green dress plaid, his vassals would not follow him blindly into wars they did not understand. And Glengarry would no longer be Glengarry without that beautiful red tartan. The glare of unmixed scarlet might be pleasing to southern eyes; to your sturdy Scot of the hills it was a hated color and not fit to inspire any gentleman to fight.

So England told Scotland to change its clothes; and Scotland, prostrate, was obliged to obey. The law was rigorously enforced. Back in the remote glens where they had not heard of it, where, indeed, they had heard only vaguely of Bonnie Prince Charlie himself, the peasants continued to wear the tartan. The redcoats came, asked no questions, and filled the jails. And many a wondering fellow, twice convicted of he knew not what, was thrust into a slave ship, kept under decks for weeks, starved, left to rot, because he had never learned that he must wear trousers.*

Charles might lay all the plots he wanted, there in France. But Scotland was down. The nation was like a boxer who has taken a solar plexus punch: he can move the upper part of his body, his arm muscles and chest muscles are still functioning, and he is conscious and willing to go on fighting, but his legs are paralyzed and he cannot rise from the canvas.

The clan system had been broken up, legally and actually. Ancient usages were proscribed or forgotten. The old chiefs, who had been the patriarchs of their tribes, were now in exile, or else had been frightened into conformity with southern customs. The new generation of chiefs were educated in England. They did not know the Gaelic, and did not have any understanding of the needs of their childlike vassals, being intent rather upon getting as much rent as possible in order to keep up appearances in London. Consequently the chiefs declined in power. The government had recompensed with silver those who had not taken up arms for Charles (Argyle, chief of the Clan Campbell, received £25,000) for the loss of their hereditary jurisdiction. But all the silver in the world could not have

* Enforcement of this law, never absolutely successful, was relaxed somewhat in 1757; but the law itself was not repealed until 1782. By that time it had exercised the effect for which it had been designed. Not many of the Highlanders resumed the dress which was older than history, older even than tradition. And today it is worn only on dress occasions and for military purposes.

killed the clan spirit if the clansmen had been permitted to wear their kilts.

All this Charles was in no position to understand. But he understood, and fully, the calamity which befell him in France at this time—a blow which was the more painful because it came from an unexpected quarter.

One night his brother invited him to dinner, and the Prince, always punctual, found Henry out of the house. But there was every evidence that Henry would soon appear: the table was laid for a sumptuous repast (the Duke, even then, was a *bon vivant*), the house was brilliantly lighted, the servants wore their most splendid liveries. Charles waited, probably not very patiently. There was no sign of Henry. The servants were mysteriously ignorant. Charles fumed and sputtered and stamped; but Henry did not come.

This was not Henry's way. The older brother knew intuitively that something had gone wrong. Had the Duke of York been assassinated? or kidnaped? Had agents of the British government, taking him for Charles, laid violent hands upon him?

At midnight, Charles went back to his own home, and his mind was a swirl of terrible apprehensions. Not until two days later did he hear from his brother. Henry had gone to Rome to see their father. Henry had feared that Charles might disapprove the trip.

That only deepened the mystery. Why should Henry sneak away to Rome? His was not a plotting nature. He was no man to be concocting schemes against his brother or any of his brother's friends. And why should he suppose that Charles would object? Charles thought it bad policy to be near Rome at any time, because of the prejudices of the English people; but that would hardly explain this surreptitious departure. Something was still wrong. Charles waited, in agonizing suspense, for the next news. It came in the form of a letter from James, and the first words were a thunderbolt:

"I know not whether you will be surprised, my dearest Carluccio, when I tell you that your brother will be made a Cardinal the first day of next month. . . ."

Surprised! Why, this was the deathblow to the Stuart cause! This was fatal. Culloden had been a trifling set-back compared with it.

". . . and we foresaw that you might probably not approve of it. . . ."

Now that required very little perspicacity. Charles had only one passion in life, one desire which swamped every other emotion in his soul; and the biggest obstacle in his way toward this—for many years the only obstacle—was the Stuart adherence to the Roman Catholic Church. Time and again, Charles' father or his grandfather might have recovered the crown of England, Ireland and Scotland, if they had been willing to give up their faith and conform to the teachings of the Episcopal Church. Time and time again they had refused to do so. The Englishmen and the Scots, generally, had only this one thing against the Stuarts. And now Henry was to become a Cardinal!

A Cardinal! A member of the Sacred College, an intimate of the Pope, whom the Englishmen and the Scots regarded as nothing less than the devil sans horns! It tied the family irrevocably to the Church. There could be no soft-pedaling this issue now. For Henry was to become a Cardinal.

A Cardinal! Few enough of the Stuart men there had been left: James, the father, moping through the corridors in Rome, writing fruitless letters, doing nothing; and Henry, a Cardinal. James might as well be dead. Henry might much better be dead. For where now could the White Rose bloom again? Now Charles must marry or the line was lost. Charles must carry upon his shoulders the responsibility, and must do all the work, the sacred work, himself. If they had but left him alone, these men who called themselves Stuarts, he might have placed them in St. James' in spite of themselves. He was beloved in Scotland and England—the more beloved because he had lost. He did not need help from James and Henry. All he needed was a promise not to interfere. But what could one person do against the congregated might of the Holy Roman Church?

Charles got drunk.

And from that day, the tearful letters Henry sent him Charles ignored. His brother was dead. Policy dictated that he abstain from open hostility to his father also, for James, after all, held the purse strings. But Charles' letters to James underwent a decided change. A few curt words to say that he was in good health: that was all. He never told his father of his whereabouts, his plans, his passions, his companions.

Well, Henry was invested at a super-spectacular ceremony. Twenty-three years old, pale, very serious, he was at once a Prince Royal and a Prince of the Church. He wore ermine on his upper cloak; and his arms were the royal arms of England, the tasseled Cardinal's hat replacing the ducal coronet above them.

The other Cardinals were peeved because of the Pope's favoritism. Henry was to have the title of Altesse Royale et Eminentissime, and he was to receive ceremonial visits from the other Cardinals without being expected to return them. Moreover, the other Cardinals, when they called upon Henry, were required to wear the red Soustanna, or cassock, instead of their ordinary black habits.

Now these were very, very important matters, comparable with the placing of the Macdonalds on the left wing at Culloden. Because of them, Henry started his ecclesiastical career with many enemies—though none of them was more bitter than the tall young Prince in Paris who was his brother.

The Pope was highly pleased, and shaved Henry's scalp personally. The new Cardinal's official family, according to Sir Horace Mann, consisted of "a Monsignore Leigh for a *Maestro di Camera*, a very noble Irishman born at Cadiz of a little merchant there; two Sicilian Marquises for his Major-Domo and Cupbearer; and the Abbe Falingieri for *Segretario dell' Embasciata. . . .*" The formal reception into the religious state took place in the Sistine Chapel, the Holy Father afterwards making a flattering speech about the Stuarts. Henry was given the usual sapphire ring, and was given also the parish church of Santa

Maria in Campitelli, although he was only a layman.* The young Cardinal, however, started to study for orders as soon as he had the Red Hat, and within a year he had been ordained a priest. Mann, in another of his gossipy letters to Walpole, suggests that he did this "from a desire to get some rich bishoprick," but the correspondent belittles Henry, who, however much he might have lacked his brother's martial spirit, was always, like their father, sincerely pious—and was, incidentally, as poor a business man.

* Somehow, James forgot to have the customary medal struck off in honor of this event. But he did set aside a sum of money for the holding of special services at Henry's church for the conversion of the British people to the Roman faith. And although James and Henry and Charles and Benedict IV and all the others, are gone now and practically forgotten, the fund still survives, so that you may witness in this little church, any Saturday morning at 11 o'clock, the lighting of thirty candles and the recitation of litanies that James Francis Stuart is still paying for.

CHAPTER SEVENTEEN

The Darling Disappears

MEANWHILE, Charles was leading a wild life in Paris. At first glance it would seem that he had determined to forget his troubles by plunging headlong into the whirl of Parisian vice, as King Louis had originally suggested. He was drunk much of the time; and although not naturally a Lothario, he was now much in the company of women.

But in justice to the boy, who is now about to disappear—or rather to change for the worse, as though by reverse metamorphosis, butterfly into caterpillar—some explanation of his turning to these familiar failings is only decent.

Whiskey, it will be remembered, was invented in Scotland; and in Scotland that much-discussed liquor is a requisite rather than a luxury. There is this to be said for whiskey, and that to be said against it; but the prohibitionist who, when exposed to the cold wet winds of the western Highlands, would not, in his heart of hearts, long for one prolonged swallow of the fiery fluid, is either more than an angel or less than a fool.*

Anciently patriotic persons protest that the national drink of Scotland is, or rather was, claret, not whiskey. Moreover, any Scot will tell you today that he does not really drink whiskey. He takes a wee nip now and then for some specific purpose. For example, if he is very cold he will take perhaps half a pint to warm him up; or if he is very hot he might take a bit to cool off; or if he is tired another nip will stimulate him; or if he feels he has had too much excitement, a little nip, he estimates, will do much to quiet his nerves; and there are many other occa-

* For example, Bishop Forbes (who cannot be accused of levity) in describing the "Cage" in Ben Alder, mentions that there were two chambers, one above the other; the upper one served as a dining room and bedroom, he writes, while the lower one served "to contain liquors *and other necessities*."

sions on which whiskey is not merely advisable but actually necessary—as a medicine, a tonic, you understand, not as a beverage.

In the Highlands, whiskey seems as natural and substantial a part of life as air, earth, or rain. This was even more true in the old days whereof I write, and before the spread of the heretical, Mohammedan idea that alcoholic beverages are reprehensible *per se*. Highlanders prescribed whiskey for everything, and still do in the remoter glens. Was a man ill? They gave him a drink of spirits, since physicians were few and far between. And if that didn't cure him? Then they gave him more spirits. Eventually the patient either died or recovered. If he died, then all that whiskey was wasted, but at least he had died happy. If he recovered, he could look back on his illness not with a wry face but rather with the smile of a man who recalls a pleasant experience. It was a simple system, and was applied with equal impartiality to all ills of the flesh and soul.

And truly, the climate seems to demand it. When you feel the peculiar chill of that west wind, you believe that whiskey is a beverage especially granted to mankind by an all-wise Providence for consumption in large quantities in the Highlands.

The Prince had been exposed to that wind many times. For hours, for days, he had shivered as only a stranger in Scotland can shiver; and he had, quite naturally, acquired the habit of drinking strong spirits to brace him against cold and fatigue.

This is offered as an explanation, not as an apology. No doubt, the Prince would have been a heavy drinker anyway. Some persons seem born to be drunkards, just as some are born to be poets, or Republicans. Charles must have been one of these. Otherwise he would never have been able to outdrink the Caledonians themselves: for we have seen how he was left drinking, on at least one occasion, long after the sturdiest topers of Lochaber and the Long Island had had enough. When he went back to Paris, and was forced into idleness by the shilly-shallying of Versailles, he naturally resumed his potations where he had left off in Scotland. And since the average companion, taking drink for drink with him, succumbed so much sooner to the inevitable effects of alcohol, it was easy for Charles to believe that he was not, himself, going too far. So long as he had something to keep him busy, so long as there was any work he could do toward building up another expedition into Britain, he kept away from the bottle, or at least did not consult it too frequently. But when matters had reached a temporary standstill, and it remained only to wait, hoping, he killed time in the most familiar fashion; so that he became one of the heaviest drinkers in an age of heavy drinkers. Bear in mind in judging any incident of his future conduct, that he was probably drunk at the time!

Nor in the matter of women is it difficult to understand Charles' behavior. He was not intended by Nature to be a Casanova. We have seen that he was shy and boyish in the presence of women, and that he preferred the camp to the court, the claymore to the courtesan. But in Paris he was hardly given a chance to refuse. He was just then the idol of the hour, the world's darling. Always he had a fatal fascination for women. His money, his rank, his grand smile and handsome eyes made him a singularly attractive young man. His romantic adventures and the possibilities of his peculiar position added to this attraction. Whenever he appeared in a box—and he was indulging to the fullest his old love of the opera and the play—there was prolonged applause, and the whole house rose to cheer him. French women worshiped him. English women braved the channel and haunted the playhouses in the hope of getting a glimpse of him. Damsels of high degree wrote him absurd letters, begging him to accept their love.

Charles did not retreat from this adulation. Instead, he accepted it with princely urbanity. He was in some theater practically every night. He rode abroad in an open carriage. He went frequently to court—the French court that he hated—and was a great favorite there. He was almost violently gay.

What was his purpose? Possibly it was, as most persons guessed at the time, merely an attempt to drown undesirable memories and to kill a pride always too acute for comfort. Possibly it was a sort of let-up after the nervous strain of the 'Forty-five and that game of hare-and-hounds with the British army and navy.

James himself had a more specious explanation. He believed that his son was playing a game for the English public: that Charles, unable to win by means of his virtues, was now trying to win by means of his vices, that he was scheming to gain the admiration and love of the Londoners by being, to all appearances, a good loser, a good sport, the kind of man the English have always most admired. James knew his son well and was much worried about Charles' conduct at this time. He wrote to chide the Prince for neglecting his religious duties, openly accusing him of striving to appear lovable in the eyes of the English. This is likely enough, in view of what happened afterwards. Charles, we know, was flirting with Anglicanism: he was considering marriage to a Protestant noblewoman—any Protestant—thus to offset, if possible, the effect of Henry's presence in the Sacred College. It was a wild plan and, like most of Charles' plans, it was never carried into effect. But Charles was prepared at least to consider anything. He was desperate. He dabbled in the most extraordinary schemes, and sometimes, from this distance and with our superior knowledge, he seems a bit mad: perhaps sometimes he *was* a bit mad. But he never lost sight of that high chair, all gilt and red velvet, over the Stone of Scone in London. His brother might fall into the warm bath of ecclesiasticism; his father might flicker out, in mid-career, like a defective candle; but Charles, drunk or sober, in bedroom, in court, on parade, or in council, was always a pretender to the British throne.

He quarreled with his friends, yet he continued to play with friendships across the channel. With Lochiel, Lord George Murray and others who had helped him in the past and might help him in the future, he had fallen out. King Louis XV was, of course, the most powerful individual in France; but Louis was ruled by the Pompadour, that extraordinary woman who forced sovereigns to call her "cousin" and governed the greatest empire of the time by means of sex appeal. Charles had no use for the Pompadour. The French Queen was a kinswoman of Charles' mother, and the Prince felt himself obliged to cut the King's mistress on this account. She sent him exquisite *billets*, on vellum, sealed with the royal arms; but Charles threw them into the fire. Another potential friend lost to him!

And now he was about to make an enemy of Louis himself and all his ministers and, at the same time, to increase his popularity with the rank and file of Frenchmen and Englishmen.

Things were going badly with the Sun King. War, always an expensive sport, had all but ruined the finances of France; and the peasants were not contributing enough to keep the court going properly. It was imperative that some sort of peace be patched up, in order to give His Most Christian Majesty an opportunity to save money for the next war. The nation was in a bad way, for all the splendor of Versailles. There were ominous rumblings, and the purse was dangerously low. So Louis sent envoys here and there; and in the course of time red-heeled representatives of Britain, France and the Low Countries foregathered at Aix-la-Chapelle for the purpose of drafting a treaty of peace.

Now it is obvious that the party most eager for peace is the party most willing to make concessions on such occasions. And Britain, as everybody knew, did not like the presence of Charles so close to London. So it was assumed by the public on both sides of the channel, that Britain would not be a signer of any treaty which did not contain a proviso that all Stuarts be forbidden to live in France or the Netherlands. It was the plan of the British government to force the Young Pretender to live in Switzerland, where he would be insignificant and harmless, or in Rome, where his proximity to the dreaded Pope would discredit him with the English people. It meant only a trifling point of honor to France, but it meant a great deal to England.

When they mentioned the approaching treaty in his presence, Charles sneered—and called for a song.

The treaty, which was signed in October, 1748, contained the clause everyone had guessed it would contain, and the delicate question arose of how to get rid of Charles Edward Stuart.

He was approached circuitously at first, and then, when he did not respond, more directly. He was offered a magnificent residence in Switzerland, that convenient dumping ground for undesired Royalty. He was offered a generous pension, too. "No," said Charles.

Ministers and courtiers and other personages waited upon him at St. Antoine. They pointed out to him that the King had been obliged to sign the treaty, and that, as a gentleman, the King was now obliged to live up to what he had signed. "I have a prior treaty with His Majesty," snapped Charles.

No less a personage than the Duc de Gesvres, Governor of Paris, called to remonstrate with this stubborn young man, and to offer a higher pension and handsomer furnishings in the proposed Swiss home. Charles showed the Duke the door, and then proceeded to have medals struck off in praise of the British fleet—a direct insult to French national pride, since it was the fleet, as usual, which had forced France to suggest a peace.

By this time all Europe was interested. How was this duel going to end? Would Charles bend his pride and go; or would Louis break his reputation for politeness and hospitality, not to say honor, and kick him out? It was a favorite topic of conversation on both sides of the channel, and a matter of much concern to all parties interested—excepting, apparently, Charles Edward himself, who pretended to be not the least disturbed.

Charles, when the news of the treaty reached him, had penned a protest. Meant to be impressive, this was merely pathetic. It was signed by the Prince Regent of Great Britain and Ireland, and denounced as illegal any pact entered upon by the Hanoverian usurper in his false capacity as King, with any other nation.

The Comte de Maurepas, a close personal friend of Charles, waited upon the Prince at St. Antoine and pleaded with him as de Gesvres had done. Again and again this nobleman called. Again and again Charles refused to listen.

Louis wrote privately to James; and James, realizing that his son was alienating the sympathy of official France, wrote to Charles. The Prince ignored the letter.

James spoke to the Pope, and His Holiness, through one of the Cardinals, wrote to Charles. This letter, too, the Prince ignored.

Then His Most Christian Majesty, waxing desperate, wrote to Charles personally, addressing him in the most affectionate terms, practically promising him that his political exile would be brief, and enclosing an order for money with the amount space left blank for Charles to fill in. The money chest of an Empire was opened for him, and he was invited to help himself. He read the letter twice, slowly, and then threw it into the fire —along with the money order.

This sort of thing could not go on forever. The British government, growing restive, pressed for action. It was all very well to be gallant, but Louis, the British government reminded him, had signed a treaty pledging himself to throw this young man out, and what was the matter?

Charles purchased a house in the Quai Theatin, in order to be nearer to the opera and the theaters; and set about furnishing and decorating it in elaborate fashion, as though for a permanent stay.

At last Louis signed an order for his arrest. The King shook his head as he did so, and exclaimed, when he had finished, "*Qu'il est difficile pour un roi d'etre un veritable ami!*"

This happened at 3 o'clock in the afternoon. It was supposed to be a secret; but secrets are slippery in Paris, and within an hour the news was all over the city. Of course it was brought to Charles. He sniffed, when he heard it, and turning to one of his retainers, commanded the fellow to engage a box for him that night at the opera.

And to the opera he went. Paris was in a hubbub; and as Charles' carriage rolled along the Rue St. Honore, somebody called out to him to go back—the Palais Royale was surrounded —they were going to arrest him! The Prince yawned. He was play-acting with a vengeance now. The greater the violence they might offer him, he knew well, the greater would be his popularity. He stepped out of his carriage and started into the opera house. . . .

JAMES FRANCIS STUART

From the Painting by Alexis Belle

What a reception! It is doubtful whether any man has ever been arrested with greater pomp and splendor. The Duc de Biron, Colonel of the swanky Household Guards, had been assigned to the unpleasant task. He took no chances and spared no expense. Knowing that the Prince had engaged a box at the opera, and guessing that Charles would attend the performance if only out of sheer bravado, the Duke had the opera house surrounded. No less than 1,000 of the King's own guardsmen were employed, besides a goodly percentage of the Paris police force. Every avenue leading to the opera house was blockaded. The building itself was packed with soldiers, armed to the teeth. In the event the Prince broke away and took refuge in some house, there were locksmiths on hand, and men with scaling ladders; there were even three surgeons and a physician in attendance.

Six sergeants in plain clothes seized the Prince from behind as he walked into the lobby. Two grabbed his arms, two his wrists, one held his middle, and the sixth threw his arms around the Prince's legs. In this manner they hurried him down a dark alleyway adjoining the theater. They confronted Major de Vaudreuil, who cried, "I arrest you in the name of the King, my master!"

Charles said quietly, "The manner is a bit violent."

They took him to a private room and searched him. The Prince had always gone well armed after his Highland experiences: he never knew when to expect assassins. The sergeants deprived him of two loaded pistols, a dagger, and his dress sword. De Vaudreuil, very nervous, went out looking for his colonel, to report. "Don't try to kill yourself," he begged, from the doorway. "I won't," said Charles coldly.

But the Duc de Biron, consulted, said that it was advisable to bind the prisoner anyway: he must be a madman, the Duke reasoned, and he might attempt suicide in spite of his promise. Everything had been anticipated. They tied Charles' arms and legs with many yards of silk ribbon, and carried him out to a coach.

There rose a great howl when he appeared in the street.

Only the bayonets of the guardsmen held back the crowd, which would have rescued its darling. It scarcely seemed possible. Bonnie Prince Charlie, that gallant boy, had been arrested; seized by policemen; bound like a common thief!

De Vaudreuil was apologizing, assuring Charles that he had never been so embarrassed in his life. "It must be very mortifying for an officer," said the Prince. They drove off.

Of the many painful things that happened to Charles Edward, this was one of the worst: it was an insult he never could erase from his memory. Yet he realized that he must play-act still. For a Prince there is no rest from the pose he must assume. He chatted with the officers, a trifle cold, rather aloof, but not the least bit disconcerted, to all appearances. When they stopped for a change of horses at St. Antoine, Charles asked, "Are you taking me to Hanover?"

With him was his old friend, Neal MacEachain, who had escaped to France on the same ship with Charles and had remained attached to his Prince ever since.

They rolled up to the prison at Vincennes, where the governor, the Marquis de Chatelet, was an old and dear friend of Charles. "I should be glad to embrace you," the prisoner said with a wry smile, "but you see, I can't move." De Chatelet was in tears; he commanded that the ribbons be cut immediately, and begged Charles, on his knees, to forgive him. Charles raised him. "I hope I shall always know the friend from the Governor. You have a duty. I cannot blame you for doing it."

Cold, quiet, head-high he was, when they led him to a bare room on the top floor—a room ten feet square, lighted by one little window in the roof. Charles looked around and smiled; he turned to Neal MacEachain. "We've seen worse, haven't we?" De Chatelet mentioned a larger room with side windows, and started, "If Your Royal Highness will give his word—" But Charles stopped him, raising his hand. "I have given my word for something already, and it was not taken." Those silk ribbons, unwound now from his body, were still tightly wound about his mind: he was never able to shake them off.

When the door closed after the jailors, Charles sank down

on the bed, weeping as though his heart would break. MacEachain tells us that he cried out, again and again, "Oh, my brave mountaineers, you would not have treated me like this! Would I were with you still!"

The next morning while de Puysieux apologized to the English minister, explained the cause of the delay, and stated that the young man would be kept at Vincennes for a few days and then sent out of the confines of France, the rest of the city was wild with indignation. A fine king was this who betrayed his cousin, his ally, his guest—and at the dictation of England! It was a matter which reflected upon the honor of all France, and of every individual Frenchman. The pamphleteers wrote tirades against Louis. The press openly sneered at His Majesty—a man who would dally with mistresses while he broke the laws of hospitality, of *noblisse oblige,* of national honor, and of common decency. The Duc de Biron, Major Vaudreuil, and the other officers who had participated in the shameful arrest, were hardly safe in the streets, so angry was Paris. De Puysieux and his ministers were condemned in the most violent terms. Poets and playwrights came to the assistance of the writers of pamphlets, and the government was assailed on all sides. One of the most popular persons in France at the time—as popular as Charles himself—was the Dauphin. The Dauphin waited upon his father at the levee the next morning and complained indignantly about the treatment accorded to Prince Charles Edward. Louis tried to tut-tut him. "He is no more than a boy," Louis said to courtiers near him. But the Dauphin, infuriated, returned to the argument with such frankness that all the courtiers felt that discretion demanded their departure, at least to the nearest keyholes.

The court attempted to justify itself with a weak lie. Charles, it was given out, had promised to surrender his arms, and when he had failed to fulfill this promise, he was seized because Louis feared that he would kill himself. Nobody believed this. Moreover, the officers who had taken part in the arrest had already told their honest stories, and they refused to change these to conform with the official account.

"Such contempt for Louis was excited, that a nail was knocked into the coffin of French royalty," writes Lang.

Five days Charles was kept in prison. Then he was taken by carriage to Beauvoisin, in the company of one French officer. From there he went quietly to Avignon, which, although in France, was Papal territory still. He was received with much pomp by the Archbishop and other dignitaries of the city, and established himself in a comfortable house.

Merciless England was not yet satisfied. Even Avignon was too close for comfort. Years before, England had driven the Old Pretender first from Paris, then from Bar-le-Duc in Lorraine, and then from Avignon, settling him finally in Rome. Now it wanted to do the same with Charles. The French court was appealed to; but Versailles had already experienced enough trouble with the lad, and would not risk more internal antagonism, besides the displeasure of the Pope, by pushing Charles further south.

The Prince moped, although he attended many brilliant social functions—for they made much of him in Avignon. But these affairs did not interest him. Shooting was more to his taste. But what to do at night? For amusement he was inspired to introduce prize fighting into Avignon, as years before he had introduced golf into Italy. This caused trouble. The Archbishop protested, on the ground that prize fighting had been specifically prohibited by Sixtus V. Charles insisted that it had not. After an acrimonious argument, they referred the matter to the Pope, who decided in favor of the Archbishop. Charles, in a huff, called off the fights. So, at least, goes one version of the story. Another version has it that Charles refused to cancel the fights, and that His Holiness himself ordered the Prince out of Avignon.

It seems improbable that the Pope would do this; and yet it seems improbable that Charles, at this of all times, would consent to forego any pleasure even at the express command of the Holy See. For Charles was by now desperately flirting with Protestantism in its most ornate form, Anglicanism, and would hardly disappoint his English well-wishers by taking dictation from Rome.

Meanwhile, England, failing to get France to drive the Prince out of the Papal city, is supposed to have threatened Rome itself with gunboats. Faced with the possibility of a bombardment of the Civita Vecchio, the Pope, it is said, finally commanded Charles to quit Avignon and return to his father's palace. There may be truth in this, England had not yet recovered from the fright the Highlanders had given her, and was not beyond adopting such measures.

Yet, after all the resistance he had put up in Paris, it does not seem likely that Charles would have quit Avignon without a word of protest. It seems much more probable that his amazing plan of future conduct had already been forced in his mind, and that the boxing fracas and England's threats were no more than coincidental with the putting of that plan into practice.

Be that as it may, Charles now disappeared. He vanished from the face of the earth abruptly, without warning.

Where was he? Nobody knew. Europe in general, omitting England, had almost forgotten the Prince, who now that he had been ejected from Paris was not a formidable figure on the great political chessboard. But when the Prince disappeared, his name once more was on everybody's lips. Europe could not believe the news. Such a thing might be possible in the wilderness of northern Scotland, but it was hardly possible in civilized Europe, where the face of a Stuart would certainly be recognized in any court, or by any courtier or official, and by many servants. How *could* he disappear? Every foreign office sent to Avignon for details.

There were not many to give. Notice had been given that Charles Edward was ill, and nobody was allowed to see him. Otherwise, in his household the routine continued. Charles' private physician called regularly every day for several days, and when questioned said that he did not want to discuss the case. Then some busybody took a telescope to an upper window of a house near that of the Prince's, and peered into Charles' bedroom. There was no light in the fireplace, although this was

February. Confronted with this discovery, such followers of the Prince as had remained with him, confessed that they themselves did not know where he was. He had gone out of the city on horseback, in company with one of his most devoted adherents, Colonel Henry Goring, of the Austrian service, in disguise and traveling under an assumed name. That was all they knew. That was all the world knew.

CHAPTER EIGHTEEN

In the Lion's Mouth

SPIES rushed all over the Continent. Where was the Prince? By day they poked their noses into everything, went eavesdropping, whispered importantly to sub-spies, grasped at every morsel of information which might have any bearing on any of the Stuarts anywhere and pigeonholed it in their memories; and by night they pieced together their results —and got nothing. No matter how hard they worked, they could not seem to find Charles.

But a spy must justify his existence; and, after some weeks of not finding him anywhere, they began to find him everywhere. The British Foreign Office was perplexed by numerous reports. Was this Young Pretender a real man, or was he a spirit? For behold! he was simultaneously in Moscow, Venice, Berlin, Warsaw, Lubeck. . . .

He had been seen entering a gate of Paris, disguised as a Capuchin friar. No, he was in Stockholm, closeted with King Charles. The two were concocting another plan to invade Great Britain; for the Swedish King had always been friendly to the Stuarts and during the 'Forty-five had seriously considered sending an army to assist the Highlanders. In Stockholm? No! That spy was misinformed. For the agent at Leipzig had seen the Young Pretender passing through that city.

Frederick the Great, with the brothers, the Earl Marischal and Marshal Keith, and all the other English, Scottish and Irish Jacobites of Germany, had greeted Charles warmly when the Young Pretender had arrived at Potsdam to perfect plans for a German invasion of Great Britain. But perhaps it was another person they greeted. For Charles, as a matter of fact, had never quit Avignon, but was still lingering in the Papal city, in hiding.

He was really dead. He was also in a prison in France, under another name.

But where *was* he? Why, that was easily answered. A spy from Italy reported that the Young Pretender was traveling through Piedmont disguised as a Benedictine monk! And yet this hardly fitted in with the positive information the British Foreign Office had received, that the Young Pretender was visiting the Great General of Lithuania. It seems he was in love with the General's daughter, the Princess Radzivil (who, incidentally, was only 11 years old at the time, and very plain) and was arranging to be married to her as soon as he regained the throne of his ancestors by means of a Russian army which the Czarina was going to lend him.

It was all very confusing. And the gentlemen of the British Foreign Office lost no little sleep over it. For how could you force into Rome, or into Switzerland, a young man you couldn't even find? And if Prussia and Russia and Sweden and all those other nations really were going to attack England, then the safety of that celebrated island was not so certain after all.

It was the more confusing because these reports, as listed above, were not reported as mere rumors: they were definite facts, according to the spies, who were each convinced of their truth. The mere rumors, of course, were without number, and they had the Prince everywhere this side of the moon.

They called him "The Boy That Cannot Be Found." His father's secretary, Edgar, once called him "l'homme sauvage" —the wild man. He was now a Royal Vagabond, flitting about Europe under a dozen different names, appearing and disappearing before anybody could recognize him, writing letters in sympathetic ink, scribbling messages in a code that was revised every few weeks, changing clothes, changing wigs, changing names. He was John Douglas; he was also Williams, Penn, Smith, Mildmay, Burton, and so on without end. He knew the art of keeping a secret, and he could travel hard in any weather.

At Avignon they were entirely in the dark. Sheridan and Stafford were there to watch out for the Prince's interests, but

Sheridan and Stafford had no idea where their master was keeping himself, or how.

Paris did not know. The ministers so protested to the indignant English government representatives, who were obliged to believe them after a while. King Louis, really angry, declared that if Charles Edward showed his face in Paris again there would be no Household Guards to arrest him with ceremony, but that he would be expelled from the kingdom.

Rome did not know. James was almost hysterical with anxiety; he hurried to the Vatican and asked the Pope. "I was just going to send somebody to ask you," said His Holiness. Charles had scribbled James a brief note when he quit Avignon; but he had given no address, and had said nothing about his plans for the future. What was known in Rome was known soon afterwards in London, and of this Charles was aware. James was informed that he could write to his son through Waters, the Stuart banker in Paris.

But even Waters did not know where the boy was. Waters gave the letters to another person, who gave them to another, and so on, until eventually they reached the ubiquitous Prince.

Charles' best friends did not know where he was—at least not for more than a short time. He shifted constantly, changing his companions as readily as he changed his costumes and his name.

One English statesman tried inserting a false notice in the newspapers of that country, to the effect that the Young Pretender had died of pneumonia. He hoped to draw a denial from the Jacobites, and through this to trace the lad.

But the Jacobites made no denial, for the simple reason that they themselves didn't know where Charles was hiding. A few of them would know, for a short time, and then they, too, would be in ignorance. The Prince was playing a strange game. He was keeping out of sight so that he would not be forced too far away from England, so that his plans for a Restoration would remain secret, and so that the spies would have no chance to "kidnap" him. For England, it seems, really was ready to "kidnap" the young man. That meant killing him, of course: they could hardly hope to take Charles alive.

The Stuarts had several times refused to tolerate plans for "kidnaping" Cumberland and other members of the royal family in London. Just after Culloden, the Macdonald of Lochgarry had submitted such a plan to Charles, and there was another of the same sort being concocted in London at this very time. Twelve fanatical Jacobites, who called themselves the Bloody Butcher Club—the Bloody Butcher being one of the nicknames Cumberland had earned for himself—had organized to attack the Duke some night when he returned from the play in his sedan chair. There was a somewhat similar plot against the life of George the Second. This was the Eilbank Plot, which fell through, perhaps because Charles would not sanction it, perhaps because the perpetrators disagreed among themselves.

But where *was* Charles Edward at this time? Even today we cannot be sure. Until very recently his whereabouts at this period were an absolute mystery; then Mr. Andrew Lang set himself to the study of the Stuart Papers, the notes Charles had scribbled to this person and that, and the notes those persons sent to one another. Out of this bewildering mass of pseudonyms, false handwritings, codes, erasures, and hidden meanings, Mr. Lang has managed to reconstruct in a general way the life of our hero between the years 1749 and 1751. But even Mr. Lang is not certain of all the details and admits that some of his reports are little more than shrewd guesses or probabilities. Still, most of this chapter is necessarily based upon his findings.

It seems that Charles went through Lyons with Goring. This far the French police traced them. After that they appear to have stepped out of the world, leaving no trace. Lang says that Charles rode through Lorraine where he probably saw the Princess Talmond, his favorite Parisian mistress, and then doubled back through Burgundy, finally returning to the Paris from which he had been ejected. So it is possible that the spy who reported that the Young Pretender had been seen in the garb of a Capuchin entering a gate of Paris, was correct after all. And in Paris he lived in the last place you would have thought of looking for him—a convent.

The Princess de Talmond, Madame de Vasse and Mademoiselle de Ferrand, all had rooms in this convent—apartments in the retreat section of the building, apart from the quarters of the nuns. This was the convent of St. Joseph, in the Rue St. Dominique. While all the Foreign Offices in Europe were wildly seeking Charles, here he remained, hidden by day in a closet in Madame de Vasse's apartment, and by night going down a secret stair to the Princess' bedroom.

Here he was, probably, at the time when the Austrian ambassador to Berlin, who was in the habit of meeting a young lady in a garden just outside the city, thought he recognized the Young Pretender in the person of a Polish gentleman who lingered quietly at an inn nearby; the ambassador reported his discovery, and spies ran around feverishly investigating all sorts of imaginary plots.

The Prussian rumor, like some of the others, was at least backed by a reasonable motive. Frederick the Great and George the Second never did get along well together: at one time they had gone so far as to challenge each other to a duel. Frederick was building his power in central Europe; and next to France, perhaps even before France, England was logically his most powerful opponent. Moreover, the Earl Marischal and Marshal Keith, two Scots who had always been active Jacobites, were much in the Kaiser's confidence. And in addition, there was some truth to the report that Charles was trying to arrange a marriage with one of Frederick's daughters. Similarly, for reasons explained in a previous chapter, there was some basis for the belief that Charles was in Poland.

Another report was made correct when, some time in April, Charles went to Venice, attended by a single footman. Here, after about a month, he was traced, and the Republic, being on good terms with Great Britain at this time, ejected him without hesitation. Charles probably returned to the Princess at the convent.

But Charles did not stay all the time at this convenient retreat. He was always plotting, always doing something in an effort to bring about the Restoration. From time to time he sent notes to his father. They said only that he was in perfect health and that he remained James' most humble and most obedient son. They never gave a hint about his plans or his travels. He wrote to friends, too, but his letters, as a rule, were strictly business epistles. In one he asked, "What can a bird do that has not found a right nest? He must flit from bough to bough."

The fourth Duke of Beaufort, Sir Watkin Wynd and other influential Jacobites in London, sent word to James, in the fall of 1749, that although their leader, Lord Barrymore, was now dead, they stood ready to do anything they could toward a Restoration when the occasion arose. They were sincere men, but timid; they had promised much on a previous occasion, but it had taken them too long to get up their courage to act.

Cluny Macpherson of Cluny wrote to Charles with some regularity, through the Parisian banker, Waters. He urged another uprising: he was optimistic. Macpherson, with a few other Highland gentlemen, was in charge of the buried treasure of 40,000 louis d'or. A good part of the money was found to be in spurious coin. Some of it was sent to Charles. And some of it disappeared. There were all sorts of squabbles about it, and the business is still a mystery: it is not known yet who was innocent and who guilty, and it probably will never be learned.

In the Spring of 1750, a deputation from Scotland waited upon James in Rome, with a list of the clans believed to be still loyal to the Stuart cause and a proposal for another uprising. James informed them that his son, the Prince of Wales, was now in charge of the family's affairs and he forwarded the news of the proposal to Charles. The Prince replied, asking through a messenger for more detailed information and, at the same time, requesting a fresh Commission of Regency. The messenger knew nothing of the whereabouts of his master; and James, sick with grief and disappointment, refused to see him personally. However, James supplied the information and also the new Commission.

James wrote to Charles, "The treatment you give me is a

continual heartbreak to me. . . . If you seem to forget that I am your father, I can never forget that you are my son."

In another letter, James begged Charles not to "treat others as you do me, by expecting friendship and favors from them, while you do all that is necessary to disgust them for you must not expect that anybody else will make you the returns I do."

James had made over to his son the income from Mary of Modena's properties in France, but this accumulated at Waters' office and Charles did not claim it. Neither did Charles make any attempt to touch his own money at Avignon, or the money he might have had from Rome. He was living on allowances sent him by faithful Jacobites in England, amounts sometimes as little as £10 apiece.

The idea of carrying on alone, without any assistance from foreign nations, was strong in Charles again now. It was the same idea, in effect, which had sent him to Scotland in the first place. If France or Spain would not help him, he would help himself. He had friends in London who loved him and would assist him if he appeared in their midst. His father's friends he would no longer count upon; they were cautious, doddering old fools who had failed him once and would probably fail him again. But he had his own friends. And the people generally, he believed, were ready to rise and support him. At a colliers' strike in Newcastle that year a mob orator had proclaimed Charles as King. It was trifling in itself, but it was an indication of the trend of thought in England—at least, so Charles supposed. The bird was about to flit to the strangest branch of all.

Lady Primrose was entertaining at cards in her town house in St. James' Square, London, when a servant announced a gentleman whose name her ladyship could not seem to recall. But she rose to receive him. When she saw the new guest her face went dead white and she almost swooned. She had known him in Paris; she had corresponded with him; she was always prepared to assist him, for she believed in his cause with all her heart—and besides, he was so good-looking. But to have him walk right into her drawing-room, of a quiet September afternoon, was almost too much for her ladyship.

Nevertheless, she greeted him with politeness, and had the presence of mind to call him by the name by which he had been announced. She asked when he had arrived from Paris, exchanged a few bits of gossip with him and, in general, carried on like a woman of the world. After he had gone, the servants seemed a bit suspicious, but the guests apparently had no idea that this visitor had been Charles Edward Stuart.

Now he was in the lion's mouth. George the Second was at Hanover. Charles strolled around London in no particular disguise, escaping suspicion by the very boldness of his manner. He had tea with Dr. King, another leading Jacobite. He viewed the Tower of London with great interest, remarking that one of the gates might be battered down with a petard. He met a little group of conspirators in Pall Mall and discussed activities with them.

We do not know just what he was plotting to do at this time. Probably it was a scheme by which Frederick, the Prince of Wales, was to be induced to call a "free parliament" which would declare a Restoration of the Stuart line with Charles as king. Frederick and his father were bitter enemies, keeping up the old Guelph tradition. Who courted one was not permitted to enter the presence of the other. They occupied different houses in different parts of the city and, of the two, there is no doubt that the weak but good-natured Frederick was the more popular. The people did not like George the Second. If the Prince of Wales did call a "free parliament" and it could be packed with Jacobites, while George was in Hanover, it was barely possible that this body could restore the Stuarts. Stranger things had happened in England.

Nothing ever came of the scheme. Probably they were not able to persuade Frederick to go through with it. He was not a bad man, only a fool; and doubtless had enough common decency, if not enough common sense, to fight shy of such an action.

Anyway, the titular Prince of Wales, our hero Charles, wandered about London, strolled through Hyde Park and down the Strand, across Clerkenwell Green . . . and dreamed, no doubt, how he would be driven along these places if ever he was successful. Once he had been within 127 miles of this city, with an army at his back. He must have wondered, when people hurried past him without a back glance, as though he were only an ordinary gentleman, instead of the prince who had frightened them all so badly a few years before—he must have wondered how it all would have gone if that council at Derby had obeyed his wish and made the last mad dash; if the Macleod had not gone back on his promise; if Lovat had come out in the first place with all his strength; if France had helped; if the left wing had charged at Culloden. . . .

His desires were boundless. He would stop at nothing. Before he quit London (he was in the city less than a week) he had renounced the Roman Catholic faith and joined the Church of England.

Details are lacking. We do not even know for certain in what chapel or church Charles took this step. What a scene it must have been! A minister pledged to the profoundest secrecy, a handful of Jacobites who were nervous merely at being in the presence of the distinguished outlaw, and the Prince himself, pale as death, repeating the words mechanically. . . . No doubt Charles even then was defending himself in his own conscience: he was telling himself that he loved God and was free to worship God as he saw fit; that he had been made a member of the Romish church when he was a mere infant; and that, having come to a man's estate, he was within his moral and legal rights in selecting for himself what was after all no more than a *form* of worship; and that he owed a divine debt to Protestant Britain which he could not repay unless he himself did the things the British did and went through their own rituals at church. He must have been telling himself all this rather furiously.

And he must have realized the quality of this act himself, although he would not admit it. From this time on his manner was even more embittered, and the humiliation he felt showed itself in a furious, stubborn spite. He had changed since the old Highland days, since the time when he sat in front of the fire drinking with those dour gentlemen from the hills. He had become an angry, self-willed person, with very little of his former high-mindedness left. When he transferred his allegiance from the Vatican to the politically preferable Westminster he completed the destruction of the youth who had inspired poets and fluttered the hearts of fair ladies.

Back on the Continent, only his intimates (and not all of them) were aware that Charles was now a Protestant. He did not inform James. He was afraid that James would learn of it anyway. He tried to be Roman to this person, and Anglican to that.

The following year, 1751, the Earl Marischal was appointed Prussian minister to Paris. This created a tremendous stir. For Prussia and Britain, for all the personal enmity of their respective monarchs, were at least technically friendly nations, and the Earl was a Jacobite, an avowed enemy of the reigning house in England. It was as though the United States today were to appoint an Italian exile, one of Mussolini's stoutest opponents, to be ambassador to France. It was a direct challenge to England, a half-insult. Frederick the Great appeared to be saying, "If you don't like it, you know what you can do." And England traditionally hates to be defied.

The Earl Marischal was an old, humorous, conscientious man. The elaborate mysteriousness of Charles, the aliases, the disguises, the strange letters, the codes, the backstairs diplomacy, were not in the manner natural to him. But although he disliked Charles personally he still regarded James as his rightful king and Charles as his rightful regent. His reputation for honesty was absolute. All the Jacobites trusted him, and most of them liked him; and as much could not be said of any other man, perhaps, at that time.

So Charles, to lend respectability to his designs, tried to get the Earl Marischal to act as a sort of public representative of the Stuart cause in Paris. He communicated with him through Goring—no easy matter, since the Earl was hounded by English spies day and night and did not dare to receive or send any message pertaining to Jacobites.

Uncertain relations between the two were kept up for some time, though nothing was accomplished. Then Charles quarreled with Goring, one of his most faithful adherents, and the Earl Marischal, probably glad of this excuse, refused to receive the substitute Charles appointed. For the Prince was giving himself over to very bad company, and was still alienating those of his followers who were wise and faithful and willing to serve him unselfishly.

Goring, like Lord George in earlier days, did not hesitate to speak frankly to the Prince on personal but important matters. He knew that Charles' attitude was going to be ruinous to the Stuart cause unless there was an immediate and emphatic change. Once he wrote to the Prince that ". . . they (the people of Britain) expect a Prince who will take advice and rule according to law, and not one that thinks his will is sufficient . . . without the assistance of your friends it is impossible to succeed, and if you disgust them there is an end of all . . ." To which Charles replied, in a huff, that he himself was familiar with the law, and obeyed it, but that "a man is not obliged to let himself be Bambousled."

This was not the direct cause of the break. Perhaps it was because Goring refused, as a man of honor, to discharge Charles' servants at Avignon simply because they were Catholics while Charles wanted to put up a strong show of Protestantism. Perhaps it was because he refused to escort Miss Clementina Walkinshaw to the Prince. The servants were not discharged, Charles changing his mind. But Miss Walkinshaw entered His Royal Highness' bed soon afterwards, Goring or no Goring.

Do you remember her? She is the tall, fair woman, a few years younger than the Prince, who helped to entertain him at Bannockburn just before and just after the Battle of Falkirk and during the siege of Stirling. At that time she promised to go to Charles whenever he wanted her, whatever his fortunes, whatever his condition of life. Subsequently she had retired to a convent on the Continent, where she became a canoness. She was tall, with a thin sweet face, of no great beauty, and had freckles. She was well educated. We know very little more about her. Of course Charles could not marry her because, although she came of good stock, she carried no political weight at all. Besides, there is nothing to indicate that he was ever very fond of Clementina. She was at the convent, Charles had nothing to do at the moment, was bored, remembered her, and sent for her.

The romance, if one could call it that, is vague in history, shrouded in a Scotch mist. Clementina was a quiet young woman. What effect she had on Charles we have no way of learning. We do know that she herself drank heavily; but this may be because Charles insisted upon her joining him in his own libations. We also know that the two fought like wildcats much of the time, and that their union was blessed, or cursed, with a female baby about a year after they came together. Lord Elcho reports seeing them, in deep disguise, leering at one another over a table in a cheap café: they were both very drunk then, he writes, and swearing at one another like a couple of sailors. But Charles owed Elcho money, and his lordship could never forgive the Prince for not paying the debt, so that this report may be set down as vituperative gossip, or at least a great exaggeration.

Charles was as secretive about his mistress as he was about his religion. She went everywhere with him, but he never mentioned her in his brief notes to James. Still, the Jacobites in England, with whom Charles was plotting almost exclusively now, knew about the lady, and objected. This was no time to be thinking about the pleasures of the bedroom, the Jacobites cried; and besides, Miss Walkinshaw's own sister (she was a tenth child) was a lady-in-waiting on Princess Amelia, daughter of George the Second. A master-spy was busy somewhere in the camp: whatever they were doing now was known in London almost before they had made up their own minds to do it, and Charles' whereabouts, after several years, were no longer a secret in official circles. The most elaborate precautions were ineffective. Who was the traitor? Why, obviously, Miss Walkinshaw, the English Jacobites declared.

Now as a matter of fact, if she was spying, there is not a shred of evidence left to prove or even to suggest it. She seems to have been a woman who really loved Charles and who remained faithful to him for eight or nine years, leading a life of odious secrecy, with no official standing, with no home, with suspicion and sometimes with physical beatings for reward.

But the Jacobites were angry. Charles was hiding on the Continent: he was safe enough, all things considered. But his friends in England were men of family and men of property, too, and, if they were found out, the best they could hope for would be confiscation and permanent exile. Naturally they were cautious! They did not now have even the French government to fall back upon. And as late as 1753, Archie Cameron, a brother of Young Donald of Lochiel, had been discovered to be participating in a plot of some sort for a Restoration and, although this was more than seven years after Culloden, he was publicly beheaded. The terrible lesson Cumberland had taught them had not been forgotten by Charles' friends; and it is common knowledge that neither Englishmen nor Scotsmen have ever liked to have women meddling in their political affairs.

So they sent a deputation to the Prince to protest against the company he kept. And Charles Edward showed in his answer to this, how low he had sunk. He said, in effect, that although he did not love Miss Walkinshaw at all, he would keep her just because some of his own subjects had shown the temerity to object to the alliance. So Miss Walkinshaw stayed. And the Royal Vagabond now was always accompanied by at least two other persons as he flitted from bough to bough—a mother and child. The child was named Charlotte.

Poor James constantly strove to give his son good advice and James' political sagacity, his temperance, his graciousness and loyalty to his friends, coupled with Charles' courage, resourcefulness, high spirit and determination, should have made a winning combination. In one person, they would have been irresistible. But that was not to be. Charles rarely took advice from any but bad friends. He threw himself furiously into every scheme for a Restoration, and as these schemes fell through, one after the other, he became more and more bitter at the world at large. James had been through all that and had emerged with a sweet temper. But then, James was made of different stuff.

"I have myself been expecting such things all my life," he wrote once to his son, "and they have never happened with success."

James observed that Charles was banking everything on the Englishmen devoted to his cause, and was trying to win through them and without the assistance of any Continental court. This would be excellent, if it were possible, James wrote. But "foreigners make the most of us for their own ends, and why should we debar ourselves from making use of them?"

Most of this time Charles was hiding in or near Paris. It has been reported that he made a second trip to London in 1753, but this has never been confirmed. Trips to Scotland and Ireland are also mentioned vaguely: they might have occurred, but we lack real information regarding them.

Evidently the British government did not care now. For it had caught the scent at last. The boy had been found, and was being watched. That mysterious spy was doing his work well; and Charles' affairs were almost as well known in the Foreign Office as the affairs of his father. No longer did England have to run excitedly from nation to nation, crying "Have you seen that young fellow? Is he hiding here?" and receiving solemn and usually honest assurances that this king or that grand duke was ignorant of the whereabouts of *l'homme sauvage*. Charles redoubled his precautions. But the game was up now. England was on his trail.

Lang says that the spy was no other than Young Glengarry, scion of one of the proudest Highland families, who was imprisoned in the Tower during the 'Forty-five, and who was one of Charles' few confidants abroad. Archie Cameron accused Young Glengarry, and so did Cameron's widow. But he was not otherwise suspected at the time. The Jacobites continued to believe that Clementina Walkinshaw was the leak; and so persistently did they beg Charles to quit her, that he himself commenced to suspect the poor woman.

England no longer gave thought to plans for "kidnaping" the Young Pretender. He was killing himself more effectively than any hired assassins could kill him, and he was destroying Jacobitism into the bargain. He was drinking himself to death, antagonizing his friends, alienating those who really wished him well and were ready to help him with more than words. What could he expect from Rome now? And George the Second and Frederick the Great had made an alliance, so that nothing was to be feared from Prussia. The Earl Marischal had been pardoned by the British government. Most of the old clan leaders were dead, and their successors were friendly to the court in London. One never knew when France might try something. But England was watching France closely.

Still, the Peace of Aix-la-Chapelle had settled definitely only one thing, and that was the expulsion from France and the Low Countries of the Young Pretender, who, incidentally, was still in France most of the time. Otherwise, Europe was in a slow-seething state, with boundaries unstable, monarchs uncertain, diplomats unscrupulous, and anything at all quite possible and even probable. England alone knew what she wanted. She was sitting down now, regaining strength like a patient after an operation. Her house had been thoroughly cleaned after the last Stuart insurrection; and the long and costly wars in Flanders were at an end. She wanted peace, and more peace. But there was no telling when some unexpected twist of politics would force her hand, and this audacious young man might come bounding back over the horizon.

In fact, something like that was definitely threatened when the statesmen of the two nations, bored with peace, found a fresh cause for quarrel in the American colonies, and France and England once again declared war against each other. That was on May 7, 1756.

CHAPTER NINETEEN

A Change of Georges

IT was an irritating sort of war, with colonists and regulars marching and countermarching, and generals getting things all mixed up, and Indians romping in now and then to remove all available scalps. It gave a young Virginian named George Washington a chance to learn something about organized fighting; and it presented Wolfe, a veteran of Culloden, with his first real military opportunity, and also with his death bullet. For it was all fought in the wilderness of America, though directed, or misdirected, by personages thousands of miles away.

But it was another chance for Charles. A Stuart uprising would cause England to rush troops back across the Atlantic for the defense of her proper borders, and leave France practically free to take and clinch possession of the Atlantic coast colonies. Moreover, if the Stuart uprising, once launched, moved with the celerity which had characterized the previous one, it might be successful before those regulars got back from America at all, and thus the government of King George would be defeated both ways.

Charles went to Luneville, in Lorraine, to see his kinsman Stanislaus, the exiled King of Poland. This gentleman was father-in-law of King Louis XV, and after a chat with Charles, who delighted him, he promised to use his good offices with Louis in an effort to persuade His Most Christian Majesty to back Charles Edward in another invasion.*

* Stanislaus himself had great personal charm. It had carried him to the bed of Catherine of Russia: he was one of the first men to share that bed. Later it carried him to the throne of Poland. He didn't want either job, but Catherine wanted him to have them, so he took them. He was a weak and amiable king. He reigned a little while; and then Catherine, Marie Theresa, and Frederick the Great, chopped up Poland for their own pur

The Prince only demanded 30,000 men—25,000 for England and 5,000 for Scotland. With this force, he said, "there would be little bludshed."

This demand seemed excessive to France. Probably Charles realized that if he asked for 30,000 he would be granted 20,000 (if he was granted any at all) and that this force would be found actually to number about 10,000 at the time of embarkation. Charles by now was reasonably familiar with French methods. And he was in a good position. He was the only man in the world capable of inflaming the Highlands, where the natives still worshiped his memory and, groaning under the barbarous laws imposed by England, prayed nightly for his return. When it came to invading Great Britain, Charles knew his business. They had to come to him. He could afford to talk big now.

But France dragged along, and the uncomfortable war in America dragged along also, and nothing much was done.

Charles was at Bouillon, where he still received letters from his fond father. James was weak and knew that death was near. He continued to beg his son to return to Rome. "You would not grudge this one journey to see your father, that he may embrace you, bless you, and give you his best advice once more before his death, which, naturally speaking, cannot be far off."

James was hearing alarming things about Charles. He wrote to Waters concerning Clementina Walkinshaw, asking for details. Waters, pledged to secrecy, told what he could in honor; it was obvious that the banker, too, disapproved of the liaison.

"It is really time to finish that scene," James wrote to the Prince. But Miss Walkinshaw remained at Bouillon.

James was hearing, too, stray whispers about Charles' conversion to the Anglican faith. How they must have troubled him! Late in 1758, while Charles was still dickering with the French court concerning the projected invasion, James sent his

poses, and Stanislaus wearily became a private citizen again. There was a story at the time that Catherine, to show her contempt for Poland, purchased the nation's throne, had a hole cut in the bottom of it, and used it the rest of her life as a toilet seat in her apartment at Czarskoe Selo.

private secretary, Andrew Lumisden, to Bouillon for more definite information. Lumisden, himself a Protestant, remained with Charles until April of 1759, when he returned to Rome and reported. Exactly what he reported we do not know. But when James heard it his habitual calm gave way and he sank into a chair, sobbing.

"I am far from dissuading you to seek a Temporal Kingdom," James wrote, when he had recovered; but, he asked, what good will all the kingdoms of the world do to a man who has lost his own soul? He insisted that there could be no trimming of the religious issue. "You equally renounce your religion whether you conceal it, or embrace another."

But Charles still had hopes of a second invasion. The Marshal de Belle-Isle had conferred with him. France was building flat-bottomed boats at Rouen for the purpose of transporting troops across the channel: they sent Charles a model of one of these. In February he was asked to appear before the ministers in Paris. He did appear—but he was so drunk that he could not stand and had to be supported by two servants.

If Charles had been sober that day, if France had carried through this project in the right way, the history not only of Europe but of America probably would have been different; France probably would have seized at least a few of the English colonies along the coast, and there might have been a briefer and bloodier American revolution, or no such revolution at all. It is useless to speculate on these things, however. France made one feeble attempt: Admiral Thurot landed 1,000 men in Ireland, and almost immediately afterwards loaded them back on the transports and returned them to the Continent, convinced of the impracticability of *that* plan, with which Charles had wisely refused to have any connection.

The war was ended in King George's favor when General Wolfe stormed and took Quebec, losing his own life in the attempt. That ended, too, Charles' last chance of a Restoration.

Now for a time Charles again disappears from our ken. This is not because he was eluding the English spies, but merely because he was not of enough importance to bother about, and the London Foreign Office had practically forgotten him. He lingered at Bouillon, near Sedan, drinking, drinking, and drinking. His little plots burst like soap bubbles, one by one. His English friends, disgusted and discouraged, had fallen away from him; his mistress was worn, cowed, no longer exciting to his senses; his father was dying slowly in that gloomy Roman palace; his brother, who was getting fat, had risen high in the Church; his Highland friends prayed for him still, but in trousers and without pipes they were impotent. The statesmen of Europe had lost interest in the Cause. England was on good terms with Prussia, with the Austrian Empire, with Russia, and Sweden, and practically all the other nations, and was even thawing out a trifle in its attitude toward the Vatican. There was peace with France, and the sad state of the finances of that nation, as well as international good taste, required that the peace be maintained at least for a few years longer. Who would help Charles?

Perhaps he enjoyed a flutter of hope when George the Second died on the morning of October 25, 1760. Walpole describes the scene. George awoke about 6 o'clock, "looked, I suppose, if all the money was in his purse," and called for his chocolate. About 7 o'clock he got up, went to a window, remarked on the excellency of the weather, said he thought he would take a stroll on the grounds that morning, and inquired whether the mails from the Continent had yet arrived. Then he went into his closet "for some private purpose." A few minutes later his *valet de chambre*, hearing groans, hurried into the small anteroom between the closet and the bedroom, and found his master unconscious on the floor. They later learned that the right ventricle of the heart had burst. The King in falling had gashed his right temple against a corner of the bureau.

They summoned Princess Amelia, who was creaky with rheumatism, "very purblind and more than a little deaf." By now the King was dead, but she did not know this. She talked to him, and supposed that she heard him answer or, at any rate, nodded, with the self-consciousness of deaf persons, and pretended she had heard an answer. Not until later did they break the news to her.

George the Second was buried with the customary pomp. His grandson, George, was next in line, the wild and wayward Frederick, Prince of Wales, having died several years previous. George the Third was twenty-three years old, a tall, well-built fellow, with large features, a good complexion, and handsome but rather stupid eyes. He was at Kew when he heard that his grandfather was ailing, and at once started for London. Just outside of Kew his scarlet outriders came upon a cloud of dust from which presently emerged the blue-and-silver liveries of the servants of Mr. Pitt, who brought the news of the King's death. Mr. Pitt had his carriage turned, and fell behind that of the new King, and in this fashion they returned to London. The picture fascinated George Meredith, who called the trip "a supreme ironic procession," since stupidity, inexperience, and ignorance, rode in front, while wisdom, ability, and true greatness, followed in the rear.

The coronation is of particular interest to us, for reasons which you will hear presently. It was the grandest England at that time had ever witnessed. Walpole called it "a puppet show that cost a million." It was super-splendid, very long, very hot, and tedious. Westminster, brilliantly lighted by sconces, was packed to suffocation with important personages in their very best clothes. The women had given up hoopskirts: now their passion was for headdresses: they wore great hanks of false hair pasted together with pomatum, smothered with powder, and stuck with feathers, bits of lace, tinsel, artificial flowers, anything at all. These monstrous erections look well in pictures, but they must have been rather horrible on close view. They were so much trouble and expense to construct that they were allowed to remain untouched, and unwashed, for many days. As for the gentlemen, they never before had gone in for such punctilio of dress, and they never have since. The quietest wore bottle green, murrey, plum, claret; but the real dandies, beaux, fribbles and bucks, wore crimson, scarlet, orange, yellow, blue, in any combination their imaginations could conceive or their tailors execute. They reveled in gold-headed canes, chased sword hilts, ribbons, orders, jewels, seals, silver buckles, red-heeled shoes, and stately, slow-swinging epaulettes. The Abbey was airless that day, but heavy with perfumery. Fabulous prices had been paid for places. The center of it all was the blank-faced young man, who was earnest, stolid, well-intentioned, more like a country squire than a king. "This paragon of somewhat negative virtues," however, was not without a sense of humor. The persons in charge of the top-heavy ceremonies got things dreadfully mixed: the wrong names were called off, and the wrong titles: the Lord High Chancellor was placed in front of the Archbishop of Canterbury, or the Lord Great Chamberlain was permitted to walk in ahead of the Lord Privy Seal, with the Master of Horse in front of both—or something to that effect. At any rate, there was much confusion and considerable hushed profanity. George, under his breath, censured the Earl Marshal, Lord Effingham, and received in reply the amazing apology that at the *next* coronation, positively Your Majesty, everything would be carried through in perfect order! George the First or George the Second would have exploded with rage at such an answer—if they had been able to understand it. But George the Third found the incident diverting.

And now this great mass of frippery and fine lace shifted uneasily, and waited expectantly. Dymoke, the King's Champion, strode to the front. His part in the proceedings was similar to that of the clergyman when he says, ". . . if there be any man or woman here who knows any good reason why these two persons should not be joined in lawful wedlock," and so on. Well, Dymoke, after the ancient custom, hurled upon the floor a glove, and in stentorian tones demanded to know whether any person challenged the right of this man to be King. He did his part impressively. The embarrassment came when somebody darted out of the crowd, picked up the glove, and whisked away with it before he could be identified.

Nobody knows who did it. The culprit was never discovered. But many say that it was Charles Edward Stuart!

Perhaps. It was the sort of thing Charles *would* have been likely to do if he had been present at the ceremony, as some writers declare. Or if he were not there, it might well have been some person commissioned by him, or, more likely, some spirited Jacobite who of his own volition decided to defy this latest "Hanoverian usurper." But it is more pleasant to believe that it was Prince Charles himself.

Soon afterwards, the young King was wedded to the second daughter of a poor and not very important German nobleman, Charles Lewis Frederick, Duke of Mecklenburg-Strelitz. She was Charlotte Sophia, an amiable young lady with a very large mouth. Then George settled down to the task of being a real king. It was a task too big for him. His subjects did not want a real king: they wanted their sovereign to sign things now and then, appear in public at the proper time, have portraits painted in befitting robes, and receive foreign ambassadors when called upon to do so. The first two Hanoverian monarchs had more or less established such a precedent and, although neither of them was quite so much of a gilded figurehead as their present descendant, George the Fifth, yet they were far from being kings as the word was defined in those days. Before them, unambitious Anne had permitted the statesmen to do much as they pleased. And before *her* William of Orange had given Parliament plenty of leeway at least in domestic matters, which didn't interest him, with the understanding that Parliament give him corresponding leeway in foreign affairs.

But George had other ideas. Monarchs in the second half of the eighteenth century were bestirring themselves, and putting forth an unexampled display of magnificence, and of authority, too. France, as usual, set the pace with the unparalleled pomp of Versailles; the Spanish king and his consort were taking back a few powers from their haughty nobles; Frederick the Great of Prussia was making central Europe do the as yet unfamiliar goose step, and writing his name in blood across the Continent; and Marie Theresa and Catherine of Russia were enjoying more or less absolute powers. George wanted to be in fashion.

Poor George! He did not understand—probably he could not understand, any more than could Prince Charles—that all this was no more than the brilliance of a sunset, the high glow that a candle gives just before it goes out. Arbitrary kingship was already doomed.

He should have been popular, too, for he was quiet, patriotic, conscientious and, above all, he was the first really English king in half a century. He had been born in England, of a father born in England, and he spoke English, wrote in English and read English. For a ruler of Great Britain this was extraordinary! He even went so far as to announce, at the very beginning of his reign, that he "glories in the name of Briton." But England wanted him to glory only in the name of "Englishman," and didn't want the sister kingdom included. "Briton" sounded as though Lord Bute had told him to say that. Probably Lord Bute had. He was a suave Scot (a descendant of the Stuarts, incidentally, on the left hand) who had great influence over the Dowager Queen, Frederick's widow; many people said that he was her lover. At any rate, the Dowager Queen ruled George the Third, her son, and handsome Lord Bute ruled the Dowager Queen, and England didn't like that at all. Scotsmen were being appointed to all the good offices. In London, there was a strong wave of jealous feeling against the Scots.

Somewhere, no doubt—whether in Lady Primrose's house in St. James' Square, or in the Duc de Bouillon's fine chateau—Charles Edward was consulting with a few faithful followers on the possibility of taking advantage of this feeling. He was ready to snatch at any straw of hope. But nothing came of it. George the Third stumbled along somehow; and, as in the case of his immediate predecessors, when he fell he was picked up promptly, brushed off by capable ministers, and hidden from sight long enough to give him a chance to recover his dignity.

Charles Edward was as badly off, then, as ever. He lacked even the consolations of a dubious love affair, for Clementina, weary of beatings and cursings, and made a nervous wreck by Charles' fanatical suspicions, had, late on the night of July 22 or early the next morning, slipped out of his house and made for Paris with their eight-year-old daughter. She knew she would at least enjoy the technical protection of her lover's father, who had been trying for some time to persuade her to leave Charles. She established herself, with her child, in a convent at Meaux. Charles boiled over, cursed his servants, cursed his friends and everybody else, cursed his late mistress most of all, and demanded right and left that she be brought back to him. For he was still behaving as though he were possessed of unquestioned power. However, she was not brought back.

We cannot either like or dislike Clementina Walkinshaw. Men fought about her, and around her, but she herself seemed to take no part in the quarrels. She must have been a weak, tired woman, frail, colorless, lacking in definition. No word that she ever said has come down to us: there is not even a good description of her personal appearances. Like Enoch Soames, she was vague. Portraits of her are purely formal and give no clear indication of what she actually looked like. The only word picture we have of her is that unlovely one Lord Elcho has left us—the picture of her drunk, leering across the table in a cheap café at her drunken lover—and this was painted by a partial hand, and is probably a caricature if not entirely false.

Still, she must have known life, for men quarreled about her, and she bore a child, and when she went into a convent Charles went into a rage. Childish always, Charles determined to shut himself up in Bouillon and ignore everything and everybody else in the world until the mistress he did not desire was restored to him and his sore pride soothed. So he locked himself in at Bouillon, never quitting the estate, receiving nobody, doing nothing in politics, not writing, not heeding the letters that were written to him. He kept a few drinking companions with him, and said "Damn the world." The world didn't mind, for it had been damned very often before, and by better men. The world rolled around in its usual way. But Charles did only two things—hunt in the forest of Ardennes by day, and drink and drink and drink by night.

CHAPTER TWENTY

King Charles the Third

JAMES was ailing. He had never been strong. He wrote to Charles when the Prince was first in Paris, before the Great Adventure, that he could not read or write without feeling an ominous giddiness . . . "so you see, My Dear Child, that you are likely to have but a useless old Father in me, but still my Heart is good, and if it's being yours could be of any help to you, that will never faill you."

The nervous strain of waiting for news from that inexplicable young man—a strain which had been upon him for almost twenty years now—must have weakened him still more. He could do nothing when George the Second died; and nothing when England declared war upon Spain, except to write to Charles in warning of the peace to come and the effect it would probably have (but didn't) upon Charles' person. "Will you not run straight to your Father?" he begged, in that letter. "Is it possible that you would rather be a Vagabond on the face of the earth than return to a Father who is all love and tenderness for you?"

It was not only possible, but a fact. Charles answered evasively, sometimes with a half promise to return, sometimes with no reference to the touching entreaties. For Charles still feared that a trip to Rome and what must inevitably follow, an audience with the Pope, would be fatal to his cause.

When the treaty was signed, in 1763, it contained no reference to the exiled royal line. It was the first treaty since 1688 of which this was true. Well . . . the Stuarts and their claims were a dead issue. Everybody but Charles admitted that. He would never admit it.

He continued to hunt and to drink at Bouillon, ignoring his

family and usually insulting his friends. The year after the signing of the treaty, James became seriously ill, and wrote again to Charles, begging him to return. More than that, his brother wrote to the Prince for the first time in many years, enclosing an invitation from the Pope to visit the Eternal City. Perhaps Henry had been informed, circuitously, that Charles would not ignore another letter from him now. Perhaps Henry only chanced it. At any rate, Charles answered that letter, and answered it politely, assuring Henry that it was his greatest desire to return to his family, and even going so far as to regret that he was not a bird with wings, so that he could fly to Rome at once.

And he seemed really to mean it, for a while. He began to pack his things. Then he dismissed the idea again, or it may be that he got drunk and forgot it, or perhaps he remembered the irreparable damage Henry had done by becoming a Cardinal, and was not yet prepared to forgive him. Again, he might have been assisting in the layout of one more scheme, with the encouragement of his drinking companions and a hint or two from some Court; for there were still a few statesmen left in Europe who had not altogether tired of the old and unfashionable game of playing with the Stuart pretensions.

Anyway, Charles did not go to Rome. And on January 1, 1764, James died, seventy-eight years old.

They wrapped the corpse in purple and ermine, put a crown on its head, the orb and scepter in its hands, and carried it with great solemnity to the Church of St. Peter where it rested in state for three days. Swiss guards, standard bearers, torch bearers, chamberlains and equerries to the Holy See, halberdiers with flat velvet bonnets, twenty-two cardinals and five hundred clergymen and members of the guilds and confraternities, each holding a lighted taper, marched to the slow music.

There is something extraordinary about the Stuarts. It is not merely that they glow in the pages of history because of the things they did and the things that happened around them: they glowed in their own persons with a light we can never explain. Always they impressed people. Realistic historians may, and do, point to the fact that this one was a fool, that one a drunkard, the third a weakling and a bumptious ass. It makes little difference. The fact remains that they were all Stuarts, and that even this James now in the cypress coffin, perhaps the least picturesque personality of them all, had something about him which made men give up their lives for him without a murmur—good men, too, wise and sensible men, who were not otherwise inclined to dabble in chivalry. In those exiles who trudged through the Roman streets beside the State hearse lies the real tragedy of this tale; or rather, it lies in the devotion, the unselfishness, the courage they displayed in the service of the man they believed to be by right their King. The spirit of Jacobitism has baffled psychologists. There is only one possible explanation for it, and that is an explanation which, in these cynical times, we find it difficult to believe: that these men, most of them anyway, had in them a store of goodness, bravery, honesty and chivalry, which strove to find expression and found it in the hopeless cause of an exiled king. Now and then the fire of an erratic genius would flash up in their midst—the rake Wharton, drunk of course, and looking for greater excitement; Bolingbroke, fascinated by plotting, who wanted a new set of political toys to play with; cautious Marlborough, without a conscience, always eager to have something to fall back upon. Into their midst, too, came persons who were disgraced in England, or disgruntled there; and persons to whom the Stuart cause was only a new form of gambling; and persons who were merely stupid and avaricious, and who guessed wrong. But the rank and file, it is safe enough to say, were in love with that vague, inexplicable something there always was about the Stuarts. . . .

James himself was a gentleman. There are few characters in history who have been more maligned without justice. He is dismissed by one writer with a shrug and a few condescending sentences about "this colorless Pretender, weak, irresolute, stupid"; while another sets him down as a low schemer, an adulterer, ambitious, selfish, bigoted. He was none of these things. He didn't ask to be born the son of James the Second of England and the Seventh of Scotland. He was totally unconscious, in the shadow of old Lambeth Church that night, in Mary of Modena's arms, that a single cry from him would have saved his race much bloodshed. Men told him he had a mission in life, and he believed them; and although he was never a powerful, commanding personality, he was faithful to that mission.

Courage? Omitting mention of the battlefields—which mean little enough when matters of real bravery are being discussed—James fought all his life for one thing, fought against terrific odds, and never faltered, never turned aside. He was not born a warrior. But he did everything it was within his power to do. Men usually aren't asked to do more, even by historians.

Ambition? He didn't want the throne. He sought it only because he believed the search to be his sacred duty to his God and his ancestors. So soon as Charles was old enough to qualify, James made him Prince Regent; and if Charles had succeeded in 1745 there is little doubt that James would have abdicated in his favor.

Unfaithful? James was obliged to face the ridicule of all Europe because of a lie, in all probability concocted by a British government spy, and certainly carried on by the hysterical behavior of a well-meaning but stupid woman; but James, even then, did not lose his dignity in spite. The lie stuck because the public has always delighted to believe unpleasant things about well-born persons, and also because Thackeray, requiring such a character for "Henry Esmond," found James convenient and gave him to posterity disguised as a rake. Yet few persons of royal blood have been so moderate in their habits.

Bigoted? He was extraordinarily faithful to his religion. He might well be rated as a saint for steadfastness. Time and again, had he cared to, he could have abjured his faith and thereby become one of the greatest potentates in the civilized world. As between duty to his ancestors and duty to his God, however, he chose God. Of his father it was said (and said by a Cardinal too) that he was the man who "threw away three

Anglicanism on the Pope as a secret bit of policy undertaken for the hour alone: but it is difficult to believe that he could deceive the Vatican.

There was some attempt at pomp—but not much—when Charles returned to the gloomy Palazzo Santa Apostola. The servants called him "Your Majesty." Henry called him "Your Majesty." And now and then there was a visitor, a grim and unrelenting old Jacobite, who did the same.

He was confined to the palace for a few days recovering from the fatigue of the journey. Bonnie Prince Charlie forced to take to his bed to recover from the effects of travel in a carriage! Meanwhile, the Pope sent out an order that nobody in Rome was to hail Charles as King. But when Charles did get out, and visited the English and Scots colleges in Rome, and the Irish Franciscans and Dominicans, he was treated as a reigning monarch and accorded royal honors. And Henry, with a display of insubordination such as he had never before been guilty of and was never guilty of again, rode out in public with Charles seated on his right side—an honor a Cardinal should grant only to a crowned head.

Henry was severely censured and soon recommended to Charles that no further attempt be made for the present to gain official recognition. It would be better, he told his brother, to let the matter rest a while. England and France would be fighting again soon: those two nations were so much in the habit of being at war with one another that they could hardly endure a very lengthy peace. And who could tell what might happen when the muskets started crashing again? The statesmen had not forgotten the Stuarts entirely. The club was still on the wall, and it was still heavy enough to give England concern. Why not live quietly for a time, Henry suggested, and wait in hope for further developments?

Charles would not tolerate such a plan. He was King of Great Britain and Ireland now—the Pope, the crowned heads of every capital, and the people of Great Britain and Ireland themselves, to the contrary notwithstanding! He would refuse to recognize the fact that the Pope had refused to recognize him! It was a curious policy, and it didn't work well.

For His Holiness was determined. The strictest orders were sent out from the Vatican that no one was in any way to recognize Charles as King. Even outside the palace this must be the case. Charles awoke one morning to find that somebody had torn down the stone escutcheons, bearing the Royal arms of England and Scotland, from the front of the palace.

There were other troubles for Charles, too. His health was bad. Lord Elcho was dunning him for the £1,500 he had lent during the 'Forty-five. One day in December, 1767, the gentlemen in attendance refused to accompany Charles to his coach because he was too drunk. He was furious: drunk or sober, he was their king and they must accompany him. No, they said, politely but firmly. So he dismissed them, leaving himself almost unattended and without a friend. He was exasperated when Henry wrote to the dismissed attendants thanking them for their attitude. For Henry worried continually about Charles' drunkenness.

Henry had his worries, too. No Stuart could be free of them. A rumor was wandering around Europe like an unpleasant odor: it said that Charles and Clementina Walkinshaw had been secretly married, before she had left him. Charles himself never spoke Clementina's name; he was still hot with rage about the affair. So Henry, who was paying the woman a small pension, arranged through Waters, the Paris banker, to have her sign an affidavit denying that she had ever been married to Charles. The rumor died on its feet. It might have been started by Clementina or some of her friends, with an idea of getting her a larger pension; or it might have been started by British government agents, who were always eager to send out rumors which would hurt the Jacobite cause; but most likely it was started by idle persons who liked to talk about such things and who knew that the victims could not strike back.

Charles, it is possible, never even heard about the rumor. Certainly he never had a thought of responsibility for his mistress and his daughter in the convent. He went on shooting, and taking the baths at Pisa, and playing the French horn (a new musical fad of his), and drinking himself insensible night after night. And the servants called him "Your Majesty."

CHAPTER TWENTY-ONE

A Beautiful Blonde

BACK in the days of the Merry Monarch, when vice was fashionable and adultery quite the thing, the Duke of York, who later became James II of England, was carrying on an affair with Arabella Churchill—an angular, ugly female whose influence with James launched her brother up the path which led to the first Dukedom of Marlborough.

They had four children, two of them male. One son was killed fighting in Ireland. The other, created Duke of Berwick, founded the family of Fitzjames, which, like so many illegitimate houses, was destined to outshine many a respectable outfit.

In the year 1772, the head of this house was seeking a suitable wife for his son and heir, the Marquis of Jamaica. The Duke of Berwick was also the Duke of Liria in Spain, where he was a grandee, the Duke of Veragua in Portugal, and a Prince of the Empire. His son, naturally, was no mean match; and the European marriage market was all aflutter.

At fashionable St. Wandru, in Mons, Austrian Netherlands, where ladies played at religion the while they angled for husbands, lived Louise Maximilienne Caroline Emmanuele, daughter of His Highness Prince Gustave Adolph of Stolberg-Gedern, and of Elizabeth Philippine Claudia, Princess of Hornes and Countess of Baucignies. Since Louise plays a very important part in our story, we will examine her qualifications as a bride a bit more closely—not as closely as the Duke of Berwick examined them, for that is not within our power now, but as closely as we conveniently can.

You would suppose that with all those names and titles, this young lady would be a person of consequence. And so she was, in one sense. There flowed through her veins the blood of the

Nassau-Saarbrückens, the Holstein-Gottorps, the Mecklenburg-Gustrows, the Hohenlohe-Neuensteins, and of many other distinguished families. She was also descended, through her maternal grandmother, from the English Earls of Elgin and Ailesbury.

Moreover, she was not only aristocratic, but was also uncommonly good-looking. Dark and highly expressive eyes, soft, spun-gold hair, and small and regular features, a dazzling complexion, a pretty figure, wit, a good disposition—certainly a desirable bride, you would say.

But it happened, as is so often the case, that, although the family tree showed as many impressive names as a prime oak shows acorns, the family pocketbook showed nothing at all. Louise was the oldest child of a very young mother and a very gallant, although penniless, father. She was born on September 20, 1752, and she had for godfathers Prince Maximilien Emmenuel of Hornes, a Knight of the Golden Fleece of the First Class, and Prince Frederic Charles of Stolberg; and for godmothers, Princess Albertine of Hornes, née Princess of Gavre, and Alexandrine, Princess of Croy and canoness of St. Wandru, who was acting for Her Highness Princess Louise of Stolberg, née Princess of Nassau.

Such a beginning! But her father, a colonel in Marie Theresa's army, was too eager to cover himself with glory and thereby to line the empty purse; and a Prussian musket ball struck him in a fatal spot at Leuthen. The pretty mother was twenty-five years old then, and had borne him three girls after Louise.

The good-natured empress took such care of them as she conveniently could, and the pretty mother, chiefly concerned with the goings-on at court, worried about them as little as possible. When Louise was only seven years old, they sent her to St. Wandru to be educated. Being educated, in those days, didn't mean much for a man: for a woman it meant even less. Louise learned to read and to write, after a fashion, and how to be lovely. That was enough.

In 1767, she was given a prebend, which meant greater

liberty and a much more conspicuous place in the marriage market. She got the stall because the Princess Marie Anne Victoria of Salm, her predecessor, had got a husband, the Duke of Lerma. The pretty mother purred. *There* was a brilliant match, and Louise would do well to profit by the example it set her.

Then came the distinguished Duke of Berwick. Imagine the chagrin of Louise when, instead of picking her, he selected her sister Caroline Augusta!

But the Duke had not overlooked the older girl. A studious matchmaker in his declining years, he was still on the lookout for a suitable mate for a personage even more exalted than his own son—a personage who, as a boy, had enjoyed his first taste of warfare under the Duke's tutelage. Princess Marie Louise of Salm-Kyrburg didn't fit. Neither did Princess Isabella of Mansfield. Negotiations with the Duc de Deux Ponts for his daughter Marie-Anne, fell through. Then His Grace suggested to certain French politicians the name of Louise of Stolberg-Gedern; and all sorts of plotting began.

The boy who had gone down into the trenches before Gaeta was now fifty years old, a pudgy, sodden wretch, possessed of little besides an imperishable name, a few pensions, a highly placed ecclesiastical brother, and some slow-music memories. He was peevishly drinking himself to death in Rome, when he heard of the plans to present him with a bride. Once, in a magnanimous mood, he had sworn that he would never marry, that the legitimate Stuart line would end in his person, never to trouble Britain again. But the mood didn't last; and when he learned that France was enough interested in him, again, to help him to a wife and present him with a pension calculated to enable him to keep her in proper state, he bestirred himself suddenly, remembering again his sacred duty to uphold forever the honor of his house. He went to Paris, anxiously inquiring how far the new plan had advanced.

There had been a time when Paris was at his feet. Now it scarcely paid him any attention. He was denied an audience with the King; no one cared for his indignation. There was a time when the task of ejecting Charles Edward from the French

PRINCESS LOUISE OF STOLBERG
(The Countess of Albany)

capital had called out the entire regiment of Household Guards and half the Parisian police. Now, after a time, some underling informed him that Great Britain was complaining again, and would Charles please efface himself as quietly as possible. Charles went, obediently, back to Rome. There he waited.

Great Britain sniffed suspiciously. Wasn't this Stuart business ever going to end? Must there be more of this chasing and spying? Great Britain demanded to know whether France was seeking a bride for the Pretender. France spread palms in eloquent denial, but when Great Britain wasn't looking went right on with the marriage plans.

Louise was asked whether she would like to become Queen of England, Scotland and Ireland. She was delighted. So was her pretty mother, who, although she wasted little enough affection on Louise or any of her other daughters, was eager to see the girls marry well. The Empress would be angry, for England had proved a good friend of the Empire. But Louise's mother decided to risk that; and after the proper messages had been whispered back and forth, the proper contracts signed and understandings reached, Her Highness Louise Maximilienne Caroline Emmenuele, Princess of Stolberg-Gedern, was married on March 28, 1772, in Paris, by proxy to Charles Edward Stuart.

Louise, a pretty doll of a girl, was different from hundreds of other young gentlewomen of her day only in the fact that she was better looking and that she possessed an inexplicable desire to read and write and learn something. She wanted to meet interesting people; she aspired to bigger and better things. She dressed nicely, and talked engagingly. Much later, when she began better to understand the world, she was wont to upbraid her mother for having neglected her; but although there is no doubt that the widow esteemed minuets and flirtations to be of far greater importance than her daughters—still, when she put Louise into the convent she did all that Louise could reasonably have expected, and in fact all the girl, for many years, *did* expect.

Nor was this childlike creature at all adverse to uniting herself with a decaying gentleman who was more than twice her age, a King without a Country, almost without a friend. On the contrary, she appeared to be highly pleased with the arrangement. A Queen! Many years earlier, a charming Polish girl had experienced the same thrill.

To be sure, Louise had not been out in the world. She knew very little about life. She wasn't expected to know any more. Marriage was something older people talked about; but they never got very definite about it, at least not in her presence. Vernon Lee, one of her biographers, suggests that at this time Louise "was, most likely, in a state of feeling like that which comes to us with the earliest light through the blinds: pleasant or unpleasant? we know not which; still drowsing, dreaming, but yet strongly conscious that in a moment we shall be awake to reality. . . ."

Reality was slower in coming to Louise; but when it came, its tardiness was offset by its bald starkness. Most of us, in spite of our protestations, cling to some illusions; Louise was left none at all.

However, after the ceremony by proxy, for which French politicians were soon apologizing to irate British diplomats, Louise set out for Rome to join her royal husband.

Charles was vastly excited. He begged the Pope to suspend the non-recognition rule for this occasion, and to receive him and his bride with royal honors. The Pope said no. So Charles appealed to his best friend in the Sacred College (excepting Henry), Cardinal Marefoschi, and made every preparation within his power to make this event unforgettable. Liveries were brushed, wigs combed, coaches gilded, orders removed from their velvet casings; and Charles hurried north.

Husband and wife met in the little village of Macerata, in the March of Ancona, on April 14. It was Good Friday.

Paint, powder and patches, pretty hair peeping out from either side of a pretty hat, stiff brocades accentuating the lovely girlish curves of her figure—there was the bride, with large awed eyes, all of life in front of her.

Tall, gaunt, stooped, his eyes glazed, his mouth slack, his

rufous face deeply wrinkled—there was the bridegroom, dressed in scarlet silks, the bright blue order of the garter across his breast, with all of life behind him.

Charles had given up drinking, more or less, in honor of his marriage, the anticipation of which really seems to have steadied him for the time; but it is highly unlikely that he broke off the habit entirely, and it is safe to agree with Vaughan, who writes of the harsh odor of brandy which rose through the perfume Charles used when he went to greet his bride. The hero of Prestonpans and of Falkirk! The man who had eluded the greatest navy in the world, and any number of armies! The man who had been the darling of Europe, the delight of the ladies, the despair of husbands; who had frightened a great nation half out of its wits, and with a handful of men at his back had gone swinging up to London, and who, defeated by overwhelming odds, had come away laughing and singing and eager to try again!

This man bowed to pretty Louise, and while the village folk gaped, they passed together up into the Compagnoni-Mareschi palace, where they signed the register, he as Charles Third, King of Great Britain, Ireland and France, she as Louise, Queen of Great Britain, Ireland and France; and the official, religious ceremony of marriage was performed.

They stayed at Macerata two days, amidst all sorts of celebrations. Louise was getting a wonderful thrill already at the thought of being not only a married woman but a Queen to boot. Doubtlessly Charles had led her to believe that they would be received with royal honors when they went to Rome: not because Charles had any thought to deceive her, but only because he always expected royal honors and was always amazed, and exacerbated, when they were not forthcoming. Again and again the whole world told this man, "You're not a King! NOT A KING!" but he refused to believe it.

They started for Rome on Easter day, the bridegroom beaming, the bride delightedly examining her pretty features on the medal Charles had, of course, caused to be struck to commemorate the event. They entered the Eternal City with a considerable display of circumstance—two traveling coaches with the attendants of Charles and his brother, and four outriders dressed in scarlet silks and with the white Stuart cockade on their hats. They galloped bravely through the Porta del Popolo and up the narrow Corso to the Piazza Santi Apostoli, while the crowds watched, somewhat amused and somewhat impressed.

This was the same grim old palace from whence the boy had slipped away to the Great Adventure, back in the days before Louise was born. This was the palace where King James, the "King Here," had moped, worrying about his reckless son. Now there were no Papal guards, with their brilliant polychromatic uniforms and their picturesque weapons. But the servants, inside, were garbed in the royal Stuart livery, and they bowed low before His Majesty and Her Majesty. . . . It was all very nicely done. Indoors, at least, Louise was a Queen.

The next day, Henry, Cardinal Duke of York, made his formal visit. The fat and amiable dignitary came bearing gifts for the bride: one of them was a gold box encrusted with diamonds, and when she opened this Louise found a bank draft for £10,000.

But not many others called. They were forbidden to greet Charles or Louise by their royal titles, and Charles would not tolerate greetings of any other sort. Nor would Charles permit his wife to return the visits of noblewomen. In fact, he stood on every conceivable point of etiquette, quite as sternly as though he were an actual, ruling King. A stubborn man was Charles! He said stiffly, "The Queen is entitled to the same ceremonies as the King, and as the Prince of Wales, too, when there shall be one." The last is significant. Charles was fond of his girl-wife; but he never lost sight of the fact that she was here for one purpose, and that was to provide his family with an heir. He, and hundreds, even thousands of others, waited eagerly for the advent of that infant.

Yet Louise enjoyed herself in Rome and although she later wrote bitterly about her marriage, and succeeded in making herself feel like a martyr, a Christian tossed to the lions, she was, apparently, a very happy and very gay girl during those early days in Rome. She went here and there, to the galleries, the opera, the excavations, the informal receptions, all the things which made the Rome of Clement XIV a world center of art and culture and the sciences. She was meeting interesting people at last! She was seeing the things she had always wanted to see! Everybody who was anybody got to Rome those days. It was unfortunate that her husband insisted upon his royalty pose and would not permit her to be a mere noblewoman for social purposes; it meant that only the most fervid Jacobites, of whom there were very few left, and those old men, could be entertained at the Piazza Santi Apostoli. But plenty of other excellent gentlemen, of all nationalities, were eager to be presented to the Pretender's wife; and somehow, things were usually arranged. Louise kept meeting persons fortuitously. She was forever encountering friends, accompanied by many other friends, in public places. Should they call her Queen, and be traitorous? or should they refuse to do so, and be impolite? They compromised by calling her Regina Apostolorum—until a charming young Swiss, a gay social gadfly, one Karl Victor von Bonstetten, named her the Queen of Hearts; and this title stuck.

Louise was fond of von Bonstetten. He was, like her, much more Latin in real temperament, than Teutonic. They were often together. Naturally, there was all sorts of talk. British spies were still on the scene, eager to start unpleasant rumors. And even without the spies, it was only necessary for a woman of Louise's position to smile with warmth on any man, to set tongues wagging. But it is extremely doubtful, in spite of the apparent evidence of some letters she wrote him later, that Louise had von Bonstetten as a lover. Even if we could believe it of her, at this time, we could not believe it of him. A love affair, for him, would have spoiled everything. For they got along beautifully, these two. An hour with the Swiss must have been a vast relief after the presence of her heavy husband.

But then, Louise liked all gentlemen. She had little regard for women. Nowadays she would be called "a good sport," a "man's woman."

The honeymoon had one exacerbating interruption. Clem entina Walkinshaw, who was now the Countess Alberstrof seized upon this time—of all times!—to go with her daughter Charlotte, to Rome and petition Charlotte's father for money Charles had refused to give her a penny since she had left him and both women were living on a small pension from th French court. When they came to Rome he refused even to re ceive them: he would not accept their petition, or deal wit them in any way, directly or indirectly. He did not seem a all curious to see his daughter again. The two women appeale to the fat Cardinal, and Henry, embarrassed and annoyed finally granted them a small pension and sent them back t their convent. The unpleasant incident of their coming, how ever, did not seem to disturb Charles seriously, and Louise prob ably only heard of it vaguely and without detail.

Charles still wanted his wife to be recognized as Queen While the spies and hopeful Jacobite agents were watchin breathlessly for a significant change in Louise's figure, Charle was arguing points of etiquette with the Pope. He still de manded recognition; and the Pope wearily explained again tha recognition at the present time was out of the question. More over, Henry now sided with the Pope, and with Louise, tryin repeatedly to convince Charles that he would best serve hi own interests by dropping for the present his insistence upo royal honors. His own brother again! Charles snapped back a him, like an angry mongrel. And his own wife! Was the whol world in conspiracy against him? and could he trust nobody a all?

His own wife! What was wrong with her! Where was th baby? The court of France had some plans, and wanted an in fant. The Stuart line must be continued. Henry couldn't d it. . . . Was this woman sterile? Had his enemies picked he because they had known she was incapable of bearing hin children?

Charles' voice became less tender when he addressed Louis and his once hazel eyes were leaden now with angry streaking of red. He was drinking again.

Two years they were in Rome, and then Charles decided to punish the Pope by quitting his dominions. The Pope, instead of weeping at this, was doubtless glad to be rid of such a troublesome resident. Charles dragged his pretty wife away—and how she must have hated to leave!—and they went to Pisa for a few months. The spies trailed after them. Did this mean a baby? Tongues wagged industriously. All sorts of preposterous stories were fabricated. But Louise still kept her girlish figure; she remained the sweet, good-natured child—a trifle wiser now, perhaps, but just as slim and just as amiable as on the day of her marriage. They went to Florence.

Here, for the first time, Charles had sense enough to drop the pose of royalty—in public, at least. Perhaps he was getting tired of his own aloofness. In the Casino Corsini, near the Pato Gate, which the prince of that name turned over to the couple, the empty ceremonies were continued: the servants still wore the royal liveries, and guests still called Charles and Louise "Majesty." But outside, by his own request, Charles was known as the Count of Albany. Grand Duke Peter Leopold, second son of Marie Theresa, had refused to recognize Charles and had commanded the Florentine nobility to do likewise.

It was the old story, with peculiarly Stuart settings. Charles, gouty, peevish, usually drunk, talked for hours about his past experiences, and often regaled his guests with the tale of how he had impersonated a woman; and poor Louise laughed at each recital. At all times a lover of the exercise of walking, Charles insisted upon daily strolls; while Louise, hot and sticky, and thoroughly bored, trudged faithfully along with him. Charles had no fondness for any art except music, and he wanted to fill the empty hours with talk and drink; but Louise, who wanted to improve her mind by reading and studying the galleries and discussing weighty topics with intelligent persons, appeared to like every art *but* music. In other words, they didn't get along well together.

Charles would not permit his wife to return the visits of the noblewomen and, as a natural result, they ceased to call; so that most of the visitors at the Casa Stuart were men. Louise probably shed no tears over *this* fact. But Charles became intensely jealous of her. And not entirely without reason. She was ripe for adventure, this awakening wife. She was writing to von Bonstetten, who was in Paris, "perhaps you reign with too much authority in my heart. Would that we were in the Desired Island! I do not mean England, for really I do not want to be a Queen . . ." and informing the jolly Switzer that he was "the type of lover I desire; one who will play the lover only when we two are alone." Not very discreet of her: but the poor girl had to have somebody to flirt with, and von Bonstetten was safe on the other side of the Alps.

No, Louise did not want to be a Queen. She had seen something of the world, enough to know that she would love it could she but have the opportunity to enjoy it without the appendix of a fat-faced, suspicious husband.

Nor did she want to be a mother. Charles was constantly questioning her. She hated him for that! People were constantly staring at her—estimating—counting months—wondering . . .

What she wanted was somebody who would adore her, somebody she could love without restraint and without shame. She was too shrewd, now, not to have noticed that men are on the whole a rather beastly lot. But there must be an exception *somewhere!* She wrote to von Bonstetten, describing the utter dullness of her existence, describing, though briefly, the illness and recovery of her husband, and remarking that "if I found a man who was wholly original, I should adore him forever."

What happened must have seemed like an answer from Heaven. She wanted a man who was wholly original? Very well. The orchestra, which had been playing fitfully, uncertainly, while the actors stumbled through their rôles, now swelled for a moment; people of the audience suddenly sat up and moved to the edges of their seats; the orchestra dramatically stopped; there was an expectant hush. . . .

CHAPTER TWENTY-TWO

The Red-Haired Poet

AND now there strides upon the stage the figure of a lank, gawky, red-haired young nobleman, a genius, possibly mad, certainly inspired.

This is Count Vittorio Alfieri. Before his entrance, you will vant a program note concerning his past.

He was born on January 17, 1749, in Asti, Piedmont, son f Antonio Alfieri of Cortemiglia, and of Monica-Maillard de 'ournon, widow of the Marquis Catherano. His father, sixty t the time of Vittorio's birth, died when the boy was barely a ear old; and his mother married a third time—a cousin, the hevalier Giacinto Alfieri of Magliano.

Vittorio lived at emotional high speed. Everything he did, ll his life, he did with terrific intensity. His joy was incredibly igh, his despair incredibly low; he seemed unaware of the inetween emotions. His boyhood and youth were a series of pasonate attachments, violent hatreds, quarrels, loves, attempts t suicide, and bursts of reckless desire which he invariably inulged. And so it was also with his manhood. He was always oectacular, always white-hot about something.

His stepfather dying when Vittorio was only fourteen ears old, the lad came in for more money than was good for im. He was then a student at the University of Turin, where, e tells us in his autobiography, he learned almost nothing. He ad a mad desire to pose as a great man, in state; and he spent ecklessly for clothes, servants, and equipage. He developed a assion for horses, kept a stud when he was only fifteen years ld, fell furiously in love with one of these beasts, rode like a nadman, did anything to produce a thrill. Something was

continually driving him from madness to madness. He coul
not even sneeze without being sensational about it.

His education, when he quit the Turin college, was negli
gible. A person of his blood, he thought, should not degrad
himself by study. But there were hours when he did not feel thi
way about it—when, overcome by remorse, he forced himsel
to read huge tomes on the dullest subjects. But for the most par
he did not care for reading, Montaigne and Plutarch being th
only authors for whom he expressed any fondness; and o
course, he was extravagantly enthusiastic about them.

He was an officer in the Sardinian army. He liked his uni
form, but he didn't like the discipline: all bowing to authorit
was hateful to this fiery young Republican. He wanted t
travel. He must be on the move! He set out for a Grand Tour
and a short while after his return, still burning with the wan
derlust, he set out for a second and grander tour. He visite
France, the Italian cities, England, Austria, Denmark, Sweden
Germany, Spain, Finland, Russia. He met Louis XV, and late
Frederick of Prussia; but he refused an invitation to be pre
sented to Catherine of Russia because he did not like her natio
and the despotism he found there. Nor would he accept an in
vitation to meet Metastasio, the fashionable poet; and this wa
because he had seen Metastasio bow low before the Empres
Marie Therese—and such actions disgusted the count.

In the Hague, he fell in love with a young woman who be
came, when her husband was not in town, his mistress. He ha
been in love with a married woman when he was a mere boy
and had attempted to kill himself when he had been forced t
avoid her presence. But this was a more dangerous case. Force
to separate from the object of this later adoration, he almos
did manage to commit suicide. His valet prevented him. Bu
for weeks afterwards Alfieri never lifted his eyes, never spoke
never changed expression. Such was his grief.

A little later, in London, he fell in love with another mar
ried woman—Penelope, Lady Ligonier. They enjoyed a hecti
affair. But Alfieri was miserable. To be in love was to be boun
to something: and he hated all fetters. There came a time whe

he could not see the lady for two days. Two days! Two centuries rather! He went riding, as always, like a madman. But he was wilder than ever this day. Perhaps he was trying again to commit suicide. At all events he was thrown heavily, dislocating his left shoulder and fracturing his collar bone. In spite of the pain, he sprang back on his horse and rode on.

In spite of the pain, too, he insisted upon going to the opera the following night. He was to meet HER after the opera. But that rendezvous was never fulfilled. Before the performance was ended—indeed, in the middle of the first act—there came a knock on the door of his box, and who should it be but Lord Ligonier!

The husband had heard: this much Alfieri understood at a glance. "I want to speak to you," said his lordship, who was calm and quiet-spoken. "I am at your service," said the count. They slipped outside without attracting attention, crossed the Grassmarket, and selected a secluded spot in Green Park. It was still daylight; even sunlight; for in those days, in the summer, the opera used to open at 6 o'clock. When the gentlemen drew and faced one another, Ligonier noticed the sling and suggested that they postpone the encounter until his opponent was in better condition to defend himself. But the Piedmontese insisted that they fight it out on the spot. The swords crossed, slithering together in the preliminary feel-out; and then Alfieri went in. He duelled as he did everything else. He advanced recklessly, in bounds; he beat the blade, disengaged, lunged, forcing the contest all the time. Lord Ligonier, perfectly cool, might have run him through a dozen times, but he backed away, parrying, until a proper opening appeared; and then his lordship thrust, pinking the count on the right forearm.

Alfieri did not even notice it. He would have fought on—but the Englishman's point went down. "You are wounded, sir." Alfieri was satisfied. Blood had been drawn, so Ligonier was satisfied. The duel was finished. Ligonier would have summoned a surgeon, but Alfieri refused assistance. Ligonier bowed and departed, breathing a bit heavily perhaps but not otherwise show-

ing any evidence that he had been engaged in mortal combat
He returned to enjoy the rest of the opera.

The fire-eater from Asti, with one shoulder dislocated an
the other disabled, drew a pocket handkerchief with his teet
and somehow managed to bind his wound sufficiently to sto
the flow of blood. Then, less than an hour from the time he ha
quit the place, he too returned to the opera house. He had n
animosity for Ligonier. On the contrary, he admired that fin
ished gentleman. Later he wrote, "I cannot sufficiently extol
the conduct of this worthy husband . . . this intrepid and gen
erous man acted throughout the whole affair in a manner I ver
little deserved."

It was all done quietly, politely, in the approved Eighteent
Century style. And yet, the next day it was all over town. Lor
Ligonier had filed suit for divorce, with damning evidence
Alfieri, in an agony of humiliation, flew to the home of hi
lady-love. Of course he was going to marry her! He was
gentleman. He could not be anything else. But the lady, whe
he told her it was only a question of waiting for the completio
of the divorce proceedings, wept and acted strangely, pushin
him gently away, and sobbing that she was not worthy of suc
an honorable man. What was the trouble? Hours afterwards
she confessed to him that he had not been her first love sinc
Ligonier. It seems that he had only succeeded the family groom

A servant! What a blow for this aristocrat! He left her; bu
he could not stay away. So he lived with her a little longer, ex
quisitely miserable, torturing himself purposely, while fashion
able London buzzed with gossip about the affair. Finally he qui
England, again meditating suicide.

In May of 1772, after various wanderings, he returned t
Turin. And there he fell violently in love with the Marchesa d
Prie—another married woman—a woman, moreover, who ha
not been as conservative in her choice of lovers as Lady Ligo
nier. Alfieri knew that: everybody in that part of the worl
knew it. And the thought of the previous men, a thought whic
was with him all the time, was like the pressure of an inquisi
torial machine.

But he was her slave. He could not stay away from her. From eight o'clock in the morning until midnight he was by her side. Then he went to his home across the street—a house he had taken in order to be always near her. He was lost. He tried, again and again, to break away; for he hated this slavery, and despised himself because of it. He fled to Rome. But within eighteen days he was back in Turin and at the feet of the enchantress. He hated her, but he loved her. He hated her personality, her loose morals, all that she was and all that she represented; but he loved her smooth white skin with such a fury that he was ready to die for her, and almost did.

This lasted for two years. He tried many things. He tried travel, but soon returned. He tried horses, and could get none of the old thrill from them. He tried reading, and although Dante, Tasso, Ariosto, Machiavelli and Petrarch fascinated and delighted him, yet they were not sufficient to keep him from that fair flesh. He decided, abruptly, to write, and to write in Italian.

Now this was characteristic of him. For, in the first place, he didn't know Italian, which at that time was considered an inferior tongue. He thought in French, and talked a barbarous mixture of French and Piedmontese. But he had decided, in a burst of patriotic sentiment, to rescue Italian literature from the slough of neglect into which it had fallen; so he set himself to study that language. Incidentally, he also began to study Latin.

If all this sounds ridiculous, you must remember, that this eccentric young man became the greatest Italian poet and dramatist of his time.

He must write, and he must cure himself of his passion for the Marchesa di Prie. He caused himself to be tied to a chair at a table; his right arm was free, and with this he wrote. Purposely he faced a window, and across the street was the home of his paramour, who was doubtless wondering by this time what had happened to her latest and strangest lover. He watched her come and go, watched her as she walked, the while he strained at his ropes, writhing, struggling to free himself and to be at his detested passion again; and finally fainted in his chair

—to revive soon afterwards, seize his pen, and write furiously until sheer exhaustion overcame him and he fell asleep.

He wrote and wrote, and at last began to write tolerably well. Cured of his mania for the Marchesa, he retired to a little Alpine village, and there he wrote and studied and studied and wrote. When he came down into the lowlands again he was, to all appearances, a little calmer, a little nearer to sanity. But he was close to another breakdown too: nervous breakdowns were comparatively frequent with him. But for the moment, anyway, he was free.

He drifted to Florence; and there, as you have already guessed, he met the beautiful and accomplished Louise, Countess of Albany.

Alfieri did not want to fall in love again. His experience had taught him that love is a disturbing and often degrading state; and now that he had an Aim in Life, a genuine purpose, he was afraid of amatory arrows and avoided the company of women who, should he cultivate their intimacy, might prove distracting. Of course, he could not conceive of being quietly in love. He was at all times a complete egotist, and believed that posterity would suffer if he were diverted from literature by any further philandering.

Consequently, when the lady was pointed out to him, in some public place, he decided not to trust himself. He declined to be introduced to her, contenting himself with gazing upon her, Dante-fashion, as she passed on the arm of her disgusting husband.

Another visit to his beloved, restful Sienna, however, so quieted his mind that when he was next in Florence he believed himself sufficiently strong to risk a meeting. The salon of the Count and Countess of Albany, quite the thing in Florence, was now conducted at the Casa Stuart, a house Charles had purchased from the Guadagni family, and which still stands, although closed to the public, near the famous church of Santissima Annunziata: today this house is the property of the ducal family of San Clemente, and has the distinction of being the only residence on the Continent ever actually purchased by any of the exiled Stuarts. Here, then, the red-haired poet met Louise, and fell instantly in love.

The fall, however, was not announced to the world by a fanfare of trumpets. Alfieri was on dangerous ground now, and must be careful. Remembering his duty to Art, he was at first panic-stricken. Ordinarily he had two recourses under these circumstances. He might buy wild horses and ride them like a lunatic in the hope of breaking his neck; or he might travel. He tried both. He rode as far as Rome, and turned around and rode back again. He couldn't stay away from Louise. He was gone only twelve days.

"The first impression she made upon me was infinitely agreeable," he wrote, much later, in his autobiography. "Large black eyes, full of fire and gentleness, joined to a fair complexion and flaxen hair, gave to her beauty a brilliancy it was difficult to withstand. Twenty-five years of age, possessing a taste for letters and the fine arts, an amiable character, an immense fortune, and placed in domestic circumstances of a very painful nature, how was it possible to escape where so many reasons existed for loving?"

Perhaps it *was* possible, but Alfieri did not try very hard. That gallop to Rome and back was his only effort. Thereafter he surrendered himself completely; and he was doubly delighted when he learned that Louise would not only not interfere with his writing, but actually was interested in that work and eager to assist him in every possible way. In this, Alfieri was not signally honored; for Louise was always being sweet to some struggling poet or painter, and always saying encouraging things.

The one objection to this love affair, then, was removed. The fact that the lady happened to be married did not distress Alfieri. He went to the Casa Stuart frequently, and was wined and dined and entertained by the lord and master of the house.

This affair, at first glance, appears to have something extraordinary about it; and has fascinated many an historian as an example of something very like perfect mutual love. Yet it was founded on deceit. Alfieri, for all his high words and supposedly high purpose, was willing to be a daily guest of Charles

Edward, to accept his food and wine, to listen to Charles' story about how he had dressed as a woman in order to escape the English soldiers, and to whisper, in their brief moments together, words of love to Charles' pretty young wife.

Just when she first began to return this affection we do not know. Alfieri talks little about this stage of the liaison, in his *Vita*. But they must have been very intimate friends from the beginning. He was annoyed because she did not know Italian and they were obliged to converse in French, the language he hated as he hated everything French. He used to force himself to read good fourteenth century Italian for several hours every night, in order to counteract any Gallicisms he might have picked up during the afternoon. He was writing full-speed now, for he found Louise a true inspiration. Sonnets, prose, tragedies, comedies fairly flew from his pen. He was also building up a fine private library. To please him, Louise studied Italian. Anything to advance the cause of *belles lettres*.

As for Charles, he became a worse husband every day. He drank more and more; his health was bad; he took almost no exercise except his hot walks in the sun when Louise was dragged along; and he was furiously suspicious, keeping his wife always in sight or, when he was obliged to leave her for a short time, locking her in her chambers and keeping the key in his own pocket. We do not know whether Louise had done or said anything to justify this suspicion. She was, of course, immensely popular among the men of Florence; but she had been popular with men in the early days of the marriage, in Rome, where Charles had been not suspicious but rather proud. Now, however, he watched every movement she made. He was not distrustful of Alfieri in particular. At least, we have no evidence that he was. It is possible, in view of what happened later, that he knew about the love plot from the beginning and kept silence only because of his pride. At any rate, the red-haired poet was only one of the many regular masculine visitors at the Casa Stuart, and Charles, to all appearances, distributed his distrust evenly among them.

As the months rolled by and the lovely young blonde still

was without child, Charles' rancor increased. What did she think he had married her for? Was a doll-faced girl going to block the continuation of one of the oldest lines of kings the world had ever known? Charles did his part: we know that from confidential letters Louise wrote to friends. For all his excesses, the Stuart had a frame essentially sturdy; and in a purely biological sense, he was still a good husband.

Because of Charles' behavior, it was impossible for the lovers to snatch more than a few minutes together at this time. For they were lovers now. Alfieri had written, "How can I attack that tower of virtue?" but he had found the task easy enough, after all. It is unlikely that they had joined themselves physically, for they lacked an opportunity. But Louise had submitted in every other sense. She was receiving the true adoration she had craved, and from a man who was "wholly original." Alfieri played a careful game well, with diabolical cleverness, always greeting Charles with a smile and a warm handshake, chatting with the other guests, reading his poems aloud.

They were both hoping that the body which had endured such hardships in the Highlands would succumb to the assaults of alcohol. Charles was ailing. He couldn't last much longer. Yet somehow, he did. And Louise, desperate, wrote of "this man of iron." They had called him that in Scotland, too, but they blessed the iron of which God had constructed him; whilst Louise and Alfieri cursed it.

Louise got Alfieri to write a drama about Mary Queen of Scots, one of Charles' ancestors and one of Louise's favorite heroines of history. That was how *Maria Stuarda* came into existence. It was a convenient job; for Alfieri made a great show of having to check up on many small points, and frequently read parts of the manuscript to Charles and Louise. On these occasions, very often, the drunken Charles would fall asleep, and the lovers would enjoy themselves to the accompaniment of his thick snoring. A pretty picture! Yet Alfieri wrote a poem on those, to him, blessed spells of sleepiness; and instead of taking umbrage because the husband did not seem to appreciate the poetry, he felt delighted because, for the time, the husband was not watching. Alfieri appears to have been very proud about all this.

One day the poet told Louise that he had renounced his title and given all his property to his sister, Julia, wife of the Count Cumiana. The reason was characteristic. As a Piedmontese nobleman, he was obliged to get the permission of the King every time he wanted to leave the country. The passports had always been granted to him, but not always with a good grace. Moreover, he was liable to the censorship laws imposed upon authors in that nation. He would ask no man's permission for the publication of a book, and apologize to no man if that book was objectionable. He wanted to write, as he wanted to travel just when the fancy took him; and he wanted to write *what* his fancy dictated too, and not what the laws of his nation prescribed. So he gave away his lands.

He got, in return, an annuity which amounted to about half of his previous income. "I would even have been contented to resign the other half," he wrote, "to have purchased the freedom of thinking and writing, and the liberty of choosing my own place of residence." For a time, he thought he was going to lose everything. The technical, legal delays irritated him almost beyond endurance, and he was tempted to throw away everything and make an insane dash for freedom. He diverted himself with the idea of making a living as a horse breaker. Not only was he happy among horses, but "I could join it with poetry, as it is easier to write tragedies in a stable than in a court." However, the King of Sardinia at last signed the papers, "and we were both well pleased, he to lose such a subject, and I to acquire my liberty."

Still wealthy, Alfieri now was seized with the notion that he was poverty-stricken, and adopted an elaborate program of economy. He spent great sums still for books; but otherwise he was frugal. He dismissed all his servants, sold or gave away all his horses, gave his clothes to his valet, limiting himself for the rest of his life to dark blue in the daytime and black at night, and eliminated from his diet all rich foods and all strong drinks, even coffee.

All this he explained to Louise, who loved him the more for it. This was so very like Alfieri. . . . An impulsive fool, perhaps but magnificently, fiercely a fool. She smiled upon him; and he went home and wrote a tragedy so touching that Byron, the poet, wept when he witnessed its stage production.

Life dragged for a time in Florence; but Alfieri and Louise kept right on being in love, and prayed daily that Charles would die. Charles grew more offensive every day. He had a fistula now, and great sores on his legs. He smelled of more than brandy, too, as a result. Worn down by life with him, Louise was growing pale: she had lost her convent complexion: but this only made her the more picturesque, and the Florentines watched her sadly, and believed everything that Alfieri circulated about the ill-treatment she was accorded by her husband. Alfieri called her "a rose, pure, fresh and blooming, crushed in the fingers of a filthy clown." But Alfieri, it must be remembered always, was every day willing to accept the hospitality of this filthy clown, and was smiling to his face, and nodding and laughing with him. Daily, too, the poet was urging Louise to run away from her husband; although desertion was perhaps the cardinal crime in Italy at this time, ranking below drunkenness, gambling, adultery, or even brutality.

This continued for three years. Outwardly, all was smooth. The Count and Countess of Albany received, entertained, smiled, went through all their usual daily routine. They attended the opera, where the Count, as a rule, fell asleep from excess of wine or brandy; it was customary for his servants to stretch him out on a sofa in his box, where he snored loudly while Louise tried to pretend that nothing was wrong. In the morning they would walk, he hobbling, she protesting inwardly but with a smile on her face. Whenever Charles walked abroad at night there was a servant on each side: not because he was feeble, but because he was drunk. There are those who declare, as confidently as though they had been in the Casa Stuart at the time, that Charles was in the habit of beating his wife. This seems unlikely. Louise was too high-spirited to tolerate such treatment. The English spies reported only one such incident, which is related below; and if there had been other instances of violence, the spies would certainly have heard of it and capitalized it. Alfieri hints darkly, but cites no specific facts; and Alfieri, who enjoyed the completest confidence of Louise, and who hated Charles, would surely have been delighted to let posterity know about any such brutality.

However, the climax came. On St. Andrew's Day, November 30, 1780, Charles was drunk from early morning, in honor of the patron saint of Scotland. By night, he was a raging beast. Louise went to bed early, afraid to be near him. But he got it into his drink-sodden brain that his wife was not alone. He burst into her bedrom, accused her of infidelity and, at her denial, tried to choke her. To this had the Stuart chivalry come! Servants, brought by her screams, dragged him away and put him to bed at last.

This was a last straw. It gave Alfieri his winning argument. He wrote, later, in his *Vita,* that "the barbarous treatment she suffered from her unrelenting husband, induced her at length, in order to save her health and life, to consider by what means she might emancipate herself from the dominion of her cruel prosecutor." He intimates that his own part amounted to almost nothing, and that his activity, such as it was, was prompted by purely unselfish motives. As a matter of fact, he is undoubtedly the person who took up the matter at the court of the Grand Duke Leopold, and persuaded that personage to extend to Louise his protection. The Grand Duke, as we know, had little love for Charles, who was no more than an embarrassment to him in Florence. So they concocted a plan to take the "fresh and blooming rose" out of the fingers of the "filthy clown."

One noon, the Albanys had for luncheon guests Madame Orlandini, an Irish lady, and her lover and *cavaliere servente,* Mr. Gehegan, a gay young adventurer from the same native soil. Madame Orlandini suggested that they go to the convent of the White Nuns in the Via del Mandorlo, to examine some needlework. Louise thought that would be very interesting. The proposal was acceptable to Charles, too; so the carriage, with the royal arms of England emblazoned on its doors, was ordered around, and the party set out.

Soon the ladies were climbing the long steps up to the convent, in the heavy yellow sunlight, while Charles and the Irishman waited in the carriage below.

They waited a long time, and the ladies did not return. Charles waxed impatient. It was hot sitting there. He sent Gehegan up to inquire; and Gehegan soon returned with the information that the door had been shut in his face. Charles was huffed. He would go up himself. They would never dare to keep a door shut in the face of the King of England!

Charles hobbled up the steps, and his grotesque shadow hobbled beside him. He was old and very stooped, and the sun was hot.

He demanded to know what was keeping his wife. A face appeared in a little square of latticework, and Charles was informed that his wife had sought and had been granted the protection of the Grand Duchess, and would remain in this convent.

Charles, we read in the *Vita,* was "very much astonished." That was putting it mildly. He shouted for them to open the door for him and to open it immediately. The face disappeared, the little latticework was shut. Charles yelled and screamed, kicked on the door, pounded on it with his feeble old fists. "*Let me in!*" He drew the two pistols he always carried. "*Let me in! Open this door!*"

But silence rested over the convent of the White Nuns, bathed in heavy yellow sunshine.

CHAPTER TWENTY-THREE

In Spite of Himself

IT IS impossible not to pity him as he limps back to the splendidly gilded carriage and is driven the bumpy, dusty way to Florence. Picture him, scowling, muttering curses, his face as red as though it had been scraped raw with dull knives, his eyes bloodshot and watery, his hands trembling—an angry, gouty, smelly, disagreeable old man. Vernon Lee remarks of him that he was "branded with God's own brand of unworthiness, which signifies that a people, or a class, or a family, is doomed to extinction." And certainly there seems to have been some satanic fate hanging over this unluckiest of all houses: a fate which had been climaxed, in a last grand explosion, in the life of Charles Edward—as a piece of firework, streaking a golden, liquid stream across the skies, bursts magnificently into a thousand bright, polychromatic portions high in air, and then dissolves into nothingness.

He was not even despicable now, this old man. He had somehow gone below that—down to a place where the shadows were so deep that his meanness, his brutality, his intense selfishness, were blotted from sight, and nothing was left but a flabby, diseased, asthmatic remnant of an ancient line of gentlemen-kings, long since gone rotten.

It would hardly be possible to hate him now, and hardly sporting to despise him. He was no more than a mass of bruises and scars, tottering, fumbling in the darkness; the world had long since left him, as his wife had left him, screaming at a gate which would never be opened to him. We read without emotion that he refused to send to the convent his wife's linen and clothes, until he was ordered to do so by the Pope. It means nothing to us that he got blind drunk again, and swore at his servants, and called Alfieri a "seducer," and threatened to hire assassins to kill Gehegan. These things, like all the other things Charles did after this episode, seem meaningless. I relate them, such as they are, only because I have undertaken to tell the whole tale through.

"The "filthy clown" now had no friends at all. Of course, he appealed to the Grand Duke and to the Pope, but both had previously promised Louise their protection and they were as good as their words. Charles appealed also to Henry, but his brother sided with the wife. Florentine society ordinarily would have condemned the action of any woman in leaving her husband, no matter what the provocation; but somehow Florentine society made an exception in this case, and it was Charles, not Louise, who was blamed. And not only blamed—but laughed at! That was the greatest offense. A bullet would have been more welcome than a sly grin, a coffin more desirable than that cartoon, published in London, of the Young Pretender gazing glumly at a burnt-out Cupid's torch.

He had no friends. Grand Duke Leopold refused to listen to him. The Pope was cold. The Stuart adherents in the Sacred College—the few who were left—acted as Henry suggested in ignoring the older brother. Louise's mother, the flighty Princess at the Imperial court, did send one tepid protest to His Holiness; but this had no effect.

The world was treating Charles as thoughtless street boys sometimes treat an aged half-wit—throwing stones at him, calling him names, laughing shrilly and dancing away, filled with delight, when he turned to swear at them and to wave his stick in impotent fury.

The English agent in Florence wrote to his government recommending that Louise be awarded a pension for having left the Pretender! The correspondent stated that she had long since ceased to expect that "officially negotiated infant," and that this separation meant that there would no longer be an occasion to worry about the possibility of a false heir to the Stuart line—another warming-pan baby.

Gehegan scribbled a right spirited note to the master of the

Casa Stuart, in which he demanded a retraction of Charles' threat to have him waylaid and assassinated. Charles evidently apologized, or in some manner satisfied the Irishman. But Alfieri, who had engineered the whole business—who had never loved any woman not already pledged to another man—Alfieri, the high-souled, suddenly discovered that he had been insulted because Charles had called him a "seducer." And through Gehegan, he wrote demanding satisfaction.

Lang suggests that Alfieri, who was always his own best press agent, worked on the belief that a duel with an exiled king would be an excellent advertisement for a young and enterprising poet. This may be so. Certainly the challenge was no credit to the Italian, who was in the prime of life, whilst his intended opponent was nearly sixty and in poor health.

At any rate, they never met. Nor is there any record to show how the matter was settled, if it was settled at all. It seems likeliest that Charles ignored the challenge; and that Alfieri became somewhat less dignified as he meditated upon the glorious hours to come, when he would have that beautiful woman for his own without any worry about her husband, and so forgot the challenge.

Oddly enough, the public did not suspect Alfieri of anything but the most altruistic motives; although in Italy, in those days, it was common practice to deduce a love affair from every friendly smile, and to take it for granted that every wife was deceived and every husband a cuckold. Yet Alfieri seems to have escaped all the rumors customary in such cases. Charles Edward knew, whether from instinct or from some previously obtained information, where the greatest guilt lay; but nobody heeded what Charles Edward said.

Louise wrote to her brother-in-law, and gentle Henry replied promptly and graciously, promising Louise full protection and urging her to come to Rome. He had already given orders that the same suite of rooms Clementina Sobieski Stuart, James' wife, had occupied in the Ursuline convent in the Via Vittorio, should be prepared for the reception of Louise. Indeed, Henry treated Louise with marvelous kindness, now as previously, for

CHARLES EDWARD
(About the Time of his Marriage)

he had at all times a genuine affection for her. He did not, of course, suspect for a moment that there was a love affair behind this escapade: any such thought would have horrified him.

When Louise set out for Rome, her carriage was under heavy guard, for fear Charles would engage bravos to attack it and take back his wife by force. The common story has it that both Alfieri and Gehegan, disguised, rode at least part of the way with this guard; but there is no evidence to prove this, and Alfieri makes no mention of it.

Life in a fashionable convent such as that in the Via Vittorio was quiet and comfortable enough, but it must have been monotonous for the social-spirited Louise. Very soon she was begging Cardinal Stuart for permission to live outside the convent, somewhere in Rome; and he took up this matter with the Pope. The runaway wife was granted a pension by the French court, and Henry halved the allowance the Holy See made yearly to Charles—it all passed through Henry's hands—and saw that Louise got her share.

Charles protested in vain. It was characteristic of him that he made no attempt to get into direct communication with Louise, and did not try to win her back by an appeal to her sentimentality, her religion, or her sense of duty. Instead he tried to force her back by means purely legal; and in this he failed.

The red-haired poet, if he did ride with the carriage, returned promptly to Florence. There, for appearances' sake, he lingered for four weeks, which, he informs us, seemed like four years. Then he made a trip to Naples, and just happened to go by way of Rome and, while he was going through Rome, he just happened to stop at the convent to see his "Donna Amata." He learned at a glance that there could be no effective lovemaking *here:* they were obliged to converse through a grating! But there were happier days ahead. Louise finally got permission to live outside of the convent. Henry offered her full use of his beautiful early Renaissance town house, the Palazzo della Cancelleria, with the carriages and servants and everything that went with it. He rarely used the place himself, preferring to spend most of his hours at his Frascati palace. Alfieri, deliriously happy, bought fourteen horses, wrote four heavy tragedies, and rented out the Villa Strozzi on the Esquiline, at that time one of the quietest places in Rome.

They were having their own little golden age now, and true love was being satisfied at last. Louise prudently saw her lover only occasionally in public, for it would not do to have the Cardinal, whose hospitality she was accepting, know that such an affair was in progress. But they were often together in secret. They used to go riding over the rolling sward of the Campagna, and Alfieri was a frequent visitor at the palace.

Even so, people talked a bit. Charles was writing letters from Florence, demanding that his wife be returned to him, that his full allowance be sent him, and that Alfieri be banished from the Papal states. It was possible that somebody might begin to believe Charles, if this continued. So Alfieri unbent that stiff spine of his, and fairly wore his knees callous groveling before certain dignitaries, notably the unsuspecting and altogether kindly Cardinal Stuart. Louise wanted him to be particularly nice to Henry, for she was using Henry's palace, spending Henry's money, commanding Henry's servants, riding in Henry's carriages, and, what was most important, enjoying the enormous prestige Henry's protection and influence at the Vatican meant to her. "Love taught me cowardice and dissimulation," the poet wrote, afterwards; but one suspects that he had been possessed of an inherent talent for these ways. He bowed profoundly before the fat, good-natured Cardinal, and later wrote ugly and altogether false things about him. And Louise fluttered about Rome, entertained everywhere, having a wonderful time. She was in her element again, meeting so many interesting people and improving her mind. The surreptitious love affair simply lent spice to the dish.

Yet Charles continued to insist that Alfieri was the villain of the piece and himself the innocent victim. So the lovers decided that it might be well if Alfieri did a bit of groveling before the Pope too, since you never could tell what would happen. Alfieri had written unpleasant things about the Pope, but evidently His Holiness, Gian-Angelo Braschi of Cesena, hadn't happened to read them. So Alfieri stifled his republicanism, and kissed the Holy Father's feet, and was patted on the cheek. He presented the Pope with a specially bound copy of his tragedy *Saul.* He offered to dedicate one of his tragedies to him, but the Pope diplomatically declined, explaining that it would scarcely be politic to associate so directly the Vatican with the abhorred stage.

This audience had its effect. The Pope thought Alfieri a charming young fellow, and so, of course, did the proud, blandly smiling Cardinal Henry, who would agree with anything His Holiness or Louise said. And so everybody was happy.

Everybody, that is, except the wreck in Florence—the "man of iron" who wouldn't die. Charles, alone, moped mournfully. He rarely walked now. He did not even have the heart to do much heavy drinking. Out-of-doors he keenly felt the humiliation of his position; and even inside, he probably suspected the servants of snickering at him behind his back. He had two non-liquid consolations—his music and the occasional noblemen who visited him. We are left a picture of him sitting at night in the middle of a great square room, two candles casting a dubious light around him, two loaded pistols on the table in front of him, while he played, hour after hour, on his violincello. Sometimes a music master was there to accompany him on the harpsichord, and together they would improvise melodies and go over old favorites. But Charles could never hear "Lochaber No More" without tears, for that was the old Jacobite song so many of his brave clansmen had sung on the scaffold.

His other diversion was intermittent. He could not, from the nature of his position, receive every visitor to Florence. Nor could every visitor, noble or otherwise, venture to visit a man the British government called an enemy. But curiosity brought some, and Charles played the host to these with some warming-up of his ancient charm.

The most distinguished visitor he had was King Gustavus III of Sweden, who was making the Grand Tour. They were cousins of some sort: Charles was a cousin to almost every sovereign in Europe. Charles begged the Swedish monarch for a considerable loan, or a pension, explaining that he was poverty-stricken. His allowance from the Holy See was cut in half, and he was obliged to pay the so-called "pin money" to his wife, a large sum stipulated in the marriage contract. Lord Elcho, now Lord Wemyss, was vainly dunning for that £1,500 he had lent Charles during the 'Forty-five.

Gustavus took pity on him, went to Rome, saw Louise, and saw the Pope too, and finally succeeded in arranging for the wife a formal separation. Louise was eager to be free, and she agreed to give up her "pin money" and her share of the Pope's pension. That relieved the financial strain, at least, for Charles. Louise was still getting money from Henry and from Versailles.

In March of 1784, Charles was taken seriously ill. They thought he was going to die; Charles thought so too, and wrote his will. Now he had forgotten, apparently, his natural daughter by Clementina Walkinshaw, until his wife had left him alone in the Casa Stuart and the need for some feminine company became increasingly evident. He remembered her on what he believed to be his deathbed. He left her all his jewels, his house, all his property. Another official (for him) document made his daughter legitimate, this being a prerogative of great kings like Charles the Third; and still another created her Duchess of Albany.

Meanwhile, Henry had been notified of the serious illness, and had come quickly to Florence. By the time he arrived, Charles was up and hobbling around again, grumbling, muttering.

Henry stayed several days. They discussed at great length the subject of Louise and her lover. What information Charles possessed to damn these two, is not known and probably never will be known. But he must have had definite proofs against them, for he convinced the gentle Henry of their guilt.

Imagine Henry then! He quivered with horror and indignation. A love affair in his palace! Tapestries that were his, screening the embraces of adulterers! His home a rendezvous, an assignation place! He went choking, sputtering, back to Rome, where, never discreet, he told everybody he met about the affair, so that it soon was all over the city. It is doubtful whether any other person was quite as shocked as Henry, who had loved Louise and trusted Alfieri, and who had sided with them against his own brother whom he now perceived to have been cruelly wronged. Henry, waving his white, pudgy, beautifully kept hands, went to see the Pope about it. And Louise doubtless summoned her lover to hasty conference.

Alfieri states explicitly in his *Vita* that he was not banished from the Eternal City, but that, hearing these false and malicious reports—which he pretends to attribute wholly to the malevolence of Charles—he voluntarily appeared before the Pope and informed His Holiness of his intention to go atraveling again. Historians refuse to believe that, and almost uniformly assert that Alfieri was banished. It doesn't much matter. Louise kept her handsome city residence, but she lost her red-haired lover and lost also the confidence of Henry, Cardinal.

She bore these losses with fortitude, remaining in Rome, living more quietly now. But Alfieri, of course, went wild. He wandered back and forth across Europe a few more times, meditating suicide, writing letters to his "Donna Amata" and receiving letters from her, buying horses by the dozen, breaking them in, grooming them himself. This lasted for about eighteen months, when, her separation arranged, Louise, no longer obliged to remain within the Papal domain, went to Colmar and sent for her lover. He dashed across Europe, riding horses almost to death, writing sonnets by the dozens in his exuberance; and after the joyful reunion, with a few necessary interruptions, they lived openly together as mistress and lover, later removing to Paris.

Somehow, Charles lived on. He was now meditating a plan to summon his natural daughter to him: the Casa Stuart needed a woman, and Charles was lonesome. He got into communication with her, and she, of course, was delighted. Her father was her one hope in life; her mother, almost penniless, could do nothing for her, and unless Charles recognized her and provided for her, she had no place in society at all. She, too, was lonesome—a healthy woman of thirty cooped up all her life in a convent but always hearing whispered tales of the magnificence of court life. She agreed readily to go to Florence—the more readily, no doubt, because Charles promised to make her his heiress; indeed, he had already done so, although he apparently had not, up until this time, notified her of that interesting fact. He had legitimated her, and created her Duchess of Albany, a title he was very anxious to have the high world recognize. Henry was annoyed, but Charles went ahead with the business, making elaborate preparations for her reception.

She came in July of 1785. She was a handsome young woman, tall, well-built, coarse-skinned, and rather masculine, but the soul of sweetness and tact. There were no airs about her. She was glad to be mistress of the Casa Stuart, and she did nothing that was not calculated to win the affection of her father. Charles, indeed, was delighted with her. She brought him out of the dank, dreary valley of despondency, gave him a comfortable seat in the sun, and danced attendance upon him in a most flattering fashion. Poor King Charles the Third! It had been many a long year since anybody had flattered him.

He was not, in this case, ungrateful. He loaded her with gifts, bestowed the Order of the Garter upon her, bought her beautiful gowns, entertained lavishly in her honor, and beamed proudly when they went out together for rides. It delighted him to see how popular she was with the stiff Florentine aristocrats —although it annoyed him to observe that no one of any importance recognized her title, most of the guests calling her simply "Lady Charlotte."

And so there comes, belatedly, this happy note in Charles' life. These two were mutually pleased with one another. He took her everywhere, to banquets, State balls, dances, card parties; and she, for the first time in her life, began to have a good time. She did not neglect her duties, either. As quietly and as tactfully as she could, she tried to keep him away from the bottle. She seems never to have nagged, never to have lost her temper, but merely to have tried to wean him away from liquor by interesting him in other things. She started a correspondence with Cardinal Henry, and soon she had won him over to her side. He realized that she was cheering the last months of his brother's life, and keeping Charles comparatively sober. And although he did not formally recognize her title as Duchess of Albany, he did warm considerably. And when Charles and Charlotte, on their way to the baths at Pisa, fortuitously encountered the Cardinal at Perugia, she clinched the matter: Henry could not resist her, and from that time on he was her best friend.

Not only in Florence did they love this tall, dark lady, but all over Europe where men and women still remembered Bonnie Prince Charlie with a sigh. At last he was happy! At last he was safe in the hands of a good woman who would care for him, nurse him, guard him against drunkenness, be kind to him, and cheer his last days. Thousands of persons who would not dare to mention the subject in public, privately toasted the Duchess of Albany and prayed to God to be good to her and keep her alive and happy. A good-looking young man in Edinburgh, in a sober hour, wrote a poem to her: and although Charlotte probably never even heard of Bobbie Burns, she is known to this generation chiefly as the subject of "The Bonnie Lass of Albany."

On St. Andrew's Day, Charles staged a sumptuous State dinner in her honor, and before a large company formally invested her with the Order of St. Andrew.

But he could no longer keep up the social pace with a young and healthy woman. He was ailing. A Mr. Greathead, an Englishman who visited Charles, foolishly induced the Stuart to relate again the whole story of the 'Forty-five. Charles' eyes, glazed for many a month, were lit with youthful fire when he described the charge at Prestonpans, the behavior of the right wing at Falkirk, the bullet-spattered water through which they escaped to the mainland with Flora Macdonald. . . . But when he began to tell of the butchery that followed Culloden, the hangings, the exiles, the attainders, it was too much for him, and he slipped off his chair and fell to the floor in a fit.

Charlotte came hurrying in. She understood, at a glance. "You must never talk to him about the Highlanders," she told Mr. Greathead. "He cannot bear to talk about them."

Henry was urging him to return to Rome. At first Charles' physicians would not permit this move, but they finally consented on the proviso that the carriage travel only about twenty miles a day. Charles gave up his plan to strike a medal in honor of Charlotte and, late in 1785, they went carefully to the Eternal City. Here, through the good offices of Henry, they were well received. Henry was prepared to call Charlotte, Duchess, now, and even got the Pope to do the same. It was the greatest concession the Holy See had made to the family for many years.

Charles struggled along somehow. He required constant nursing now, and he was always in pain. But he did not drink much: Charlotte's work was having its effect.

One day a distinguished Frenchman, whose name was not given, requested and was granted an audience. Now this was the Comte de Vaudreuil, son of that officer of the Household Troops who had arrested Charles at the opera house in Paris many years earlier. Moreover, the Count looked exactly like his father. Charles, who had not been given his name, or had not heard it, sprang to his feet when the count entered the room: his eyes grew big with amazement and horror as the memory of that humiliating night came crashing back into his brain: and before he could utter a word to the bowing Vaudreuil, he dropped in a faint upon the floor. The Frenchman was hustled outside, and Charlotte again took care of the invalid.

In the Spring of 1786 he suffered a serious relapse. To hasten his recovery he went to the baths at Albano. But the end was near at hand. It was seldom that he could be taken outside the gloomy old palace. And early in January of 1788 he suffered a paralytic stroke which deprived him of the use of half his body. He was now altogether helpless. Between 9 and 10 o'clock on the morning of January 31st, 1788, he died in his daughter's arms.

Henry went to the Pope and requested permission for a

royal funeral. This was denied. And yet a Stuart could not be buried without the proper pomp. King Charles the Third could not be dragged away to his grave like any commoner. Henry caused the body to be transported to Frascati, his own see, where his word was the law. And here they buried Charles as became a man of his blood. They clothed him in purple and ermine, put a scepter in his hand, a sword at his side, orders and medals on his breast. They placed him in a coffin of cypress wood, and this they put into a leaden outer coffin. The whole was placed on a huge catafalque in the nave of the Frascati cathedral. A heavy purple pall with the royal arms embroidered on it in many places was draped over it. The church was filled with enormous waxen tapers which were kept lighted all the time, and was hung with gold lace and black cloth into which had been woven a profusion of gold and silver tissue. On either side of the coffin stood three gentlemen of the household: they were in mourning cloaks, and each carried a banner. Thus the body lay in state.

At 10 o'clock in the morning of the funeral day, Cardinal Stuart was brought to the cathedral in a black-draped sedan chair; he was attended by his entire ecclesiastical suite, the most numerous in the Church at that time. He seated himself in the Cardinal's throne on the right of the altar and, with the choir joining in now and then, sang the funeral office for his brother. There were tears in his eyes, and his voice was not steady. For although Henry was effeminate, compared with Charles, he was of the same blood, and he was singing the swan song of that noble line.

They buried Charles at Frascati, but the body was later disinterred and taken to the crypt at St. Peter's, where it rested beside the body of James.

He left annuities to all those faithful servants who had so often supported his drunken frame. He left his private secretary 100 ducats, and Henry 2,000 ounces of silver. Everything else, including all the Stuart and Sobieski jewels which Charles had possessed, went to Charlotte.

Anatomically, then, he was dead. Actually we can hardly

consider him dead at all. He lives still, and will always live, so long as there are men and women who believe that courage and high spirit and a heart for adventure are sometimes to be preferred to the safety of common sense.

The male line of the Stuarts was extinct, yet Jacobitism struggled on, degenerating into a sort of polite, parlor patriotism. There were even men and women in England who refused to call Victoria 'Queen'; but they were little better than cranks and poseurs. There were men and women, too, who believed an astonishing story told by the brothers Allen, who said they were the grandchildren of Charles Edward Stuart. They called themselves Sobieski-Stuart, and fluttered around in good company. They were a handsome, talented pair of young men, and they got a lot of fun out of life. They wrote a book called "The Tales of a Century," in which they set forth their claims under the guise of fiction. Louise, they said, had borne a child, a boy, shortly after she had quit Rome and before she and Charles had taken up their residence in Florence. This was at Leghorn. Fearing that the agents of King George would attempt to kill the baby, the parents turned it over to Admiral Allen (who, incidentally, was a Whig) and he carried it back on his flagship to England, where he brought it up as his own son. This young man they called the Red Eagle. That was a nice touch; indeed, the whole story is a pretty one, the sort of thing many persons wanted to believe—but couldn't. The Red Eagle served with distinction in the British navy, married an English woman whom he had rescued from smugglers, and had two children—the eccentric Brothers Allen.

This preposterous tale won many believers. But the brothers never did anything about it, except write their book and address one another as "Your Royal Highness." Possibly they never believed it themselves. Perhaps they perpetrated it as a practical joke. Anyway, there can be no doubt that it was false from beginning to end.

This was the sturdiest of many such yarns. People simply would not permit Charles Edward Stuart to die. In the Highlands they confidently looked forward to his second coming, with or without an army at his back. They still thought of him as a handsome young man, who never grew up, and who would appear in all the glory of his beautiful smile and send the fiery cross over the hills to summon out the clans. He was a sort of myth, an eternal boy, who was going to come back some day and deliver Scotland from her bondage and restore the Highlands to their pristine glory. Old mountaineers told their sons and daughters about Bonnie Prince Charlie, and they could not tell the tale without tears; and the sons and daughters believed. It would not amaze me to learn that there are still peasants in Lochaber who believe that the Prince will come back one day. Hadn't he promised to do so? As for getting old and dying, how could Bonnie Prince Charlie get old? The idea is unthinkable!

But even those men who knew him in his later years as we know him now—even those men loved him. Charles was one of the best beloved men who ever lived. Ingratitude, rashness, apostasy, selfishness, arrogance, ambition, drunkenness, brutality, and all the rest of it . . . yet nobody who ever met him was able to hate him; and posterity, understanding that he was always a boy, let the good live after him and interred with his bones the evil he had done. He is thought of, not as the red-faced, watery-eyed, selfish drunkard of Rome and Florence, but as the lad who led a handful of fighters through unbelievable hardships, and who grinned while the bullets were whistling, and sang a little song. . . . We may forget the rest. *That* Charles cannot die!

He will always live. Tourists still gaze at his exquisite cenotaph in Rome. In Scotland men still point out Charles' caves (there are as many of them as there are chests of drawers carried on the *Mayflower* to New England: a visitor gets the impression that Charles lived all his life in caves, a different one every night); and locks of his hair, and cups he drank from, and beds in which he slept—these are passed down lovingly from generation to generation. Near where he landed, in Eriska, there grows a fleshy-leaved convulvulus, which he planted and which will grow forever and always bloom because of this: nor will this flower grow in any other part of Britain.

But at Glenfinnan stands the most suitable memorial. It is situated somewhere near the place where the Stuart standard was unfurled on that day of grand hopes; and it was erected by Alexander Macdonald of Glenaladale, direct descendant of the Glenaladale who fought with Charles, and the last of his name.

The Prince, in stone, stands atop a tall, smudgy column, hand on claymore hilt, and gazes fixedly across the rocky hills. At the foot of the column are two plates, one with a Latin inscription, the other with the same inscription in English—a language Charles himself never could write properly. The plates are rusty, and already the lettering is barely readable. At the bottom on each side is a tiny ornamental knight: all four knights are rusty and headless. Probably these heads, discouraged by the weather, fell off. It is not likely that anyone would wade across such a bog for the purpose of collecting souvenirs, for there is a bog now where once was a mound. The spot has all the bleak grandeur of the Scottish Highlands. It is beautiful, but infinitely lonely. Loch Sheil, smooth as glass and blue as a baby's eyes, glitters with stony coldness, and the River Finnan leaps away over unresponsive stones toward the sea. The hills roll down like the chest muscles of a giant; the clouds hang low; the Ben Bhreac, lifting a huge white half-pineapple, sullenly blocks the west.

Glenfinnan is little changed. It is much the same place today that it was when the old Marquis of Tullibardine, supported by two servants, read the proclamation which announced to the whole world that His Majesty James the Third of England and Eighth of Scotland, King, Defender of the Faith, etc., had appointed his older son, the Prince of Wales, to be Prince Regent of Scotland, England and Ireland; and the banner was unfurled while the clansmen, shouting Gaelic war-cries, flourished their swords and tossed blue bonnets into the air. It is very nearly the same place it was when Charles Edward, not stone but flesh and spirit, stood, hand on claymore hilt, and smiled with pride at the sight of these gallant Camerons and at the prospect of a gilt-and-red-velvet throne.

Up the hill, beyond the old Glenaladale estate (now owned by a Mr. Scott), there is a tiny railway station, a tiny store, a few tiny homes, and also a tiny inn. In front of the stone Prince, a mile or so away, a rather pretty little trestle escorts a couple of steel rails across a dangerous drop: there are two trains a day. Nearer are a few tiny telephone poles and, if you look closely, you can discern a few tiny wires strung between them. Otherwise, Glenfinnan is much the same. The loose crags hang precariously on the hillsides, as though posed to charge down at any moment. The flawless lake glitters like unmeltable ice. The clouds slink scowling past.

And Charles stands there and gazes across a country that he never conquered. He gazes toward the sea.

It is a cold place to stand, but Charles could endure the cold. He could endure hardship and starvation. He could grin at peril, singing a little song. . . . What he could not endure was defeat. He should have fallen at Culloden!

And yet defeat made him. One pictures Charles as he would have been had he somehow succeeded in placing his father on the throne. One pictures a sensational but altogether orthodox Prince of Wales—drinking, quarreling, entertaining assorted mistresses, scheming now with this group and now with that, meddling with matters that were none of his concern. . . .

Defeat was his forte. In victory, as all the world knows, there is glory. But there is also responsibility and all the disguised dangers of good fortune.

But in defeat there is poetry. Charles' name is not spoken as with a roll of drums. One does not pronounce it with awe, as one pronounces the names of Marlborough, Cromwell, Napoleon. His little revolution is almost forgotten. But his smile will always remain. It beams on through the years, that smile, like a material thing that father passes to son, a light that will never fail. He was not a conquering hero, but he was a poem, which may (it is barely possible) be a more desirable fate. He was not a king, as that word is defined by politicians, historians, and the men who make dictionaries. But he rules supreme in the realm of romance. Though he did not win, he fought well: he did his best, that nobody can deny. Even yet, indeed, he has not given up. He still gazes out toward the sea in the hope of seeing those French ships come at last with the money and the men that were promised him. He still keeps his hand on his claymore hilt; and when an occasional sportsman comes down the road to shoot clay pigeons across the bog, and the sniff of gunpowder ascends around the bleak column, those stone nostrils must twitch a bit and those stone feet shuffle with impatience for battle.

No, he was not a great general, and he would have made a very bad king. But he was and always will be a fighter; and he makes a good poem—a poem of stone, the sort that doesn't wear out.

APPENDIX

It hardly seemed fair, after introducing so many characters and telling a little about each, to drop them just because they did not, in after life, enter into any important relationship with our subject. The story of a man like Charles Edward Stuart reads so much like a novel that you are naturally curious to know, at the end, what happened to the subordinate parties. Did they marry? Were they ever again involved in adventure? Did their deaths come in the course of nature or by violence?

We have already seen the aged Marquis of Tullibardine dying in the Tower; and Kilmarnock, in spite of the tears of his wife, going to the gallows along with Balmerino, Derwentwater, and many another brave gentleman. Donald of Lochiel was given a lieutenant-colonelcy in the French army: he died, an exile, in 1762. Alexander Lord Forbes of Pitsligo, like Lochiel, accepted a French army commission, and he, too, died in Paris in the same year. The Duke of Perth, never strong, was unable to endure the hardships and privations of his escape: he did escape, obtaining passage to France, but died on shipboard, May 13, 1746. Sir Thomas Sheridan, when he returned to Rome, received from James such a severe reprimand for having permitted Prince Charles to embark on the foolhardy enterprise, that, in semi-disgrace, he died soon afterwards. It has been said that Sheridan died of grief because of the ire of his master; but it is difficult to believe that James, who was so quiet and gentle, could bring anyone to death by harsh words.

And there are others:

SIR JOHN COPE

This unfortunate soldier was hooted into retirement after Prestonpans. He was a typical English general of the period—one of that class to which America owes its independence. He might have won all sorts of honors if he hadn't become involved in a real war.

Back in London, he was brought before a court martial. He was accused of disobeying orders by turning aside at Corryarrack (one wonders what he would have been accused of if he had gone ahead there!), of disheartening his troops at Prestonpans by shifting them from one defensive position to another and giving them the impression that he dreaded the coming attack, and finally of not rallying his men after the battle. The court martial acquitted him. But in the eyes of the populace he was branded as both a fool and a coward, and they made life miserable for him; when he went out in his chair he was obliged to keep the curtains pulled together or else be accompanied by a jeering and often stone-throwing crowd.

They say that when the news of the battle of Falkirk reached London, only two men were undismayed—King George and Sir John Cope. Cope not only was not dismayed, but, unpatriotically, although quite naturally, he was pleased. He had been hearing about the wonderful things Hawley, a *real* general sir! would do to the miserable rebels, and he had himself insisted that Hawley, real general or not, was going to take a beating. The boasters offered to bet, and Cope scraped together every penny he could lay hands on, and got big odds as the day of the battle approached. The result was that Cope's winnings made him independently wealthy. He retired from the army and lived quietly in the country after that.

LORD GEORGE MURRAY

He escaped to the Continent, like so many others. And like so many others, he died in exile. He was not given a commission in the French service, as were Lochiel and Maxwell of Kirkconnell and others. For he still lacked the confidence of his Prince. Charles was wont to attribute his defeat to what he was pleased to consider the treachery of this the bravest soldier under his command, this model of faithfulness and loyalty. Years did not make Charles more reasonable in this respect: instead, his hatred of Lord George Murray seemed to increase.

Lord George drifted here and there, almost penniless, while his wife, of necessity, remained in Scotland and cared for the children. He went once to the big gloomy palace in Rome. The royal exile, a much better judge of character than his hot-headed son, liked Lord George and trusted him; after this visit they corresponded occasionally, and they mutually respected one another.

About a year after Culloden, Lord George was passing through Paris and, learning that Charles was in the city, he purposed to wait upon him and pay his respects. But a messenger called upon the general with the information that his royal highness "desired that I should not come near him, for that he would not see me, and that I would do well to leave Paris as soon as I could."

How that must have hurt! But Lord George bore it quietly, as he bore all his misfortunes. On the field of battle, or in the camp, stupidity infuriated him: he had a sea captain's passion for efficiency, the right thing in the right place at the right time. But personal relationships were another matter. He was a military man, and on military matters he was ready and eager to give his emphatic opinion and to cling to that opinion regardless of the exalted rank of him who opposed it. But it must have hurt him extremely to have his prince carry prejudices off the field, and to be in peace even more obstinate and even more unjustly suspicious than he was in war.

Lord George wrote to James in Rome about this incident, reporting it exactly and neither sputtering with indignation, nor begging for pity. James answered sadly and with characteristic good sense. James and Lord George seem to have understood one another. Both were exiles, both had been grievously wronged, both were doomed to a slow, sad, lonesome life, and both watched their beloved Charles making himself a butt of ridicule all over Europe. Nor did either the king or the general have a means of striking back at insulters, without descending into pettiness.

Lord George eventually got a little farm in Holland, and here he lived quietly. He could have lived no other way, for the government was relentless in its search. Lord George used the alias of De Valignie, and was very careful about his letters to his wife. He wrote once asking for "bed & table linnings, with a dozen spoons, forks, & knives, some old china, and as much bedding as serves two rooms, & a few choise books." A simple existence.

In the fall of 1747 his infant daughter, born a few days before the battle of Falkirk, died. The next month a favorite nephew followed her.

Occasionally his wife was able to visit him. After one of these visits she went to Scotland heavy with a seventh child. Lord George was fifty-seven years old at the time.

He was not allowed to see his oldest son, John, who in time succeeded to the title of Duke of Athole. The second son, like the oldest, had taken military service with the Hanoverian. That, too, must have hurt their father.

His loyalty would not die. He loved King James, and pitied and admired him from the bottom of his heart. He was ready to polish the claymore, shoulder the target, and give battle for the White Rose whenever the call came again. He wrote to one friend, "How happy would you and I be to sit over a bottle in Angus or Perthshire after a Restoration, and talk over old services. May that soon happen!"

But the Jacobites were never called out again, and the old gentleman in Holland died at last, as old gentlemen will, however brave and vigorous, and was buried in Medemblick, the town where he died. This was on October 11, 1760, fourteen years after Black Culloden Day.

NEAL MacEACHAIN

Gentle Neal MacEachain went to France with Charles and there enlisted in Lord Ogilvy's regiment of French Scots. This regiment was disbanded in 1763, and Neal retired to Sancerre, where he married a penniless girl with a sharp tongue, and tried to live with her on his small pension. But they were ill-mated: when he wanted to play the violin, or read Greek, or browse among the Latin poets, she wanted to talk, talk, talk. Moreover, she had a quick temper. They had four children, and separated. One daughter and one son lived on: the others died in infancy. The son became the celebrated Marshal Macdonald, Duke of Tarentua, who fought gallantly in the Napoleonic wars. Neal MacEachain never saw his native land again. He died in 1788.

FLORA MacDONALD

We left this heroine on the shore watching Charles' boat carry him toward the wild but hospitable island of Raasey. That scene fascinated Scottish bards, and reams of poetry and near-poetry have been written about it. It would have been almost the perfection of romance, had it not been for the fact that a heavy rain was falling.

When she quit that shore, it was to return to her mother's home at Armadale in Sleat, where she displayed the most extraordinary tact in not mentioning to any one the fact that she had assisted the young Prince. The fault wasn't hers that the secret got out. Somebody else—the traitor has been blessed with anonymity—whispered it into the ear of the notorious Captain Ferguson; and within a few days after the brave girl had returned, Ferguson, with a large company of redcoats, came knocking at Macdonald of Kingsburgh's door.

Ferguson demanded to know in what rooms Miss Macdonald and her "servant" had slept, several nights previous. Kingsburgh replied that he would be glad to show the captain the room in which Miss Macdonald had slept, but as to the servant, he said, he had asked no questions. Ferguson sneered, and addressed himself to Lady Kingsburgh:

"Did you put the wench in bed with the Young Pretender?"

He was shown the two rooms, and observed that the one in which Miss Macdonald had slept was not nearly so good as the one in which her maid had slept. It was obvious that he knew the identity of the "servant" and had come simply to trick them into confessions. They had no time to warn Flora Macdonald, who was arrested later that day and taken prisoner on the sloop-of-war *Furnace*. She was hurried off without being granted time to say farewell to her parents or even to change her clothes.

Three weeks later, when the *Furnace* was cruising near her mother's home, she was permitted to go ashore for clothes and an interview with her parents. A guard of redcoats was sent with her, and she was admonished not to talk to her parents except in the company of these men, and not, under any circumstances, to talk in Gaelic.

Soon afterwards she was transferred to the *Eltham*, and later to the *Bridgewater*, both vessels of war. She was on one or the other of these craft for five months, and was well treated by Captain Smith of the *Eltham* and Captain Knowles of the *Bridgewater*. In Leith Roads, where she spent almost three months of this time, the Jacobites came aboard in great numbers to shower her with praise and presents. These visitors were mostly women. Their adulation might have turned a less sensible girl's head, but Flora Macdonald was uniformly grave and polite; she saw nothing extraordinary about the affair, she said; it had been what any honest woman would do under the circumstances.

She was not permitted to go ashore, but was allowed to entertain any friends she wished, and was generally treated with courtesy and thoughtfulness. The orders were, in effect: "Anybody may come to see her provided she herself is willing to receive; but there shall be no vulgarly curious persons who would only annoy her." She had a sweet, clear voice, and she used to play and sing for the visitors in the cabin. But she refused to dance while her "poor Prince" was still in danger.

On November 7, 1746, the *Bridgewater* sailed for London, and there Flora Macdonald was kept a prisoner eight months in a private house, in charge of a messenger, one William Dick. Again, she was permitted visitors, and was well treated. Much of the good treatment she received here should be credited to the boisterous Prince of Wales, Frederick, the King's wayward son. He called on her, out of curiosity, and asked her how she had come to do a thing so contrary to the commands of her sovereign and so inimical to the interests of her country; to which she replied that she had only obeyed the dictates of ordinary humanity, and that "if it was you or any member of your family who had come to me in that distress, I would have done the same thing."

Frederick was so pleased with this answer that he exerted himself in every way possible to make her confinement more comfortable. It may be, too, that he was pleased with her beauty, for Frederick had a fatal fondness for women.

However, the story that she was freed, finally, because of Frederick's intercession, is not true. She was freed under the Act of Indemnity, passed in July, 1747.

The Dowager Lady Primrose (the lady who, three years later, was to entertain Prince Charles himself on the occasion of his first visit to London) took in Flora Macdonald, who for the rest of the time she stayed in London was the lion, or lioness, of the season. The Jacobites could not do her enough honor. The house in Dunnipace, Essex-street-in-the-Strand, day and night was fronted with the carriages of exalted persons who had come for a look at the "Pretender's Deliverer." They showered praise and gifts upon her, as the ladies of Edinburgh had done; and, as previously, she was modest and grave. For a girl who had never before been far from her wilderness home in Sleat, she was remarkably easy of presence: indeed, she was in every way a social success. The Jacobites raised a purse of almost £1,500 for her, when finally she left London. They also presented her with a carriage and a pair of horses. Malcolm Macleod, released from prison about the same time, rode back to Scotland with her.

On November 6, 1750, about three months after her return, she was married to Alexander Macdonald, the Younger, of Kingsburgh, oldest son of that gentleman who had helped her save the Prince. They had five sons, all of whom later won commissions in the army or navy, and two daughters. Dr. Johnson and Boswell visited them in the fall of 1773 and were impressed by both husband and wife. Dr. Johnson slept that night in the same bed which once had harbored Bonnie Prince Charlie. "I got no ambitions from it," he told Boswell the next morning. He described Flora Macdonald as "a woman of middle stature, soft features, gentle manners and elegant presence." Boswell mentions her as being "a little woman of genteel appearance, and uncommonly mild and well-bred."

Shortly after this visit, Kingsburgh's financial affairs becoming entangled, he tried his luck in the New World, going with his wife to an estate they had purchased in North Carolina. The American Revolution found Kingsburgh faithful to George the Third, and he was thrown in jail as a Tory. Later he was released, and joined a Tory regiment, the North Carolina Volunteers. Still later, he and his family returned to Scotland. The war was still in progress, and their ship was attacked by a French man-o'-war. The women were ordered below, but Flora Macdonald insisted upon staying on deck and encouraging the gunners. She is credited with so inspiring them that they drove off the Frenchmen, but this is undoubtedly pleasant fiction. At any rate, the English boat escaped, and the Kingsburghs returned to their native heath—though Flora, in the height of the battle, had been thrown to the deck and had suffered a broken arm. She was then well past middle age.

She lived to be seventy years old, a staunch Jacobite to the end. Nobody ever was permitted to call Prince Charles a "pretender" in her presence. She died March 4, 1790, and was buried wrapped in one of the sheets the Prince had slept in that memorable night, her mother-in-law, Lady Kingsburgh, having been buried in the other sheet.

MURRAY OF BROUGHTON

This plotter, it will be remembered, had betrayed his trust, turning over to the government, presumably in return for gold and a promise of immunity, all the confidential letters by means of which many a better man was sent to the gallows.

Such treachery produced its own punishment. John Murray of Broughton got what he deserved—the complete, frozen contempt of noble and vulgar, Tory and Whig, alike, both in Scotland and England. He was not hissed and booed. He simply was ignored. He was never mobbed; but probably before many months had passed he was wishing that he might have been, for the looks he saw in men's faces were more terrible, and inflicted wounds more painful, than all the brickbats and clubs in the world.

When they had brought him up to identify the men he had betrayed, his head was hung.

"Do you know this man?" they asked Sir John Douglas, in Privy Council.

"Not I," the knight snapped. "I once knew a man named Murray of Broughton, but he was a gentleman and a man of honor."

Murray frittered out a quiet, obscure life, mostly in Scotland. He showed his face in public as seldom as possible, but met with no violence except the violence of contempt. Broughton he sold; and his wife, a large and handsome Amazon, left him. He must have been something like happy when he felt death coming. Nobody wept when he was gone.

There is a story told by Lockhart in "The Life of Sir Walter Scott," which perfectly illustrates the general feeling toward this Judas.

Scott's father was a staunch Whig, a sensible, unromantic man, a writer to the signet, and a barrister, in Edinburgh. Every night, for almost a week, a sedan chair was stopped in front of his home, and a tall, well muffled man was ushered into his private office—a room open only to the master of the house and to his business associates and clients. When Mrs. Scott questioned her husband about this visitor, the answers were vague. Her curiosity increased: until she could stand it no longer. So one night, when she heard him ring for his sedan chair at the end of a conference with the barrister, she put two cups of tea on a tray and boldly ventured into the sanctum sanctorum.

"It's a chilly night. Wouldn't you gentlemen like a wee nip of tea?—particularly you, sir, because you're going out now."

The stranger bowed, thanked Mrs. Scott, and accepted the tea. But Scott coldly refused the cup his wife had prepared for him. The stranger left. And the barrister, as soon as the sedan chair was out of sight, snatched the empty cup from the table, opened a window, and threw it out.

He snapped, "I may admit to my house on a piece of business, persons wholly unworthy to be treated as guests by my wife. But neither lip of me nor of mine comes after John Murray of Broughton's!"

Scott had been arranging for the sale of the traitor's estate. Years afterwards, the Bard of the North used to keep the saucer which had belonged to this cup, hanging above a large framed picture of Prince Charles in the famous study at Abbotsford.

THE DUKE OF CUMBERLAND

William, Duke of Cumberland, Baron of Alderney, Viscount Trematon in Cornwall, Earl of Kennington in Surrey, Marquis of Berkhamsted, etc., was from the beginning his father's favorite. The reader will recall that the Hanoverian kings since George the First have, almost as though by family tradition, quarreled with their eldest sons. George the Second was no exception, and his quarrel with the Prince of Wales was one of the most spectacular in English history. But for his second son, the King always had a deep affection.

What William wanted he got, if it was possible for the King to get it for him. But William did not want fame. He was not ambitious, nor was he interested in politics. His desire was for a great military career.

However, he was a poor soldier. His conduct at Fonteroy has already been described. So has his conduct at Culloden, and afterwards. To be sure, he won the battle of Culloden; but any other leader could have done so quite as easily. No soldier, whatever his talent for doing the wrong military thing, could have lost that battle.

Nevertheless, the people of London made a great to-do about him when he returned after Culloden. You would have thought he had achieved a brilliant victory against overwhelming odds. There were salvos of artillery, regimental salutes, bonfires, ringing of church bells, and shouts by the excited populace. The people had been given a good scare when Charles had reached Derby, and—overlooking the fact that Charles never would have reached that town, nor would ever have returned therefrom, if Cumberland had known his business—they hailed him as their country's deliverer.

His official allowance was raised from £15,000 to £40,000 a year, and he was made ranger of Windsor Great Park, a chancellor of St. Andrew's University, and otherwise loaded with honors.

Gradually the English people began to learn the truth of the matter—that Culloden was won before the first shot was fired, and that what Cumberland had called "a little blood-letting" was in fact a series of the most horrible and brutal massacres ever perpetrated upon a defenseless race. They realized that, although strict measures had perhaps been necessary, cold-blooded butchery of innocent mountaineers was not necessary at all. So they swung from adulation to vituperation. They dubbed the duke "Billy the Butcher," and the opprobrious epithet stuck. Whig and Tory, they hated him.

To all this Cumberland was indifferent. Provided he was given an army to command, and a sufficient supply of harlots to entertain him when there was no war, he was happy. His disposition did not soften. Horace Walpole wrote on July 20, 1749, to George Montague: "His savage temper increases every day . . . he loves blood like a leech."

Perhaps the popular feeling against Cumberland would not have been so strong had he really been as good a general as the official panegyrists insisted. But, in spite of his rigid discipline, his studies of maneuvers and his close observation of everything about an army from the smallest pistol grip to the biggest cannon, he was always an unsuccessful leader of troops.

His military career was ended by the 1757 fiasco. In that year Hanover was threatened by a French army, and George the Second was panicky. Cumberland begged his father for the command of the allied armies, and got it. Hurrying to the scene, he placed himself at the head of some 50,000 men, and met the French at Hastenbeck. In spite of a stupidly directed battle, the allies were getting the better of it and the French commander, d'Estrées, was about to quit the field, when Cumberland unexpectedly ordered a retreat! Nobody has ever been able to learn why he did this. It could not have been lack of courage because, for all his faults, Cumberland had plenty of that. It could not have been to prevent unnecessary slaughter, because Cumberland never considered how many lives his policies cost. It must have been sheer stupidity.

D'Estrées, amazed and delighted, again took the field. His staff officers urged him to pursue the retreating duke and crush him; but the French commander shook his head.

"Why should I do that when he's sure to lose his own cause by bad generalship?"

Cumberland moved about until he had worked himself, without a skirmish, into an impossible position and there was nothing left for him to do but surrender. Moreover, the terms of the peace, made at the Convention of Closter-Seven, were peculiarly ignominious for England. Jesse asserts (though without giving his authority) that Cumberland had instructions for everything he did at this parley, his royal father being willing to make concessions because of the fear that the French might decide to retake Verdun and Bremen. If this was true, George never made the fact public, nor did Cumberland. The English public now hated Cumberland more violently than ever. He was coldly received, too, when he returned to St. James. Disgusted, he gave up his various titles and retired to private life, devoting himself, thereafter, to hunting in Windsor Great Park and to the pursuit of women.

But if his cruelty was notorious, at least he was able to bear pain. It was necessary, one night, to perform an operation on his right knee. Ranby, the celebrated surgeon, warned His Highness that it would be a very painful operation. But Cumberland refused to be bound. (It was usual to bind patients for surgical operations in those days, because, without narcotics—which were not in use then—even the strongest were likely to squirm in pain and thus to make the blade slip.) And when none of the officers in the rooms with him at the time seemed willing to hold the candle for Ranby,

Cumberland himself picked it up and held it throughout the operation, with a perfectly steady hand. In the midst of the surgeon's work he called a halt. Ranby supposed that the pain was more than the patient could bear. But Cumberland simply called for fresh cap and waistcoat for the surgeon—"Poor fellow! he's perspired right through those he's got on."

Frederick, Prince of Wales, died March 20, 1751, at the age of forty-five, in Leicester House, Leicester Square. When they gave the news to Cumberland, the duke sneered. "It is a great blow, but I hope the country will recover in time."

Frederick had been rather likable and the most popular member of his family. The street crowds were calling, "Why couldn't it have been the Butcher? Better the Butcher!" They were afraid that Cumberland would ascend to the throne, for George the Second was getting on in years and the dead prince's oldest son, George, was then only thirteen. Cumberland, at least, would probably be appointed regent in case the King died before the new Prince of Wales came of age. Cumberland himself supposed that. It was a blow to his dignity when the King named the Dowager Princess of Wales (she had been Princess Augusta, daughter of Frederick the Second, Duke of Saxe-Gotha), for Cumberland was the logical regent. He felt the slight very bitterly, not because he wanted the power, but simply because his dignity was hurt.

He died October 31, 1765, at the age of forty-five, in his town house in Upper Grosvenor Square, and nobody wept.

THE COUNTESS OF ALBANY AND ALFIERI

These lovers were together in Paris when the news came that Prince Charles was dead. Details of the scene are lacking; but Alfieri says that his mistress was genuinely affected, and he marvels at this.

The couple made it clear, however, that this death would not be the signal for a marriage between them. In letters to Alfieri's mother, Louise had hinted at a ceremony which would save the family name from extinction; and the poet himself, in his diary, had longed for the day when he could call his love holy. And yet they decided not to marry.

It was pleasanter, for both of them, to be mistress and lover rather than man and wife. It was more romantic. It also was more lucrative; for if Louise ceased to be a Stuart by marriage, presumably she would cease to collect her regular allowance from the Vatican and from the Court of France. In Paris, too, they were leading the sort of life Louise had always wanted to lead. They were entertaining at the hotel in the Rue de Bourgoyne, and they were being entertained. Their irregular alliance prejudiced no one against them. Indeed the people with whom Louise associated and whom lfieri tolerated sometimes, probably considered their liaison commendable ather than reprehensible.

Louise loved the life she was now leading. It consisted of intellectual alk, not wholly empty, and of immorality gracefully accepted and grace- ully indulged. It was fashionable but not The Fashion, gay but not vul- ar, brilliant without being magnificent, and comfortable yet not enervating.

Alfieri didn't like it at all. In the first place it was essentially a French ife, and Alfieri loathed French things. In the second place, these people hattered while he worked; and although they worked too, they didn't vork with the savage, driving force of Alfieri. He hated them: they were ike mosquitoes buzzing around him while he was writing.

But he and his mistress stayed at Paris. This was not simply because ouise wanted to stay: Alfieri was never henpecked. It was because a good art of her income came from the Court of France, and a good part of his noney was invested in French bonds; and, in those days, with the fuse of evolution well lighted, it was advisable for people who wanted French noney to stay near the source.

In 1791 they visited England. This beautiful lady, who still had her ervants call her "Your Majesty," who still used table plate on which was ngraved the royal arms of England, who still kept in her home a royal hrone on which those arms were emblazoned—this beautiful lady had con- eived the idea that she might also get an allowance from the Court of t. James!

She did not like England. She wrote in her notebook: "The nation is nelancholy, without any imagination, even without wit; *the dominant haracteristic is a desire for money.*"

Through the young Countess of Aylesbury, she had herself presented to he royal family at a private audience. It must have been an amusing scene. Iorace Walpole learned that the Princess of Stolberg (Louise was presented nder this pre-marital title) was "well dressed and not at all embarrassed." he King seemed to be delighted with her. The young princess seemed to ke her too. And Queen Charlotte, according to Walpole's informer, "looked t her earnestly."

This was on May 19, 1791. On June 10 Louise accepted a seat at the oot of the throne when George the Third spoke to the House of Lords.

They wanted to go to Scotland, too; but the state of French finances ad by now become such that Alfieri and his mistress made an abrupt re- urn to Paris. She had not yet received her allowance from the British overnment; but she had pulled the proper strings, and the allowance ap- eared soon afterwards.

They sailed from Dover. And Alfieri, as he was about to go aboard the hannel boat, saw on the shore the former Lady Ligonier. Extraordinary man! ven now he was not free of the spell she had once cast over him. "She appeared scarcely less lovely than what she had been twenty years be-fore. . . . She cast on me a gracious smile . . ." But he did not dare t face that smile. Trembling, he hurried aboard the boat and retired to hi cabin. Later, in Calais, he wrote to her, expressing the hope that she wa well and happy, and upbraiding himself unjustly for having brought abou her ruin. She replied like a lady: ". . . You cannot doubt but that I an sensible of the marks of your remembrance, and of the interest you s kindly take in my fate, or that I received them gratefully; the more so, a I cannot regard you as the author of my misfortune, although the sensi-bility and uprightness of your heart make you fear so. You are, on the con-trary, the cause of my deliverance from a world in which I was neve formed to exist, and which I have never regretted for a single instant. . . It is said that she (Louise) fears you also. I well recognize you there! With-out desiring it, or perhaps without perceiving it, you have irresistibly tha ascendency over those who love you. . . ."

(Parenthetically, Lord Ligonier had died soon after he obtained his di-vorce, and her ladyship had married again, obscurely.)

The next summer the poet and the prince's widow were in real danger Money or no money, it was imperative that they quit France at once. Th flame had licked itself almost up to the end of the fuse: the Revolution wa about to explode: there was a horrid hush, as in fields before a thunder shower. Louise succeeded in getting a passport from the Swedish Minister Alfieri from the Venetian Resident: these two were almost the only diplo-matic personages left in Paris. They were to have moved August 20, bu Alfieri had a premonition of danger, and insisted that they move on the 18th

At the Barriere Blanche, on the road to Calais, their coach was held u by a mob. Aristocrats! Kill them! For a time it looked as though they woul be pulled to pieces because of their fine clothes. The National Guardsme were powerless to aid them, in spite of the passports. But Alfieri, in a white hot rage, plunged in and out among the people, shouting, screaming, curs ing them, wildly waving the passports over his head; and eventually th coach was permitted to pass.

At Mons they heard of the August massacres—the most famous slaugh ter in history. They heard that many of their friends had been beaten, jailed spit upon, beheaded. They heard also that an order for the arrest of th Countess of Albany had been issued on August 20. Had it not been for he lover's premonition, she would have been jailed, insulted, executed in th sight of a howling, drunken mob. And Vittorio Alfieri would not have stoo quietly by and watched this!

In November they moved to Florence. They were almost penniless. Bu they set up a home, and again Louise turned to her correspondence an her books, and Alfieri turned again to his writing.

She was getting old now, and rather fat, as will sometimes happen t even the most beautiful women. She was amiable, cynical, well-spoken; sometimes a trifle haughty, when she remembered that there were still persons who esteemed her the rightful Queen of Great Britain; but generally she was a very likable person, round and pleasant, in a red shawl. She wrote innumerable letters to intellectual people. She read vastly—Locke, Kant, Mme. DeGenlis, Lessing, Shakespeare, Milton, anything good she could get her hands on. She entertained. One of the persons she entertained often was young Francois Xavier Fabre, a south of France gentleman, handsome and witty, who had recently won the *Prix de Rome* with an oil painting. She liked Fabre.

And Alfieri worked on like mad. He always worked that way. Probably he *was* a bit mad. He wrote night and day—memoirs, comedies, tragedies, translations, poems. He grew longer, more gaunt, more darkly somber every day. Because he did not feel well, he began to take long walks; and he cut down on his diet, which had been meager enough these twenty years past.

Now he became seriously ill, but he would not admit it. That was like him. He tore off the mustard plasters Louise placed upon his legs and body. He read Homer, growling. For he had suddenly decided (at this age!) to take up the study of Greek. On the morning of October 9, 1803, at the age of fifty-four, he died, leaving everything to Louise.

The "friendship of twenty-six years" was ended. Charles' widow, who had been sailing serenely on an ocean of love, suddenly found herself cast high and dry; she was alone in the midst of intellectual friends, and childless. She wrote, in a letter to a friend, ". . . happiness has disappeared out of the world for me. . . . I take interest in nothing; the world might be completely upset without my noticing it . . . for when I return to my own thoughts and think of all that I have lost, I burst into tears and call Death to my assistance, but Death will not come."

Fabre was not so unresponsive. Very soon after the earth had been packed down over the gaunt, red-haired genius who had been her first lover, Louise accepted the company of this handsome young painter with the south of France accent, and fashionable Florence, without so much as a raised eyebrow, put them down as man and mistress.

She had always wanted a real salon. The life of Paris was the life for her. And now she had her opportunity and she took full advantage of it. Every person of ability and importance, at some time or other, dropped in to see Louise of Albany in her Florentine home. It was a rendezvous of wit and culture, celebrated all over Europe, all over the world; and Louise, bathing in its brilliance as a weary worker bathes in strong sunlight when his labors are finished, was an ideal hostess. Chateaubriand, Mme. Recamier, that beautiful Duchess of Devonshire, Lamartine, Paul Louis Courier, Mme. de Stael, Canova, Foscolo, Sismondi, Werner—these and dozens of others she

entertained. She was not herself great, but she was born to mingle well wit
great people. Louise was an ideal companion, a talking post *par excellenc*
Moreover, she corresponded continually with all manner of persons, an
many a struggling student or artist was encouraged, for a time at least, b
her letters. She did much, in her way. And she enjoyed herself whil
she did it.

When Napoleon came thundering down into Piedmont, she was ordere
back to Paris. That salon, Napoleon estimated, was a dangerous institu
tion. So that Casa Alfieri was deserted for a year, during which time Louis
renewed old acquaintanceships in France. She did not seem to mind th
exile. In fact, she enjoyed it. She was fatter and more amiable than ever
and she still wore that red shawl, when she finally returned to Florence
where she died January 29, 1824, at the age of seventy-two, leaving every
thing she owned to her lover, Fabre. She must have been a charming woman

CLEMENTINA WALKINSHAW

The latter part of the life of Charles' mistress is lost in obscurity. Clem
entina never did quite emerge into reality. As the Countess Alberstrof, sh
lived quietly in her convent and apparently took no part in any public ac
tivity. After Charles left her, she reappears only for the visit to Rome
previously described. She was alive in 1799 and still getting her 3,000 crown
annually from the personal estate of Cardinal Stuart; but when Henry died
in 1802, he made no mention of her in his will.

CHARLOTTE, DUCHESS OF ALBANY

Charles' illegitimate child did not survive her father by many years, an
the rest of her life, after his death, was uneventful, though happy. She wa
much entertained in Italian society generally, and accepted everywhere
Apparently she never put forward any sort of claim to the thrones of Grea
Britain and Ireland and, indeed, she seems to have had no interest in Jacob
itism. From time to time she rejected proposals of marriage from pett
Italian princes: it would seem she was matrimonially ambitious. At on
time (but this was before Charles' death) there was much talk of her making an alliance with the King of Sweden's brother; but this fell through
She died in Bologna, in 1789. She had been thrown from her horse whil
visiting her friend, the Princess Lambertine, and had developed an absces
in her side which proved fatal.

HENRY, CARDINAL DUKE OF YORK

Henry was prepared for the death of his brother. As early as the Sprin
of 1784 he had Cataldi, a Roman lawyer, draw up a memorial of his claim

to the British throne. There was no mention of the Duchess of Albany in this document.

The Cardinal was quiet, but firm and perfectly serious. He explained that he intended to retain the title of Duke of York, and thereafter he was wont to refer to himself as "the self-styled Duke of York." "But we have no intention of ever renouncing these rights of succession and fealty which we hold over these Kingdoms." When he died, he added, they "will pass in their full and unimpaired force to that Prince to whom they will lawfully revert by proximity of blood." Presumably he meant the King of Sardinia, who, however, never seemed to take any interest in his shadowy claims. But no name is mentioned in the memorial.

Henry made certain that the world knew he meant what he said. The silver crescent, heraldic emblem of a second son, disappeared from his escutcheon, and the ducal coronet was replaced, on his plate, coach panels, seals, etc., by the crown. His servants were instructed to call him "Majesty" in the future, and medals were struck to commemorate the succession.

Besides this, Henry touched for scrofula, or "the King's evil." This was a quaint prerogative which William of Orange and the Hanoverian monarchs never practiced. It originated, in England, according to tradition, with Edward the Confessor. After Edward, the King could touch any person afflicted with scrofula, and by this touch cure the disease. A touch piece went with the ceremony, and this was to be hung around the neck for the rest of the cured man's life: it was a small coin bearing the representation of a three-masted ship on one side, and on the other side a relief of St. Michael casually killing a dragon. The piece was set: it never changed. Henry had it struck off in silver, with white ribbons attached. He was always prepared to touch whomsoever asked the boon of him. Probably nobody was ever cured; probably, indeed, many pretended to be ill in order to obtain one of those silver pieces as a curio; but Henry considered himself a King now, and the Stuart kings had always touched.

Of course, his claims created no excitement. The 'Forty-five was a long way back, and England was definitely committed to her German rulers. What was more important, the Vatican was getting along well with the Court of St. James. The Pope had sent Monsignore (afterwards Cardinal) Thomas Erskine, a Scot, to England, as a sort of unofficial Nuncio; and the Court of St. James sent Sir John (then Mr.) Hippisley, to Rome as a sort of unofficial ambassador. Both were excellent men. The island and the Vatican smiled back and forth pleasantly, and exchanged assurances of mutual esteem. Doubtless they were honestly glad the strain had let up.

The Cardinal Duke of York got along admirably with Hippisley, who was a frequent guest at Frascati. But it was too much for Henry when, as Vice Chancellor of the Apostolic See, he was obliged to read a Papal document which officially recognized the family of Guelph as the royal family of Great Britain and Ireland. He dropped the document, and promptly framed a protest to Pius the Sixth.

That paper is pathetic enough to bring tears to the eyes. For more than a century, Henry pointed out, his family, beaten about by ill luck, had clung to a double source of hope and satisfaction: it had always been faithful and loyal to the Primacy of Peter and the Holy See, and it had always been conscious of the Vatican's devotion to the royal house of Stuart. The maxim of Clement the Fifteenth, it had seemed, had established this attitude beyond change. The Stuarts had given up everything for the Church. The Church, Henry intimated mildly, might continue to give up something for the Stuarts. It was so little. . . . He would soon be dead; and then common sense and the necessities of things political could be indulged to the fullest. Forget him when he was gone . . . but while he was alive, remember his dignity, remember what this matter meant to him. He had served the Church well. . . . "I confess that I used to flatter myself that during these very last few remaining years of my life my Royal House would be allowed to expire in me without this fresh act of humiliation . . ." The letter closed with a statement of the writer's intentions to remain for the rest of his life among his flock at Frascati. It was dated November 4, 1792.

Not even his enemies—and he had so few!—could help but feel sorry for this aged man. They knew, then, what it meant to him. No government of any sort, no official body, any longer recognized his family's claim. All the blood of the clansmen had been shed in vain. He was the last of an ancient and honorable line of kings; and he was to die unrecognized, undignified. And his whole life was in his dignity. He had nothing else. His father, at least, had held a little power and the formal recognition of several nations; his brother had been romantic. But he himself was obliged to lean on dignity alone. He could not hope for a Restoration now. All he asked was that the Church, at least, call him King Henry the Ninth for a little while. And the Church, because the common sense of politics was on the other side, refused to do so.

But Henry's protest was soon lost to sight in more important, more immediate affairs. France had gone mad; and before the fever had subsided there had come a genius to lead Frenchmen against the other peoples of the world. The Vatican, like all the rest of Europe, was in a dangerous position. Pius the Sixth openly allied himself with the First Coalition—with Great Britain, Austria and Prussia.

National breaths were held, for the tiniest false step meant the coming of a whirlwind. Hugo Basseville, a representative of the dreaded Directorate, got all excited in the streets of Rome, made a frenzied speech, waved a tricolor, stirred up a mob and, as a climax, got himself stabbed in the chest—as he well deserved.

The Vatican had not been involved in this affair. A note of regret was sent to France; some of those in the mob were punished. But the damage had been done, the false step made. France, at the time, was in a mood of exuberant belligerency: she was looking for excuses to fight: with a lunatic confidence, and the strength, too, of a lunatic, she was ready to fly at the throat of any other nation. The killing of Basseville gave her a welcome opportunity. In the summer of 1796, Napoleon crossed the Alps and the Po and started down toward the Holy City. There was panic in Rome, Ambassadors were sent north to meet the French forces, which had occupied Bologna. In that city a treaty was signed. The Papal representatives had to comply with Napoleon's wishes: they had no troops. The terms of the treaty were characteristically harsh. One clause dictated the payment of what amounted to $7,500,000 (worth three or four times as much in those days) to the French Directorate, besides many art treasures. The Vatican, in addition, was forced to cede to France all its property in that country, including, of course, Avignon.

That was bad enough. But in January of 1797, there was a minor uprising near Ferrara, and this gave the French another excellent excuse. Again Napoleon swept down toward defenseless Rome. Again there was panic, and another treaty. That treaty, signed at Tolentino on February 19, 1797, demanded $6,000,000 more.

Rome was rich, but this was a large sum for those days. Much of the Church's plate was melted down, the ladies gave up their jewels, the remainder of Sixtus the Fifth's treasure in Sant' Angelo was brought out and sent to France, and an appeal was made to the Cardinals.

Henry did more than his share. He might object to the Holy Father's attitude toward the Stuart pretensions, but he would not be parsimonious when Mother Church was needy. He gave many of his best beloved treasures, including an exquisitely embossed shield of solid gold which the Austrian Emperor had given to King John Sobieski of Poland, Henry's great-grandfather, when King John had defeated the Turks before Vienna. Henry gave, too, the famous Ruby of Poland, the size of a pigeon's egg and worth, in those days, about $250,000. He also gave other jewels, and much of his plate.

But the French Directorate had no intention of keeping out of Rome. These were merely preliminary maneuvers. When all the money had been sucked from the ancient city, another excuse was found for military action. A trifling riot in December of 1797 served the Directorate on this occasion. General Berthier, with 18,000 men, entered Rome on February 10, 1798.

The day before, the Cardinal Duke of York had fled Frascati. Such treasures as he had left were concealed there. The rest of his belongings fell to the French, who promptly sold them.

The poor Cardinal went the only way he dared to go—toward Naples by way of Terracina. In Naples he found many other exiled Cardinals. But even Naples did not remain safe. So Henry chartered a small coasting vessel and, in company with the devoted Monsignore Cesarini and his valet, Eugenio Ridolfi, set sail for Messini. The Admiral of the English fleet, Lord Nelson, on the following night transported the King and Queen of the Two Sicilies and the royal family, together with certain other personages, to a place of safety, using the flagship *Vanguard*: but Lord Nelson did not save the Cardinal Duke.

There were twenty-three days of stormy weather. At Messini, Henry met Cardinals Pignatelli, Doria and Braschi (the Pope's nephew), who like him, were fleeing before the whirlwind; and the four lived together in one house. They were very poor now. Later they chartered another vessel and set sail for Venice, then in the hands of the Austrians. However, the elements in the Adriatic were quite as fierce as in the Tyrrhene, and the boat was forced to put in at Corfu. From there, the Cardinals made their way to Trieste, and later to Vienna.

Henry was now weak, and very old. In addition to the fatigue of the journey, he was suffering from inflammation of the eyes and from a leg swollen because of a misstep in entering a carriage. He was practically penniless. He could not even afford to engage a house, but was obliged to accep the hospitality of a nearby monastery.

It was then that Stefano, Cardinal Borgia, wrote an interesting letter to Sir John Hippisley in England. Cardinal Borgia suggested, most discreetly, that the Court of St. James do something about Cardinal Stuart. We do not know whether or not Henry was informed that this letter was being sent. At any rate, the request did not come directly from him, and there is nothing to indicate that it came from him indirectly.

Hippisley took up the matter with another official, who took it up with another, and so it got to George the Third, who was a third cousin twice removed of the Cardinal Duke. In the end the sum of £2,000 was deposite with the house of Cloutts and Co., in London, for Henry to draw upon as he wished. In addition, Lord Minto, George's ambassador at Vienna, wrote t say that another £2,000 would be available the following July, if the Cardina Duke required it.

The messenger arrived just after the opening of the Conclave at Venice Pius the Sixth had died in exile, and it was necessary to elect a successor. Al over the world they were predicting that not enough Cardinals could b assembled in one place legally to hold a Conclave. But it was done. It was on of the longest Conclaves in the history of the Church. Henry acted his par as Sub-Deacon; and had he been an Italian, it is probable that he would hav been elevated the one remaining step to the Holy See. In March, Cardina Gregorio Chiaramonti, a Benedictine monk, was elected, and assumed th title of Pius the Seventh. The chair of St. Peter had been vacant for six months.

Meanwhile, Henry was writing exquisite letters of gratitude to Lord Minto and to Sir John Hippisley. The helping hand had been extended just in time.

On Wednesday, June 25, the whirlwind having departed, he arrived back in Rome, coming from Sienna where he had stopped for rest. He was greeted with wild enthusiasm; and when he returned to Frascati the bands played, flowers were thrown, bonfires were lighted, fireworks set off, and the people, with whom Henry had always been popular, shrieked themselves hoarse with delight.

He was a large, smooth, ruddy-faced man. He stooped when he walked, and his leg was troubling him more and more every day, so that he moved with a limp, a dragging step. But the servants still called him "Majesty."

He continued to entertain. The Court of St. James had granted him a life annuity and, in addition, some of his Mexican and Spanish properties were producing some revenue again. He was still poor, but it never occurred to him to save anything. He lived royally, as he had always lived, and entertained with a lavish hand. Once he received Prince Augustus Frederick, Duke of Sussex, the sixth son of George the Third. Henry and the Duke, by tactic agreement, called one another "Your Highness." Henry did not visit, except to the Vatican and the palace of Charles Emmanuel, King of Sardinia. To visit any other persons would not have been proper in a King.

When Giovanni-Francisco, Cardinal Albani, died, Henry was created Bishop of Ostia and Velletri, with which position went the deanship of the Sacred College, the second highest position in the Roman Catholic Church. But Henry remained at Frascati. He was too old to move.

In 1804, invitations to the coronation of Napoleon the First, Emperor of France, were sent to Rome. The Pope, you will remember, was to crown the new emperor. The Cardinals were invited. But Napoleon, writing to Henry, had saluted him only as "cousin," not as "brother," and Henry was indignant. He demanded that a formal complaint be made to Napoleon. He would not attend the coronation unless properly invited. He was a King—Henry the Ninth, king of Great Britain, Ireland and France, Defender of the Faith, etc.

What Napoleon might have done about this very important matter will never be known. Before the complaint was made Henry was taken ill.

Louise of Albany, she who had carried on her love affair under his nose, hurried to Rome when she learned of his illness. She did not do so in order to be present to comfort him in his dying hour. Her purpose was to inquire anxiously about her jointure. If Henry died, would she still get the money? She conferred with Monsignore Cesarini, and he relieved her fears. So she returned to Florence.

Henry recovered, but the attack left him pitifully weak. The last few years of his life were spent in constant illness. He was not able to think clearly much of the time. His eyesight began to fail. In the summer of 1807 he was taken with chills and fever. He died on July 13 of that year—on the forty-sixth anniversary of his consecration as Bishop of Frascati. He was eighty-two years and four months old, and had been a Cardinal for more than sixty years. For twenty-one years, five months and fourteen days he had called himself King Henry the Ninth.

On July 16, the body was escorted by a troop of cavalry through the streets of Rome to the Cancelleria where it rested on a catafalque in the great hall for three days, the Papal soldiers guarding it. It rested with miter and crosier and the Scarlet Hat at its feet. The royal arms were displayed, but without the crown. There was a grand requiem mass at the Church of Sant' Andrea della Valle, the Pope and twenty-two Cardinals assisting. There were also requiem masses at the cathedrals of Velletri and Frascati. The body was entombed in the Grotte Vecchie, in St. Peter's. Canova, one of the interesting friends of the Countess of Albany, designed the monument in the church which is familiar to all tourists. It is of white marble, with busts of Charles, Henry and James in low relief, and under the weeping genii. The Prince Regent of Great Britain, who was later George the Fourth, gave fifty pounds toward its construction. He is popularly credited with raising all the money, but actually his contribution was nominal, and the Pope paid the lion's share.

It was discovered that in his will, the Cardinal Duke had remembered every friend, mostly with gifts of historic interest, for he died a poor man. The Hanoverian on the throne of Great Britain was given a Cross of St. Andrew set in diamonds, which Charles the First had worn, and a ring with a single ruby engraved with a cross. The cash residue was just about sufficient to keep up the life annuity for Louise, Countess of Albany; and when she died, this money went to the Scots College in Rome.

Solemnly, at the end of the will, the last of the Royal Stuarts decrees that with his death the rights he held to the thrones of England, Scotland, Ireland, etc., should pass to his nearest blood relative. This was Emmanuel of Sardinia, but Emmanuel wasn't named. The naming might embarrass the Pope. And the Stuarts had excellent manners.

AUTHORITIES

ADAM, FRANK, *Clans, Septs and Regiments of the Scottish Highlands*

ALFIERI, *Life of Vittorio Alfieri, by Himself*, Foreword by W. D. Howells

ANONYMOUS, *Ascanius*, etc., Edinburgh, 1812

ANONYMOUS, *The Heirs of the Stuarts*, (Skene?) in Quarterly Review of June 1847

ANONYMOUS, *A Narrative of Prince Charlie's Escape, by One of His Companions*, Foreword by George Skene; in Blackwood's Edinburgh Magazine, October 1873

BLAIKIE, WALTER BIGGAR, *Itinerary of Charles Edward Stuart* with map, for the Scottish Historical Association

BLAIKIE, WALTER BIGGAR, editor, *Origins of the Forty-five, and other papers relating to that Rising*

BROUGHTON, *Memoirs of John Murray of Broughton*, for the Scottish Historical Association

BURNET, BISHOP, *History of His Own Times*, two volumes

BURTON, JOHN HILL, *History of Scotland*, eight volumes

CHAMBERS, ROBERT, *History of the Rebellions in Scotland*, five volumes

CHARLES, GEORGE, *Transactions in Scotland in the Years 1715-16 and 1745-46*, two volumes

COPPING, EDWARD, *Alfieri and Goldoni, Their Lives and Adventures*

DE RUVIGNY ET RAINEVAL, MARQUIS MASSUE, *The Jacobite Peerage*, 2 vols.

DORAN, JOHN, "*Lives of the Queens of England of the House of Hanover*, two volumes

DUKE, WINIFRED, *Lord George Murray and the Forty-five*

ELCHO, DAVID, LORD, *A Short Account of the Affairs of Scotland in the years 1744, 1745 and 1746*

EWALD, ALEXANDER CHARLES, *Life and Times of Prince Charles Edward*

FORBES, BISHOP, *The Lyon in Mourning*, edited by Henry Paton, 3 vols., for the Scottish Historical Association

FORBES, RT. REV. ROBERT, BISHOP, *Jacobite Memoirs of the Rebellion of 1745*, edited by Robert Chambers

FYFE, W. T., *Bonnie Prince Charlie*

GRANT, MRS. OF LAGGAN, *Essays on the Superstitions of the Highlanders of Scotland*

HAILE, MARTIN, *James Francis Edward, the Old Chevalier*

HENDERSON, ANDREW, *The History of the Rebellion* (5th edition, 1753)

HENDERSON, T. F., *The Royal Stewarts*

HOME, JOHN, *History of the Rebellion of 1745* (London 1820)

JESSE, JOHN HENEAGE, *Memoirs of the Jacobites and Their Adherents*, three volumes

JESSE, JOHN HENEAGE, *Memoirs of the Reigns of William and Mary, Queen Anne and the First and Second Georges*, four volumes

JOHNSTONE, CHEVALIER DE, *Memoirs of the Rebellion of 1745 and 1746* (second edition, 1821)

JONES, CHARLES C., *Recollections of Royalty, from the Death of William Rufus in 1100, to that of the Cardinal York, the last Lineal Descendant of the Stuarts, in 1807*, two volumes

KELLY, BERNARD, *Life of Cardinal Duke of York*

LANG, ANDREW, *Prince Charles Edward*

LANG, ANDREW, *Pickle the Spy, or the Incognito of Prince Charles*

LANG, ANDREW, *The Companions of Pickle*

LECKY, W. E. H., *History of England in the Eighteenth Century*, 7 vols.

LEE, VERNON, *The Countess of Albany*

MACAULAY, THOMAS BABINGTON, *History of England*, five volumes

MACLAUGHLAN, REV. THOMAS, *A History of the Scottish Highlands, Highland Clans and Highland Regiments*, edited by John S. Keltie

MAHON, LORD, *History of England from the Peace of Utrecht to the Peace of Aix-la-Chapelle*, three volumes

MAHON, LORD, *The Decline of the Last Stuarts; Extracts from the Despatches of British Envoys to the Secretary of State*, edited for the Roxburghe Club

MCCARTHY, JUSTIN, *The Reign of Queen Anne*

MACARTHY, JUSTIN AND HUNTLY, *A History of the Four Georges*, 4 vols.

MELVILLE, LEWIS, *The First George*, two volumes

RAIT, ROBERT S., *Scotland*

RAIT, ROBERT S., *Five Stuart Princesses*

RATHERY, E. J. B., *Journal and Memoirs of the Marquis D'Argenson*, 2 vols.

RAY, JAMES, *Compleat History of the Rebellion*, (1750)

SCOTT, SIR WALTER, BART., *Tales of a Grandfather*

SKENE, GEORGE, *The Highlanders of Scotland*

STANHOPE, EARL, *History of England, comprising the Reign of Queen Anne until the Peace of Utrecht*

STRICKLAND, AGNES, *The Queens of England*, twelve volumes

STUART, JOHN SOBIESKI AND CHARLES EDWARD, *Tales of the Century, or Sketches of the Romance of History between the Years 1746 and 1846*

TERRY, CHARLES SANFORD, *Life of the Young Pretender*

TERRY, CHARLES SANFORD, *The Forty-five: Contemporary Papers*

THACKERAY, WILLIAM MAKEPEACE, *The Four Georges*

VAUGHAN, HERBERT MILLINGCHAMP, *The Last of the Royal Stuarts*

VAUGHAN, HERBERT MILLINGCHAMP, *The Last Stuart Queen: Louise, Countess of Albany*

VITELLESCHI, MARCHESA, *A Court in Exile,* two volumes
WALDEGRAVE, JAMES, EARL OF, *Memoirs*
WARD, A. W., *The Electress Sophia and the Hanoverian Succession,* (second edition)

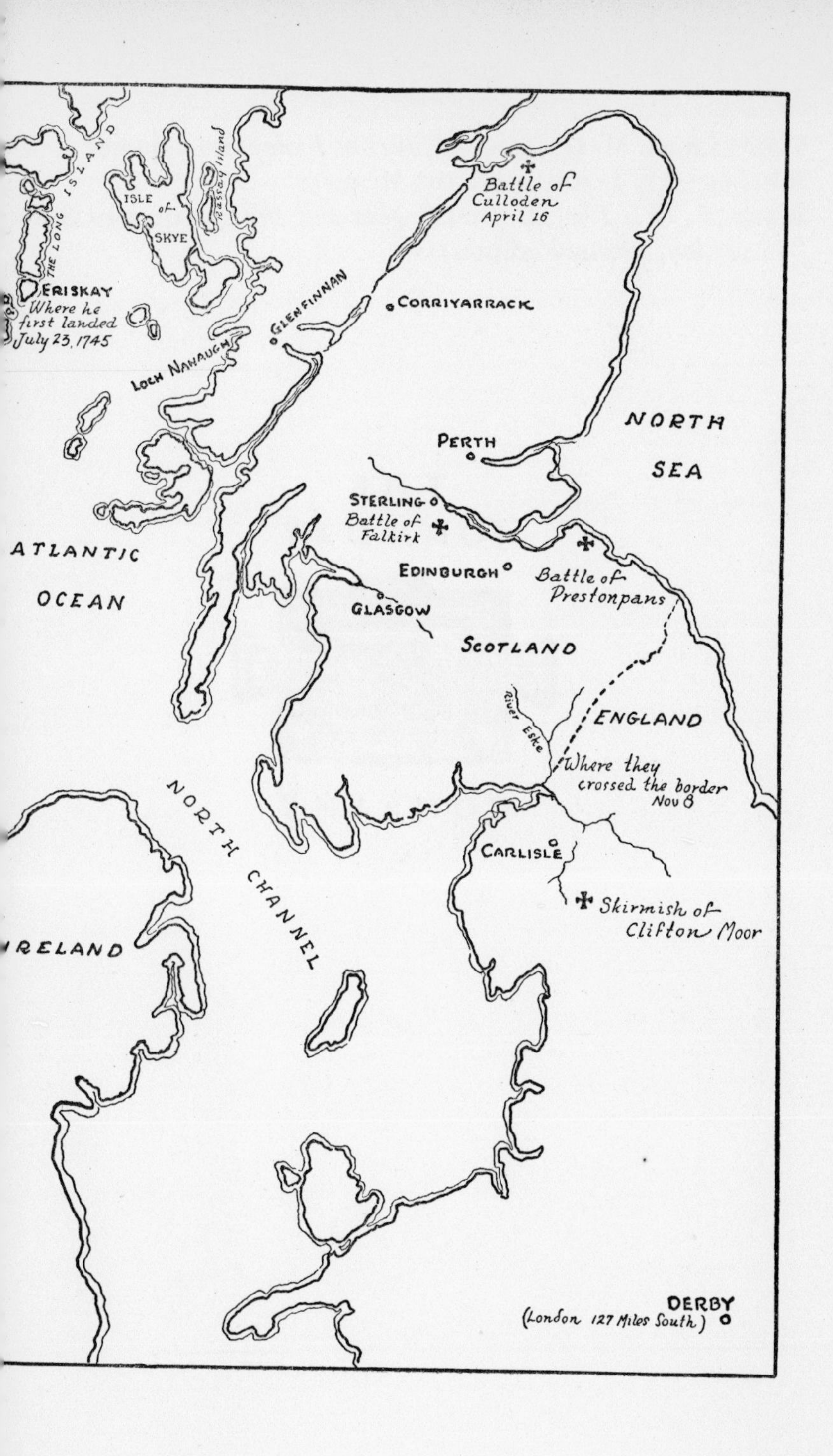

THE LONG ISLAND
ISLE of SKYE
Rasay Island
ERISKAY
Where he first landed July 23, 1745
LOCH NANAUGH
GLENFINNAN
CORRIYARRACK
Battle of Culloden April 16
NORTH SEA
PERTH
STERLING
Battle of Falkirk
ATLANTIC OCEAN
EDINBURGH
Battle of Prestonpans
GLASGOW
SCOTLAND
River Eske
ENGLAND
Where they crossed the border Nov 8
NORTH CHANNEL
CARLISLE
Skirmish of Clifton Moor
IRELAND
DERBY
(London 127 Miles South)

THE
JOHN DAY

COMPANY

INC.